**Ulrich von Schwerin** is currently a journalist with a focus on Iran, the Middle East and South Asia. He holds a PhD in History from the University of Hamburg.

# THE DISSIDENT MULLAH

Ayatollah Montazeri and the Struggle for
Reform in Revolutionary Iran

ULRICH VON SCHWERIN

I.B. TAURIS

LONDON · NEW YORK

Published in 2015 by
I.B.Tauris & Co Ltd
London • New York
www.ibtauris.com

International Library of Iranian Studies 55

ISBN: 978 1 78453 173 7
eISBN: 978 0 85773 774 8

A full CIP record for this book is available from the British Library
A full CIP record is available from the Library of Congress

Library of Congress Catalog Card Number: available

Typeset in Garamond Three by OKS Prepress Services, Chennai, India
Printed and bound by CPI Group (UK) Ltd, Croydon, CR0 4YY

130042757

*To my parents*

# CONTENTS

# LIST OF ILLUSTRATIONS

Plate 1. Having obtained the degree of *ejtehād*, Montazeri, here in a photo from 1957, wore the characteristic white turban and dark cloak of the clergy. (Source: © courtesy of the Office of Ayatollah Montazeri)

Plate 2. During the protests against the reforms of the Shah in 1963, Montazeri with other young clerics set out to mobilise the students of the seminaries in Qom. (Source: © courtesy of the Office of Ayatollah Montazeri)

Plate 3. At the opening session in August 1979, Montazeri was elected chairman of the Expert Assembly, but mostly left the chair to his deputy Beheshti. (Source: © courtesy of the Office of Ayatollah Montazeri)

Plate 4. Montazeri and Beheshti were considered the main advocates of *velayat-e faqih* in the Expert Assembly and strongly pushed for its inclusion in the constitution. (Source: © courtesy of the Office of Ayatollah Montazeri)

Plate 5. In autumn 1979, Montazeri served for several weeks as Tehran's Friday prayer leader, but after his return to Qom he left the post to Khamene'i. (Source: © courtesy of the Office of Ayatollah Montazeri)

Plate 6. Montazeri and Khamene'i had closely collaborated during the struggle against the Shah, but after the revolution maintained only a distant relationship. (Source: © courtesy of the Office of Ayatollah Montazeri)

Plate 7. Although Montazeri, here during a speech in 1980, did not hold any formal office after the revolution, he regularly intervened in the public debate. (Source: © courtesy of the Office of Ayatollah Montazeri)

Plate 8. Montazeri, here during Tehran Friday prayers in February 1980, was known as good natured, humorous and amenable. (Source: © courtesy of the Office of Ayatollah Montazeri)

Plate 9. Shortly after the revolution, Khomeini placed Montazeri in charge of choosing and training the Friday prayer leaders for whom he set up a special school in Qom. (Source: © courtesy of the Office of Ayatollah Montazeri)

Plate 10. As one of Khomeini's closest students and supporters Montazeri was chosen in 1985 as his designated successor, but during the following years, he maintained his intellectual independence. (Source: Kaveh Kazemi/Getty Images)

Plate 11. In November 1997, in his famous speech at his *hosseiniye* in Qom, Montazeri attacked Khamene'i for obstructing reforms and disputed his claim to the *marja'iyat*. (Source: © courtesy of the Office of Ayatollah Montazeri)

Plate 12. Following his release from house arrest in January 2003, Montazeri despite his advanced age and frail health continued to work on his religious and political writings. (Source: © courtesy of the Office of Ayatollah Montazeri)

# ACKNOWLEDGEMENTS

I would like to express my gratitude to Henner Fürtig and Dietrich Reetz for their guidance in my research, as well as to Katajun Amirpur, Mohsen Kadivar and Walter Posch for their helpful comments and advice. I would also like to thank Oliver, Benedikt, Just and my other friends at the Staatsbibliothek for the exchange and their company during the years of research. Thanks also to the Archiv für Forschung und Dokumentation Iran in Berlin for their assistance in sifting through their historic newspapers. Finally, I am much obliged to my parents for enabling me to continue my research – and, of course, to Charlotte for listening to the lunchtime tales of my latest troubles and my newest finds.

# NOTE ON TRANSLITERATION

The transliteration follows the system of the *International Journal for Middle Eastern Studies* (IJMES) with the exception of the short vowels, which are given as o and e, not u and i. All translations from Persian, if not taken from secondary sources in English, are my own.

# INTRODUCTION

> In the Islamic state, to determine one's fate is the people's first and
> most fundamental right. No one can appoint himself the people's
> guardian and deprive them of their right to vote. In this system
> the freedom of parties and the democratic character of the media
> must be guaranteed, and no one has the right, under any pretext,
> to deprive the people of its use.
>
> (Montazeri on the Islamic state in 2006)[1]

When the Iranian cleric and dissident Grand Ayatollah Hossein-Ali
Montazeri died in December 2009, at the height of the protests against
the controversial re-election of the hardline President Mahmud
Ahmadinejad, he was regarded by many as the spiritual guide of the
reform movement. In his view, as expressed in the citation above, the
Islamic state must be based on the will of the people. They must be free
to express their opinion in the media and to participate in government
through political parties. Montazeri fiercely criticised the violation of
civil rights by the regime and unrelentingly called for a reform of the
authoritarian system. Although Montazeri, as the only senior cleric in
Iran, endorsed the state doctrine of *velāyat-e faqih* (guardianship of the
jurist), his reading of this theory profoundly differed from the official
interpretation. In his view the *vali-ye faqih* (ruling jurist) is not
appointed by God, but elected by the people. He is not their guardian,
but their representative. Rather than exercise power himself, Montazeri
argued, he only supervises its use to assure that the government does not

violate Islamic precepts. The mandate and power of the ruling jurist must be restricted, Montazeri insisted, and the constitution must be revised accordingly. Yet in 1979, Montazeri, as the chairman of the constitutional assembly, had played a key role in writing this very constitution. While Grand Ayatollah Ruhollah Khomeini, the leader of the revolution, had remained silent on the future form of the system, Montazeri had insisted that it be based on *velāyat-e faqih* and had opposed all efforts to establish a democratic system.

> In order to be Islamic, the government must be based on a leader appointed by God [. . .]. The commands of a president who has not been approved by the *vali-ye faqih*, even if the entire population has voted for him, has no binding value,

Montazeri had declared.[2] How did this man, who had played an integral role in the founding of the Iranian regime, come to be one of its fiercest critics? What made him change his views, and how did he come to prioritise civil rights, pluralism and popular participation? What influence did his views have on others, and what does his example reveal about the political and religious discourse in Iran? Drawing on the speeches and writings of Montazeri and other central figures of the discourse, this book examines the evolution of Montazeri's political thought over the course of five decades and studies his contribution to the understanding of religion and politics in Iran. Starting from Montazeri's entry into politics in 1963 this book examines his activities in the struggle against the Shah, his role in the revolution and his position in the ensuing factional conflicts. It studies how he came to be chosen as Khomeini's successor in 1985, how he used this position to press for reforms and why he was deposed from this post in 1989. It examines how the regime sought to break his authority and to exclude him from the discourse. It then goes on to study his role in the debates on reform that unfolded in the 1990s and his relationship to other reformist clerics and intellectuals. Through the study of the life and thoughts of Montazeri this book seeks to contribute to the understanding of recent Iranian history. Furthermore, it seeks to help understand under what conditions discursive authority can change the objective structures of reality in a context shaped by force. In many ways the case of the Iranian reform movement is instructive for understanding the problems and potentials of a social movement in peacefully transforming an authoritarian regime.

In studying the Iranian discourse on politics and Islam, this book focuses on the role of religious authority and political power in defining the rules and limits of this discourse and in influencing its ability to shape reality. As this book will show, the discourse on the relationship between religion and politics in Iran was never an abstract academic debate, but its participants sought to attain discursive hegemony in order to change not only the understanding of religion but also the social and political order of society. In this book a discourse is understood in line with Pierre Bourdieu's definition, as the scene of the struggle for the legitimate interpretation, designation and definition of reality with the objective of enforcing certain visions of social order in order to change this reality.[3] In this view the discursive field is not a space free of power, but rather power, authority and discourse are in many ways interrelated: only if a person speaks from a position of authority will this person's vision of reality be accepted as legitimate. This ability to define the socially accepted perception of the world in turn confers the power to change its objective structures. However, while authority is a condition for the exercise of power, power can also exist divorced of authority. What is more, as power confers the ability to define the rules and set the limits of the discourse, it can be used to restrict the domain of the sayable.[4] According to Michel Foucault, discourses are situated in a discursive field located in time and space with certain defined rules and limits. These rules define who can take part, what can be said and in what way. Whether a statement is accepted as legitimate by others depends on the position of the speaker, the place of speaking and the form of the statement. Consequently the legitimacy, and in a more general sense the significance, of a statement depends on its context.[5] The internal rules are subject to a separate discourse in which participants try to change the game according to their particular interests. Thus, they may try to exclude certain participants or to restrict what can be said.[6] Each of the different fields, such as politics, religion, science, culture and economics, which Bourdieu conceived as autonomous but interrelated, operates according to its own rules and norms. These circumscribe the participants' actions and the way their conduct is judged.[7] These fields can be understood as spaces of conflict between different forces over the distribution of 'capital'. The recognition of a person's symbolic capital such as education, eloquence or knowledge by a social group or institution lends that person authority and gives legitimacy to his/her position in the field. Authority is less a personal quality than a relationship that cannot exist without others who are willing to recognise it. It is bestowed upon a person and can also be withdrawn.[8] It is the necessary condition for asserting perceptions of social order and the link between discourse and power, as only authority accords language the ability to shape reality. In the absence of authority, the act of speaking remains without consequence.[9] While authority and legitimacy are important conditions for the exercise of power, these concepts should not be confused. Power is classically defined as the ability to induce a person to act in a way in which he/she would not have done of his/her own accord. While authority permits a person to influence others, power confers the ability to force others to comply with one's own will. According to Bourdieu, power is the ability to produce and to manipulate the objective structures of society. It not only seeks to shape the public's conception of the social world but also the world itself.[10]

This brief introduction will help understand the theoretical approach chosen for the study of Montazeri's role in the Iranian discourse on Islam and politics. This discourse must be understood as a struggle over the authority of interpretation and discursive hegemony in order to determine the conception of politics and religion, with the ultimate goal of changing the structures of society and the State. This book begins with the rise of Khomeini's clerical movement in the 1960s when the discourse first emerged in its contemporary form. However, its origins reach further back as it must be understood as the continuation of the wider discourse on Islam's relationship to modernity, begun in the nineteenth century by Islamic clerics and scholars trying to find a response to the growing cultural and political influence of the West. Like these clerics and scholars, Khomeini sought an answer to the question of how religion could retain its relevance in a changing world. His response to the challenge of modernity was a radical redefinition of religion's relationship to politics, which, after 1979, became the guiding model for the transformation of society and the State. Yet the formation of the new system raised new questions for religious intellectuals. The disappearance of the separation between the religious and the political field forced the clergy to redefine its role vis-à-vis the State, and to adapt religious law to the exigencies of practical politics. The problems that arose from the new situation eventually led to a debate on the place of human reason, individual rights, freedom, pluralism and democracy in Islam. This in turn led religious intellectuals to reconsider the interpretation of the holy scriptures, and to seek new approaches to the formation of religious knowledge.

The example of Montazeri, who was one of the key figures in the discourse, will illustrate the causes and conditions under which it was conceived. It will highlight its changing motives and objectives and its internal rules and external limits as well as the evolving role of religious authority and political power in the shaping of the discourse. This book seeks to understand not only how Montazeri influenced the understanding of religion and politics in Iran, but also the way in which he sought to change the rules and limits of the discourse itself. Especially in his later years, much of his energy was devoted to the fight for a more open and free debate. The symbolic capital acquired both in the religious and the political field through his religious studies and his political activism lent him authority, which he could employ in the discourse in order to influence the public's conception of Islam and politics. However, while words have power, words alone cannot change the world. As we shall see, discursive authority does not directly translate into political power, and mere words remain powerless in the face of brute force. In this sense, the example of Montazeri can also help us to understand the relationship between discourse and reality in a context shaped by force both before and after the revolution.

As the subject of this study is Montazeri's role in the Iranian discourse on Islam and politics, it focuses on the debate among religious intellectuals[11] inside Iran directly related to Montazeri. The contribution of secular thinkers and thinkers in exile are not the subject of this study, and the conservative and orthodox positions will also not be treated in great detail. Documents were chosen according to both their relevance and their accessibility. For reasons of efficiency the analysis is limited to the major works of the central figures of the discourse. Apart from Montazeri himself, these include Mehdi Bazargan, Hassan Yussefi Eshkevari, Akbar Ganji, Sa'id Hajjarian, Mohsen Kadivar, Mohammad Khatami, Abdollah Nuri, Mohammad Mojtahed Shabestari and Abdolkarim Soroush. This study understands a statement as the product of a specific discursive situation, in which the speaker acts in accordance with the rules and limits of the discourse under the influence of the specific historical context and in line with his/her individual habitus. Hence, this study seeks to place the statements in their precise discursive and historical context to show the conditions of their creation. As the discourse was not an academic exercise but a fight for power and influence, to neglect the political interests that shaped the discursive positions would mean to misunderstand the agents' motives. According to Bourdieu, the extra-discursive conditions of speech are the actual sources of discursive effectiveness. Hence, much space will be dedicated to the analysis of the struggle for position and power in the religious and political field as well as to social and political developments.

Despite Montazeri's prominence in Iran, there are few studies on his life and thought by Iranian or non-Iranian scholars. Many have mentioned him in passing, but few have dedicated more than a few paragraphs to him. By far the most extensive and detailed analysis of his political thought was written by Mohsen Kadivar (see bibliography for details). Katajun Amirpur, Geneive Abdo and Navid Kermani have also written about him at length. Maziar Behrooz and Babak Rahimi have dedicated articles to specific aspects of Montazeri's work, and Yann Richard has written a biographical sketch of Montazeri. Finally, the works of Wilfried Buchta, Baqer Moin and Ziba Mir-Hosseini are also of interest. Given the lack of secondary sources on Montazeri, his book *Khaterat* (*Memoirs*) – containing hundreds of fatwas, letters, speeches, interviews and other documents – is of particular importance. Of course, the book must be read with a pinch of salt: given the fact that it was only written in the late 1990s it does not directly reflect his thoughts, motives or feelings at the time of events. As it was composed to defend and justify his actions, the depiction of events as well as the choice of documents is often one-sided. Several passages whose truth cannot be verified independently must be treated with caution. In the case of the events leading to his deposition I refer for alternative accounts to the books by Ahmad Khomeini, Mohammad Reyshahri and an anonymous group of Montazeri's students published on the internet. Additional information on crucial episodes of his life is contained in Montazeri's short book *Enteqad az khod* (*Self-Criticism*), which was published after his death and in which he answered the critical questions of his son Sa'id. Although this book too must be approached cautiously it shows that, contrary to most other leading politicians in Iran, Montazeri was ready to self-critically address his own mistakes.

Even though the current work will concentrate on the post-revolutionary period, the first chapter is dedicated to the events before the revolution as these are not only essential to understanding the social, religious and political context that gave rise to the idea of an Islamic state, but also to understanding the formative experiences that structured Montazeri's habitus and thereby shaped his later ideas and practices. An analysis of this period is also necessary because Montazeri's religious and political authority after the revolution, which enabled him to become a key figure of the regime, cannot be understood without knowledge of his early life.

The second chapter will show how the Islamists came to dominate the discourse during the revolution, while adopting the central demands of their secular rivals. It will retrace the debate on the doctrine of *velāyat-e faqih* both inside and outside the constitutional assembly, highlighting Montazeri's role and position in this debate. The new constitution made Islam the basis of politics and accorded the clerics[12] a privileged role in politics. However, as the advocates of *velāyat-e faqih* had no clear vision of the implications of this doctrine and its relation to the republican institutions, the new constitution was full of contradictions.

Political praxis soon showed that contrary to the Islamist assumption, the laws and prescriptions of Islam were neither sufficient nor well suited to administering a modern state and society. Moreover, the clerics lacked the experience for the posts they assumed after the revolution. Chaos and violence was the result. In many cases the new regime was more repressive, corrupt and inefficient than its predecessor. Chosen in 1985 as the designated successor to the leader, Montazeri in a series of lectures on *velāyat-e faqih* set out to reinterpret this doctrine in order to allow for more popular participation and political freedom.

The fourth chapter will show how Montazeri's intervention against the excesses in the courts and prisons, as well as his enthusiasm for the export of the revolution, regularly brought him into conflict with other institutions of the regime. When in 1986 his opponents intervened to cut back his power and to bring him under control, his longtime friend and mentor Khomeini refused his support. This considerably damaged their relations and embittered Montazeri. When in the summer 1988 he criticised the massacres in the country's prisons, and the following winter publicly called for the liberalisation of the system, he was deposed from his post.

Montazeri was not the only former revolutionary to be alarmed by the regime's evident failure to fulfil its promises, religion's loss of influence in society and the increasing politicisation of religion. When the pragmatists and conservatives in 1992 redrew the rules and limits of the political field to the disadvantage of the Islamic left,[13] this led a growing number of clerics, politicians and intellectuals to consider options for reform. The fifth chapter will focus on the debate regarding the understanding of religion and its relationship to politics as well as on the autonomy of the religious field which emerged in the following years.

The election of Mohammad Khatami as president in 1997 demonstrated the level of popular support for the reformers. However, as they did not control central positions of power they were unable to implement their programme. The resulting structural paralysis of the political field once again proved that legitimacy can indeed be divorced from power. When Montazeri challenged the religious authority of Ayatollah Ali Khamene'i in a speech 1997 and urged the President to confront the leader, he was placed under strict house arrest for the next five years. That the reformers were unable to prevent the sanctioning of Montazeri foreshadowed their failure.

Finally, the seventh chapter will study the causes and consequences of the rise to power of the principlist faction, before dealing with the controversial re-election of Mahmud Ahmadinejad in 2009. In the protest against the election results, Montazeri once again played a prominent role, and in the months before his death assumed the position of spiritual mentor to the Green Movement. The support for this movement proved the continuing attractiveness of the reformist discourse. Yet, as in the past, the popular legitimacy and discursive superiority of the reform movement could not prevent its repression.

# CHAPTER 1

# MONTAZERI'S PATH INTO POLITICS

## Social Modernisation and Other Challenges to Religion

At the time there were few students, and Reza Shah exerted great
pressure on the clerics. They were mistreated and their turbans were
removed. In the seminary of Isfahan, political matters were not
discussed and the students did not read any newspapers [...]. To
read newspapers was not common among the people or the students,
and only some of the senior clerics spoke about politics.

(Montazeri, from his memoirs regarding the situation during
the 1930s)[1]

The prominent role played by the clergy in the opposition to the Shah
in the 1960s and 1970s had been difficult to foresee during the
preceding decades. Disappointed and disillusioned by the failure of the
Constitutional Revolution from 1906 to 1911, which had sought to
replace the absolutist monarchy with a parliamentarian democracy, to
introduce a constitution and to reduce foreign influence, the Shi'ite
clergy had turned its back on politics and returned to its traditional
position of quietism. According to this position, only the Imams have
the legitimacy to rule. In the absence of the Twelfth Imam, who according
to Shi'ite tradition went into hiding in AD 874, all government is
considered illegitimate and the clergy is supposed to abstain from
any participation in politics. This position was notably represented

by Grand Ayatollah Abdolkarim Haeri-Yazdi (1859–1937), who on the invitation of the local clergy in 1922 had moved his seminary to Qom.[2] As the location of the tomb of Imam Reza's sister Fatemeh, this city in the arid plains south of Tehran had formerly been an important teaching centre but it had declined in importance by the 1920s. It was only on the initiative of Haeri-Yazdi that its seminaries were revived and rebuilt. In the following decades, the city attracted an increasing number of scholars and students and eventually eclipsed the other centres of Shi'ite learning such as Najaf, Isfahan or Mashhad. When in 1925 the former cavalry officer Reza Khan deposed the last Qajar ruler and proclaimed himself Shah, he initially maintained a position of polite respect towards the clergy. However, his programme of state-controlled modernisation and centralisation soon led to conflict. Inspired by the policies of the Turkish President Kemal Atatürk, he sought to modernise State and society through the adoption of modern science, technology and bureaucracy as well as certain outward forms of Western customs and culture. Central goals of this programme included the reform of the education sector and the justice system, which were traditionally controlled by the clergy.

In 1928 Reza Shah introduced a reform of the judiciary which profoundly transformed its traditional structures. Although the new code of civil law remained influenced by Islamic law, the penal and criminal law was reworked according to the Western model. Furthermore, the informal religious courts, which until then had played an important role in the judiciary, were abolished and replaced by a system of secular courts under the control of the State. This meant that the clergy not only lost an important source of income, but also one of its central functions: the interpretation of the law and the administration of justice.[3] Reza Shah also introduced a reform of the school system. With the establishment of free secular state schools, the traditional religious school (*maktab*) organised by the local *mullah*, which in most villages and towns had held the monopoly on education, lost its dominant position and was eventually abolished along with other confessional schools. The religious foundations (*waqf*) that had served to finance the schools and other religious institutions were placed under state control and their funds appropriated to finance the new school system.[4] In 1928 Reza Shah also introduced new dress rules. He prohibited the wearing of the veil in public and only allowed those clerics who conformed to the State's definition of this function to wear the traditional garment of the clergy. Prior to this reform, any person could wear a turban and cloak (*abā*) and call himself *mullah*, even if he earned his living as a farmer or trader. Henceforward, only those who had received a religious education and passed an official exam were entitled to this privilege. As recompense they were freed from the compulsory military service which had been introduced in 1925.[5]

These measures, which were violently enforced by the police if necessary, caused much resentment among the clergy who perceived them as an attack on religion and popular tradition. However, neither the State's intrusion into the religious field nor the clergy's loss of funds and important functions in the fields of education and justice led to any organised opposition on the part of the latter. On the one hand this was due to the threats and violence with which Reza Shah enforced his policies.[6] On the other hand, after the chaotic and conflictual period of the Constitutional Revolution many clerics were content to return to their traditional religious functions. Furthermore, if Reza Shah's policies led to the loss of important functions and funds, they also helped define the religious field more clearly. While before it had encompassed a wide range of self-proclaimed clerics and preachers (*rouze khan*), who earned their money leading mourning sessions for Hussein but had little or no religious education, now only those with a formal religious education in the seminaries (*madresse*) were entitled to call themselves *mullah*. Thus, the reforms of Reza Shah helped establish the clergy as a professional group with a hierarchical structure and a formal education.[7]

This was the context when Montazeri first came to Qom in 1935. Born in 1922 in the small rural city of Najafabad, some 30 kilometres north-west of Isfahan, as the eldest son of the peasant Ali Montazeri and Shah-Beigum Sobhani, he attended several religious schools as well as one of the newly founded state schools. On the initiative of his father he started learning Arabic at the age of six. Although a peasant of very modest origin, his father valued religious learning and had himself acquired some religious knowledge under the guidance of the local *mullah*, so that he knew large parts of the Qur'an by heart and sometimes led the Friday prayer in the local mosque. Only 13 years of age upon his arrival in Qom, Montazeri was not eligible for a stipend. However, having answered some questions to the satisfaction of Haeri-Yazdi he did obtain a small allowance, which enabled him to stay for ten months in the city. When this money ran out he was obliged to return to Isfahan, where he continued his studies at the local seminary and obtained a modest stipend. During these initial years his life at the seminary was hard. In the beginning he lived with an elder student who made him do the housework and beat him if he did not do it to his satisfaction. Since his allowance was too small to survive, he was obliged to travel every two weeks to Najafabad to bring back basic provisions from his parents' garden.

> Officially, each of the students obtained a monthly stipend of four silver coins from the school. In reality, however, we only got two silver coins and for the rest I was obliged to make do with the bread, yoghurt and other things I brought from Najafabad,

Montazeri wrote in his memoirs.[8] In the 1930s, the Isfahani seminaries were generally in a difficult financial situation, as income from the religious foundations was sparse and religious donations were mostly sent to Najaf. For students of Montazeri's social origin it was particularly difficult to obtain a good scholarship. Although in principle the religious field valued piety, learning and other personal merits, in reality one's position in the field often depended on genealogical descent. The posts of prayer leader, religious judge or shrine guardian were mostly held by families of clerics and *seyyeds* (descendants of the Prophet), who passed them on from one generation to the next. Related through marriage, these families formed a clerical elite into which it was difficult to penetrate. As Montazeri was not from any of these old families he remained in a marginal position, and it was only as he advanced in his studies that he was able to improve his social and financial position.

During this time, politics were discussed neither in the seminary nor in the mosque. As Montazeri critically remarked, only a few clerics were interested in political and social matters. Many were out of touch with the concerns of the people and, in the seminaries, most avoided discussing questions of current interest. Newspapers were not read among the students, and the radio was still looked upon with curiosity and suspicion.[9] The situation only began to change in 1941 when Reza Shah was forced into exile by the British and the Soviets, who suspected him of harbouring sympathies for the Germans. Under the rule of his son, Mohammad Reza, Iran experienced a decade of relative freedom. The repressive measures against critical newspapers and dissident groups were eased. The young Shah also made efforts to improve relations with the clergy, which had been greatly strained by his father. In 1946 he visited the highly respected Grand Ayatollah Hossein Borujerdi (1875 – 1961) while the latter was in hospital in Tehran, and established a sort of non-intervention agreement.[10] This tacit agreement implied that the State would refrain from meddling in religion as long as the clergy did not intervene in politics. When Borujerdi, upon the invitation of the local clergy, moved his seminary from Borujerd to Qom some months later, he imposed his position of political quietism on all other clerics. After the death of the highly respected cleric Seyyed Abolhassan Musavi-Isfahani in 1946, he advanced to become the supreme religious authority of the Shi'i world. Until his death in 1961, no cleric, with the notable exception of Ayatollah Abolqassem Kashani, dared intervene in politics.

However, not even Borujerdi could prevent the gradual politicisation of the seminaries, and during the following years his position of political quietism was increasingly challenged by the younger students. Although Montazeri had chosen Borujerdi as his *marja'-e taqlid* (source of emulation),[11] he too was discontented with his quietist stance. Having returned to Qom in 1942, Montazeri became increasingly interested in social and political developments. Upon his arrival he had made friends with the young student Morteza Motahhari who was to greatly influence his further intellectual development. Born in 1919 as the son of a cleric near Mashhad, Motahhari was three years older than Montazeri and somewhat more advanced in his studies, but he had also just arrived in Qom. During the 12 years in which they lived and studied together in Qom they not only discussed questions of religion, ethics, law and philosophy but also current social and political matters, and together became acquainted with the world of politics. In their thinking they were profoundly marked by Ayatollah Ruhollah Khomeini, whose courses they attended since their arrival in Qom. Khomeini, who with his teacher, Haeri-Yazdi, had come to Qom in 1922, did not yet count among the most senior clerics, but he was already a renowned scholar and teacher.[12] His evening lectures in ethics and poetry in the Madresse Feiziyeh, adjacent to the shrine of Hazrat Masumeh, were popular among the students but were frowned upon by the traditional clergy, who did not want mysticism, ethics, poetry and philosophy to be taught openly in the seminaries. In their view these subjects were close to the heterodox practices of Sufism and therefore suited only to the more advanced students, who were able to handle the 'dangers' of these questions. For Khomeini, however, the mystical approach to God was the foundation for all ethical and political action. He tried to overcome the traditionalist clergy's scepticism by showing that mysticism (*erfān*) and jurisprudence (*feqh*) are not contradictory, but many remained suspicious of his approach and opposed his teaching.[13]

Montazeri only read ethics (*ekhlāq*) and poetry (*manzume*) with Khomeini, but, as he recalled, all of Khomeini's teachings on philosophy were imbued with his mystical approach. Later, he and other students persuaded Khomeini to also teach jurisprudence (*feqh*) and methodology (*osul*). The first of these courses lasted for seven or eight years and was limited to no more than eight students. Later, he held another series of public lectures on *osul*, which regularly attracted 500 to 600 people.[14] After the lectures Montazeri, Motahhari and some others regularly stayed on to continue their discussions. Twenty years their elder, Khomeini was a stern and for many an intimidating teacher who often answered questions with just one word, so that many dared not pose any questions at all. Montazeri and Motahhari, however, became so close to him that they spent long hours together discussing religion and politics, and regularly accompanied Khomeini, who was fond of walking, on walks along the riverbank. Many other clerics who rose to prominence after the revolution also took part in Khomeini's lectures, but according to Montazeri none were as close as he and Motahhari.[15]

At his arrival in Qom, Montazeri initially lived in one of the cells of the Madresse Feiziyeh. Measuring approximately three by four metres, these rooms on the second storey surrounding the central courtyard are even today only sparsely furnished and mostly shared by several students. Equipped with no more than carpets, thin mattresses and perhaps a shelf for their books, the students here lived an extremely spartan life, which they often only escaped when they married. However, for Montazeri, as for many other students of his social origin and financial situation, it was not easy finding a wife. Moreover, he feared that founding a family would keep him from his studies. His friend Motahhari, however, insisted that a life of celibacy was no good, and during the summer holidays of 1942 they both set out to their respective home towns to find a suitable girl. While Motahhari returned alone from Mashhad, Montazeri eventually found a bride after having consulted the Qur'an.[16] Khadija Soltan Rabbani, as the eldest daughter of an artisan from Najafabad, was, like himself, of modest origin. After their wedding in September 1942, they together returned to Qom where he rented a small room for the two of them.[17]

As Montazeri, like most traditional Muslims, was very discreet about the female members of his household, little is known about his wife. However, she clearly played a substantial role in his life and work, staying by his side throughout the long years of exile and house arrest until his death. Over the years they had four daughters and three sons.[18] Their first son, Mohammed, was born in February 1945 followed by their daughters, Esmat in June 1947 and Eshraf in July 1951. In April 1955, their second son, Ahmad, was born, followed by Tahere in May 1960, Sa'id in August 1962 and finally their daughter Sa'ide in June 1968. All four daughters completed secondary school and Sa'ide also obtained a bachelor's degree in arts and literature. The three sons studied *feqh* and *osul* at the seminaries in Qom – in the case of Ahmad, after receiving a diploma in textile engineering at Amir Kabir University in Tehran.[19] Montazeri not only influenced his sons in the choice of their studies, but also left his mark on their political convictions. Mohammad, especially, engaged early on at the side of his father in the protests against the Shah and later played a major role of his own in the struggle, while Ahmad and Sa'id in their later years had an important part in publishing and distributing their father's writings.

In his first years in Qom, Montazeri not only studied with Khomeini but also attended the courses of Borujerdi. Although Borujerdi was recognised by the Shi'i clergy as the supreme religious authority, or *marja'-e taqlid-e 'ämme*,[20] he was cautious not to anger the other senior clerics and hesitant to allow innovation. For example, when Montazeri began giving courses in poetry, Borujerdi after a short time asked him to close them down. It eventually emerged that he had been pressured by traditionalist clerics in Mashhad who disapproved of public lectures on poetry and philosophy.[21] Borujerdi was also hesitant to allow urgently needed changes in the organisation of the seminaries. Although the number of students had risen from 800 to 3,000 since his arrival in Qom, the curriculum remained largely unchanged and was therefore increasingly unsuited to the growing number of students and to the rapidly changing world. The seminaries lacked publications to disseminate Islamic thinking and teaching, and students speaking foreign languages who could be sent abroad to preach and proselytise. Only slowly were new schools founded, new publications created and elements of the curriculum reformed. As part of these reforms official exams were introduced, which all students had to pass in order to obtain a stipend. In 1952, Borujerdi asked Khomeini and two other clerics to elaborate a plan for a more far-reaching reform, but after a short time withdrew this order. Motahhari, who had also developed ideas for a reform of the seminaries, believing that the reform of Islam must begin with the reform of the clergy, left for Tehran frustrated by the failure of this project and the general immobility of the seminaries.

During the 1950s, the clergy were worried about the growing social and political influence of the Baha'i, whom they considered apostates. They were particularly concerned that the Shah allowed numerous Baha'i to enter the administration and to rise to important positions. For Borujerdi the fight against this creed was a top priority, and during the holidays of Ramadan and Moharram he regularly sent his students to the towns and villages to preach against it. As Montazeri had studied the works and writings of the Baha'i, he played an important role in this campaign. When he was sent to Najafabad to agitate against them in 1955, he asked Borujerdi how Muslims should behave towards them. In his response, Borujerdi declared that Muslims should respect the law and maintain peace but that otherwise they should refrain from any contact with Baha'i. Montazeri disseminated this fatwa widely in Najafabad and convinced the representatives of several guilds to sign a declaration that they would no longer serve Baha'i. Thus, drivers refused to take them on their buses and bakers declined to sell them bread. The climate in Najafabad eventually became so hostile that the Baha'i were forced to go into hiding. However, when Montazeri disseminated Borujerdi's fatwa in Isfahan, the clergy and the people refused to act against the Baha'i. While initially the Shah tolerated the campaign against the Baha'i in return for Borujerdi's acceptance of his plan to join the Central Treaty Organisation (Cento), which was criticised by the nationalists, he eventually intervened to put a stop to the campaign.[22] Following complaints from Najafabad, Montazeri was summoned by the Isfahani governor, who vowed to put him on trial should he continue his campaign. Although Montazeri threatened to stir up the masses against the Baha'i, he was forced to end his agitation.[23]

Another question that worried the clergy at this time was the increasing influence of the communists. The Tudeh Party, which had been founded in September 1941 after the exile of Reza Shah, was considered by pious Muslims a threat to the traditional order of society due to its openly anti-religious and anti-clerical line. Borujerdi and the traditional clergy condemned the party as an enemy of God, but Montazeri and other politicised clerics took a more moderate position, as they saw it as a potential ally in their fight against the Shah.[24] The clergy's position towards the Jebh-e Melli (National Front) led by the landowner and aristocrat Mohammad Mosaddegh (1882–1967) was marked by the same ambivalence. While most of the clergy kept their distance from his nationalist government when he was elected prime minister in 1951, a small group around the influential politician Ayatollah Abdolqassem Kashani (1882–1962) actively supported his policies. Kashani notably welcomed the highly popular nationalisation of the Anglo-Iranian Oil Company, and when Mosaddegh was forced to resign in the ensuing conflict he called for a demonstration which significantly contributed to Mosaddegh's return to power. Montazeri had been introduced to Kashani during a visit to Tehran, and during the following years regularly returned to his house to discuss matters of religion and politics. However, he was careful to keep this contact from being known to Borujerdi who did not approve of clerics engaging in politics. For this reason, Montazeri also declined when the people of Najafabad asked him and Motahhari if they could place them on Kashani's list for the parliamentary elections.[25]

By 1953, the international sanctions imposed after the nationalisation of the oil industry had provoked an economic crisis in Iran which led to rising unemployment and growing discontent. Because of differences on the influence of communism and the place of Islam in politics, Kashani broke with Mossadeq. When in August 1953 the British and American secret services organised a military coup to overthrow Mossadeq's government, Kashani organised large demonstrations in support of the measure. The coup was also supported by the Fedaiyan-e Eslam, a militant Islamist group inspired by the Egyptian Muslim Brothers. The group had been founded in 1946 by the young radical cleric Navab Safavi (1924–55),[26] who had risen to fame when, possibly under the influence of Khomeini, he had murdered the Iranian historian and religious reformer Ahmad Kasravi in March 1946 in Tehran. In Qom the group had considerable support among the seminary students, of whom 1,000 to 1,500 regularly attended its meetings. Safavi's influence among the younger students eventually rose to such a point that they no longer

listened to Borujerdi. Even Khomeini, who sympathised with the
Fedaiyan-e Eslam, felt that things had spiralled out of control. Motahhari
tried to persuade Safavi to temper his rhetoric in order not to further
alienate the leadership of the seminary, but his words were to no avail.[27]
In November 1955, Safavi and other leaders of the Fedaiyan-e Eslam were
arrested by the police during a meeting in the Madresse Feiziyeh of Qom
and, after a brief trial, executed in January 1956. Although Borujerdi had
on another occasion loudly protested against the arrest of a student and
claimed the right of the clergy to try their own members in a special
court, his protest against the arrest in the Feiziyeh was rather muted. As
Montazeri remarked, revolutions are never supported by the upper
classes.[28] Because Khomeini, Motahhari and Montazeri had been in
contact with Safavi, Borujerdi suspected them of supporting the
Fedaiyan-e Eslam. When Motahhari, on his departure to Tehran in 1952,
wrote a letter to Borujerdi, the marja' refused to accept it, to Motahhari's
dismay.[29] On another occasion, Khomeini accompanied a friend to
Borujerdi's house to deliver donations he had received on his behalf.
When after several hours Borujerdi had still not admitted them to his
chambers, Khomeini left in a fury, swearing never to return. Until
Borujerdi's death in 1961 Khomeini never again set foot in his house.[30]

## The Failed 'Revolution' of 1963

> Be assured that your violation of the Islamic principles, the
> Constitution and the laws of parliament will make you and
> the present government responsible to God, the Muslim people
> and the law. Introducing women to parliament, the provincial
> assemblies and the municipal councils is against the principles of
> Islam. According to the Constitution these are laid out in the
> statements of the olamā and the fatwas of the marāje'. No others
> have the right to intervene in these matters.
>
> (Khomeini, in a telegram to the government of
> 20 October 1962)[31]

The death of Borujerdi in March 1961 marked a turning point for the
clergy and its relationship with the State. Until then, this had largely
been characterised by mutual toleration: as long as the State did not

interfere in the affairs of the clergy, the clergy also refrained from any interference in politics. However, after Borujerdi's death the clergy lacked an authority willing and capable of ensuring the continuing respect for this agreement. At the time of his death, there was no *marja'-e taqlid* in Iran or Iraq who could pretend to his position of *marya'iyat-e 'āmme*, and thus the *marja'iyat* was again divided, with each city and each province choosing its own source of emulation. In Qom the most senior clerics were the Grand Ayatollahs Mohammad Reza Golpayegani, Kazem Shariatmadari and Shahboddin Mar'ashi-Najafi, while Khomeini had little support. As Montazeri recalled, when on the evening after Borujerdi's burial he went to Khomeini's house to say the evening prayers not a single visitor came to express his support for Khomeini's claim to the *marja'iyat*. According to Montazeri, Khomeini at this time had no ambition to become a *marja'-e taqlid* and although his students insisted that he publish a *resāle-ye amali-ye* (religious treatise)[32] and hand out stipends to them, he remained relatively unknown outside the closed circles of the clergy. Until 1963 he was only recognised as a *marja'-e taqlid* in some small cities such as Najafabad and Rafsanjan, and it was only during the clergy's protests against the reforms of the Shah that he came to be known to the wider public.[33]

In 1961, Prime Minister Ali Amini announced the creation of provincial and regional assemblies in an attempt to decentralise power. As in the view of the clergy these assemblies were not in conformity with the laws of Islam, they fiercely opposed the bill. In the ensuing campaign, Khomeini for the first time actively engaged in politics. When the clergy wrote a letter of protest to the Shah, Khomeini sent a separate harshly worded telegram. In his reply, the Shah did not mention Khomeini in the hope of isolating him among the clergy, but this omission only contributed to his fame.[34] The opposition from the clergy eventually forced the government to withdraw the bill. However, in January 1963 the Shah called for a referendum on a more far-reaching reform – which was later propagated as the 'White Revolution'. The six-point programme included land reform, privatisation of industries, nationalisation of forests, profit sharing for workers, a literacy campaign and an electoral law that included voting rights for women.[35] Although female suffrage was perceived as being contrary to Islam and the proposed land reform directly affected numerous clerics, many were hesitant to oppose the programme. Their campaign against the provincial and regional assemblies had proved that the clergy could achieve their objectives if they remained united. However, many feared that the State would not back down on this project, which the Shah himself (rather than his prime minister) had proposed. Many were also afraid that they would alienate the peasants should they oppose land reform. As Montazeri noted, the clergy found it difficult to explain to the people why they should oppose a more egalitarian distribution of land and a campaign to provide healthcare and to spread literacy in rural areas.[36] In a cunning but somewhat opportunistic move, Khomeini therefore instructed his students not to preach against the land reform but only against the referendum, which Khomeini considered an illegitimate innovation. Ayatollah Ahmad Khonsari, who had not heeded this advice and had preached against the land reform, was subsequently attacked in the bazaar in Qom, presumably by angry peasants.[37] Although it can be assumed that Khomeini was honestly opposed to the reforms for religious reasons, it appears that he also perceived them as a welcome pretext for continuing the protests.

Montazeri was one of the most active members of the movement that during the following months set out to mobilise the students and organise the protests. On the initiative of the students, the four leading clerics – i.e. the Grand Ayatollahs Shariatmadari, Golpayegani, Mar'ashi-Najafi and Khomeini – agreed to meet once a week for tea to coordinate further steps. As Montazeri recalls, a visitor from Najaf was surprised to find all four leaders united in one room, as in Najaf quarrels and rivalries were common among the *marāj'e*. Among Montazeri's fellow activists were many clerics who later rose to prominence during the revolution. According to Montazeri, the most important activists besides himself were Abdolrahim Rabani-Shirazi, Ahmad Azari-Qomi and Hashemi-Taqriba. Ali Khamene'i and Ali Akbar Hashemi-Rafsanjani also belonged to the inner circle.[38] Montazeri, at 41 years of age, was among the most senior of these men. During this period, two separate groups of young clerics were formed in Qom and in Tehran to elaborate a plan for a reform of the seminary system. The first group, in Tehran, was composed of some of the most progressive clerics of the time, counting Motahhari, Mohammad Beheshti, Mahmud Taleqani and Allameh Mohammad-Hossein Tabataba'i as well as the layman Mehdi Bazargan among its members. In January 1963, the group published *Bahsi darbare-ye marja'iyat va ruhaniyat (A Discussion on Marja'iyat and the Clergy*), in which they outlined their plan for a reform of the seminary system as a first step towards a comprehensive Islamic reform of society.[39] The main theses of the book were: centralising the financial resources of the clergy; placing a greater focus on ethics, ideology and philosophy in the seminary; forming a central committee of mojatheds for issuing fatwas; encouraging the specialisation of the *marāj'e-ye taqlid*; propagating Islam as a comprehensive social and political system; developing *ejtehād* as an instrument for adapting Islam to the changing circumstances; and reviving the injunction to enjoin good and prohibit evil. All of these measures were designed to strengthen the clergy relative to the State, and to transform it into an efficient instrument for the reform of society.[40] The second group was founded by 11 young clerics in Qom with a similar objective. Among them were Montazeri, Rabani-Shirazi, Azari-Qomi, Rafsanjani, Ali Meshkini, Ali Khamene'i with his brother Mohammad, and Mohammad-Taqi Mesbah-Yazdi as the group's secretary. Mohammad Khamene'i wrote a 45-page manifesto in which he outlined their plan for reform. This paper was distributed to the whole group, but after the arrest of several of its members it fell into the hands of the Savak, the Shah's intelligence service, who used it in court against them.[41]

In spite of the clergy's protests, the referendum was held as planned in January 1963. The reforms were accepted with a large majority, and although the political clergy and other opposition groups accused the regime of having manipulated the vote they could not prevent the implementation of the measures.[42] Despite this setback the clergy continued its protest, which by now was no longer directed against the reforms but against the regime itself. In the months following the referendum the situation became ever more tense, and on the Iranian new year on 22 March 1963 the conflict finally came to a head. As Montazeri recalls, when in the morning he went to visit Khomeini in his house, the atmosphere in Qom was tense and thousands of policemen were posted in the streets. In this year, Golpayegani had decided to hold the prayers commemorating the death of Imam Sadeq not at his house but in the Madresse Feiziyeh. Thus, in the evening thousands of mourners assembled in the courtyard of the seminary to attend the prayers. During the ceremony violence erupted between the students and the police. No casualties were confirmed, but a large number of students were injured and the building was considerably damaged. This apparently premeditated attack was an unprecedented humiliation for the clergy. However, many clerics feared an even more violent reaction from the State should they not remain silent, and Shariatmadari asked Khomeini to refrain from any provocative action. However, Khomeini issued a strongly worded declaration condemning the attack.

During the following months he continued to agitate against the State, and on Ashura' (3 July) the conflict reached its climax when Khomeini in a fiery speech in the Feiziyeh compared the Shah to Imam Hossein's enemy, Yazid. The regime, Khomeini said, under the influence of the agents of Israel was opposing religion and its representatives, which it had violently attacked in the Feiziyeh. In a direct attack on the head of state, Khomeini warned the Shah that should he continue on this path, he would end up like his father, who had been forced to leave the country: 'I advise you wretched, miserable 45-year-old man, to stop and ponder a little. These people prefer to brand you as a Jew, in which case I am required to declare you an infidel. Then you will be kicked out of the country.'[43] Early on the morning of 5 July, Khomeini was arrested in Qom and taken to Tehran along with two other clerical leaders. On receiving this news the mourning processions in Tehran turned violent, with protests quickly spreading to Kashan, Shiraz and other cities. They could only be contained through massive use of force, which reportedly left several hundred dead. Although the protests were sparked by Khomeini's arrest, their causes lay just as much in the discontent of the poor classes, which had not profited from the recent boom and were now suffering from a faltering economy and rising inflation.[44]

When Montazeri, who usually spent the month of Moharram in Najafabad, was informed of Khomeini's arrest, he organised a sit-in in the mosque of the bazaar. Every evening for seven days large crowds assembled in the mosque to listen to the speeches of the clergy. The protests provoked the fury of the police, but they did not dare storm the assembly and arrest Montazeri for fear of provoking riots and bloodshed in Najafabad. It was only after a week that Montazeri, on the request of Shariatmadari, finally called off the protests.[45] After the bloody repression of renewed protests in Qom and Tehran, it was rumoured that the regime was planning to take Khomeini to court and sentence him to death. This would have been a heavy blow to the entire clergy, and a large number of senior clerics began to assemble in Tehran. While they were still unsure how to proceed, Montazeri drafted a declaration with

Ebrahim Amini and Morteza Teherani for the other clerics to sign. Because they were not sure that everyone would agree to the harshly worded text, they also prepared a shorter and more moderate telegram. During a meeting they appealed to the assembled clerics to make their protest public, but, as they had foreseen, the clerics found the declaration too strong. Montazeri then read out the telegram they had prepared. As it was addressed to the 'honoured marja'-e taqlid Grand Ayatollah Ruhollah Khomeini' the clerics objected that Khomeini had no right to this title, but Montazeri explained that the idea was to show that Khomeini had the clergy's full support. Moreover, as a *marja'-e taqlid* he could not be executed according to the constitution. After this meeting Montazeri, Amini and Teherani went to the *madresse* where Shariatmadari was residing and managed to convince him also to sign the declaration. As an agent of the Savak was present at the meeting, Montazeri was arrested upon leaving the seminary, but having foreseen his arrest he had passed the declaration to Amini. The police thus had no evidence against him and after a brief interrogation set him free. Other activists brought the declaration to the telegraph office where they forced an officer to send the text.[46] Shariatmadari and three other *maraje'-ye taqlid* later sent another letter of protest in which they once again addressed Khomeini as a source of emulation. In August 1963 he was finally set free and after several months under house arrest in Tehran he returned to Qom in April 1964.

According to the regime Khomeini had promised not to interfere in politics again, but he quickly shattered all hope that he would keep quiet when after a meeting with families of the victims of the Ashura' riots he delivered another scathing speech against the Shah. In the following months, Khomeini's main theme of agitation became a treaty that guaranteed immunity to all members of the US forces in Iran in return for a $200 million loan from the USA. When the text of this controversial treaty was leaked to Khomeini, Montazeri and other politically active clergy, they immediately launched a protest campaign. This culminated on 27 October in a speech in which Khomeini decried the treaty as a humiliation to Iran, which he claimed was being reduced to the status of a colony. The document, so he declared, was contrary to Islam and therefore without any validity. Its consequence would be that if an American cook ran over the Shah he would have immunity, whereas if the Shah ran over an American dog he could be put on trial.[47]

This speech was disseminated throughout the country by activists of the movement, and several thousand copies were distributed to houses of the members of the elite and the army, which particularly infuriated the regime. On 4 November 1964, Khomeini was once again arrested and directly deported to Turkey.

This time his arrest provoked little reaction among the clergy or the people. The violent suppression of the Ashura' protests had already led many to distance themselves from the movement, and in the end few were willing to risk their position by protesting against the regime. Although Montazeri spoke of their movement as a revolutionary one, the events of 1963 were not an attempted revolution. The political clergy around Khomeini neither had the intention of overthrowing the Shah nor had they a concept for an alternative system. Even during his speech of 3 June, Khomeini emphasised his support for the constitution.[48] He did not yet have a clear plan for an Islamic state, and his only concrete proposal was that the responsibility for national education and the religious foundations be given back to the clergy and that they receive a few hours' radio airtime per week.[49] The riots following his second arrest were more out of discontent about the economic crisis and in protest against an attack on the clergy than in support of an Islamic state. It was only during his exile to Najaf that Khomeini elaborated his theory of *velāyat-e faqih*, which became the core of the post-revolutionary system.

## The Idea of an Islamic State

> This slogan of separation of religion from politics and the demand that Islamic scholars should not intervene in social and political affairs have been formulated and propagated by the imperialist, it is only the irreligious who repeat them. Were religion and politics separate in the time of the Prophet? Did there exist on one side a group of clerics and opposite a group of politicians?
>
> (Khomeini, in *Velayat-e faqih*)[50]

Khomeini developed his theory on the Islamic state in the first months of 1970 during a series of lectures in Najaf, and later published it under the title *Velayat-e faqih* (*Governance of the Jurisprudent*). This theory was a radical departure from the traditional quietist position of the clergy, which holds that in the absence of the Twelfth Imam all government is illegitimate and that the clergy should refrain from participating in politics. Khomeini not only declared that even in the absence of the Imam the Islamic laws must be applied, but also that the clergy as the supreme guardian of religion has the right to assume power and to govern society. This theory was a bold reinterpretation of the scriptures, as no cleric had yet dared to claim power for the clergy. However, the role of religion in politics and the clergy's relationship with the State had long been a matter of controversy. Khomeini himself had addressed these questions in *Kashf al-Asrar* (*The Revealing of Secrets*), which was anonymously published in 1942.[51] This often highly polemical book was penned in refutation of the writings of the religious reformer Ali Akbar Hakamizadeh as well as Ahmad Kasravi and Reza Qoli Shariati Sangilaji, who had denounced the clergy as an obstacle to reform.[52] In the book, Khomeini railed against a society in which theatre, cinema, dance and alcohol have become widespread, criticising in particular the idea that 'the elevation of the state is achieved by undressing the women in the streets.' He mocked those 'whose mind and intellect have been stolen by the foreigners' to the point that they even imitate their daily routine and who believe that the world's respect can be won by wearing a certain hat, not realising how the foreigners laugh at their childish behaviour while carrying away the riches of the country.[53] Turning to politics, Khomeini emphasised that it is universally recognised that man needs laws and a ruler to enact them. However, nobody but God has the right to rule over someone else or to pass a law. It is His laws alone, which encompass regulations for all aspects of human life from the cradle to the grave, that man must obey. In order to govern a state by reason and justice it must be governed according to the divine law of Islam, Khomeini asserted. In order to ensure the correct implementation of its laws during the time of the occultation of the Mahdi, the State must be supervised by the most qualified jurists.[54] This, he emphasised, does not mean that the jurists themselves assume the administration of the State:

> That the government must be in the hands of a faqih does not mean that the faqih must become king, minister, general, soldier and sweeper, but he must have supervision over the legislative and

executive power of the Islamic state [...]. We say that the
constitutive assembly (majles-e mo'assesāni) which is set up to
found a state or reform a regime must be composed of highstanding
enlightened foqahā and mullahs [...] so that in the choice of a king
the interests of the country and the masses be taken into account and
a justice-seeking shah, obeying to the laws of the land, which are
those laws of God, be elected.[55]

For Khomeini there was no objection to a king ruling the State provided
that he ruled in accordance with Islam. In his view the clergy should have
a central role in choosing the king and in supervising the government,
but they should not assume power themselves. 'We do not say that the
government must lie in the hands of the faqih but we say that the state
must be administered by the law of God [...]. This will not be realised
without the supervision of the clergy as it was ordained by the
constitutional government.'[56] What Khomeini had in mind basically
resembled a constitutional monarchy under the supervision of a clerical
council, as laid out in the constitution of 1906. This position was close to
Borujerdi's view on the political role of the clergy. According to the script
of a lecture series compiled by Montazeri in February 1950, Borujerdi
argued that the jurists, as God's appointed representatives, should in the
absence of the Imam exercise collective guardianship (velāyat-e entesābi
'āmme foqahā) over the people. They have the duty to ensure respect of the
Islamic precepts, which are valid irrespective of time and place and hence
must be applied even in the absence of the Imams. However, Borujerdi's
ideas on this topic remained theoretical and he stopped short of advocating
that the jurists themselves assume an active role in politics.[57]

    At this time, even the Fedaiyan-e Eslam did not call for the rule of
the clergy and only accorded them a role of guidance. In their utopian
vision of an Islamic state, published in 1950 under the title Barname-ye
enqelabi-ye Fedaiyan-e Eslam, the radical Islamist group rejected the idea
of a separation of politics and religion in the absence of the Imam.
However, they accepted the Shah as the 'father of the nation' as long as he
adhered to the precepts of Islam. Thus, their concept of an Islamic state
also basically consisted of a monarchy governed by a just king who
respects the precepts of Islam and is guided by the clergy.[58] Khomeini
for the first time publicly spoke about the role of Islam in politics during
a series of lectures on osul, which was edited by Montazeri in May 1951.

Like Borujerdi he emphasised that the laws of Islam are not limited to questions of personal conduct and ritual practice, but rather concern all aspects of social life from birth to death. In his view the social and political order laid out in the scriptures cannot simply be put aside. In the absence of the Imams the jurists are appointed to assure the application of the law. However, Khomeini at this time too stopped short of calling for the clergy to assume power.[59]

The attempts at this time to develop an Islamic system were marked by the desire to create an authentic alternative to the modernist state of the Shah, which was perceived as a Western imposition alien to Iranian culture. The concern over the increasing political and cultural influence of the United States in the 1950s led to the emergence of a nativist discourse marked by an essentialising view of the West and its rejection as 'the ultimate other'.[60] One of the central figures of this discourse was the intellectual Jalal Al-e Ahmad (1923–69), who in a polemical essay in 1962 coined the term *Gharbzadegi* ('Weststruckness'), which became the rallying cry for a whole generation worried about cultural alienation and political domination.[61] In this pamphlet Al-e Ahmad decried the infatuation of many Iranians with the West and their uncritical imitation of Western culture.[62] Seeking to develop an alternative to the alien other, Al-e Ahmad and other intellectuals turned to Islam, which they perceived as the source of an authentic identity. They understood Islam as the central element of their national culture, which the State had the duty to preserve and protect against foreign influence. In this sense they were cultural nationalists rather than Islamists who approved of an Islamic state or the rule of the clergy as imagined in the theory of *velāyat-e faqih* developed by Khomeini in 1970.

Khomeini's lectures on this issue went well beyond all earlier writings on this issue. In the introduction to these lectures he reiterated his belief that Islam presents a comprehensive system of laws, norms and practices that govern all affairs of society. As this body of laws is not sufficient to ensure the reform of society it needs to be implemented by an Islamic government. This task was delegated to the Prophet during his lifetime and after his death to the Imams as his rightful successors, Khomeini declared.

A body of laws alone is not sufficient for a society to be reformed. In order for law to ensure the reform and happiness of man, there must be an executive power and an executor. For this reason, God Almighty, in addition to revealing a body of law (i.e. the ordinances of the shari'a), has laid down a particular form of government together with executive and administrative institutions [...]. It is self-evident that the necessity for the enactment of the law which necessitated the formation of a government by the Prophet, was not confined or restricted to his time, but continues after his departure from this world.[63]

Khomeini argued that Islamic precepts were not meant to be put aside in the time of occultation. To be able to live by the rules of Islam it is necessary to replace a secular regime with an Islamic government. All true believers have the duty, Khomeini wrote, 'to overthrow all treacherous, corrupt, oppressive and criminal regimes'.[64] Because in the absence of the Imam no particular individual has been appointed by God to govern society, the question arises who should assume this task, Khomeini wrote. His answer is both simple and radical: as the government should be based on the laws of Islam, those most qualified to interpret the law should govern the State, i.e. the *foqahā*, or Islamic jurists. Rather than merely serve as consultants to the ruler, 'the true rulers are the foqahā themselves, and rulership ought to be theirs, to apply to them, not to those who are obliged to follow the guidance of the foqahā on account of their own ignorance of the law'.[65] In a radical reinterpretation of the scriptures, Khomeini declared that the *foqahā* are not only the guardians of widows and orphans, as is traditionally assumed, but that their guardianship extends to the whole of society: 'With respect to duty and position, there is indeed no difference between the guardian of a nation and the guardian of a minor.'[66] Based on various passages from the hadith, Khomeini laid out why the *foqahā* must be considered the sole legitimate successors to the Prophet and why it is their duty not only to interpret but also to implement the religious laws. In his view, only then can they be considered the guardians of Islam. While Khomeini was clear about the necessity of the *foqahā* assuming government, he remained somewhat vague on the form that this government should take. At one point he wrote that the *foqahā* should merely *supervise* the functioning of government, while at other times he referred to them as the leaders and rulers of society. Clearly he had only little knowledge of the reality of a modern state and cited Imam Ali, who governed the State from a corner of a mosque, as an example to imitate. He also somewhat naively talked of the *foqahā* raising taxes and punishing criminals as if they were personally responsible for the task.[67] However, his plan for assuming power was set. He exhorted all students and clerics not to fear prison and death, and to engage in propaganda to undermine the legitimacy of the regime and to spread the message of 'true Islam'. Opposed to violence, Khomeini advocated a tactic of passive resistance and civil disobedience:

> Let us overthrow tyrannical governments by: (1) severing all relations with government institutions; (2) refusing cooperation with them; (3) refraining from any action that might be construed as aiding them; and (4) creating new judicial, financial, economic, cultural and political institutions.[68]

Khomeini's interpretation of *velāyat-e faqih* was later criticised by many scholars as an illegitimate innovation and even today is still not accepted by most traditional clerics. In 1971, Khomeini's lectures were published under a pseudonym in a small booklet, copies of which were smuggled into Iran and circulated among the population. As many Iranians could not read, Khomeini and the other politically active clerics also used cassettes with recordings of their speeches and lectures to be played in the informal religious meetings (*hey'at*) of the popular classes during which religious, social and political questions were discussed under the guidance of a mullah.[69] However, it remains a matter of controversy to what extent his theory was known to the public before the revolution. Whereas some scholars maintain that his tapes and books were widely disseminated in Iran, others deny that his theory was known to a wider public. Furthermore, the book was remarkably absent in 1979 during the discussion about the future form of the State. As will be shown later, even though the concept of *velāyat-e faqih* quickly became the central point in the debate, Khomeini's book was only mentioned once during the 67 sessions of the constitutional assembly. Generally, the importance of Khomeini's writings and their role in the political and religious discourse of the 1960s and 1970s should not be overstated. During this time the group around Khomeini was just one among many political groups, and its later rise to power was neither foreseeable nor inevitable.

## The Clergy in the Opposition to the Shah

As a result of the abnormal ways of the anti-national governments,
the situation of the Muslims has come to the point that a popular
marja' cannot publicly speak about the sacred commandments and
defend the people's freedom and the country's independence, and is
sent into exile for more than one year for the crime of protesting
against the despised capitulation.

(Letter by Montazeri and other clerics to
Prime Minister Hoveyda)[70]

The movement of the political clergy which had emerged during the
anti-reform protests in 1963 was a loosely organised and informally
structured group of mainly younger clerics. It lacked the formal
structure and hierarchy of a political party, it had no regular meetings,
no formal membership and no written statutes, and it never discussed or
published a political programme. The inner circle of the movement
consisted of politically inclined junior clerics close to Khomeini, who
had mostly first engaged in politics during the protests of 1963. While
Motahhari at the age of 45, Montazeri at 42 and Beheshti at 36 were
already respected scholars and teachers, Rafsanjani (30), Khamene'i (25)
and many others were still quite young and not yet very advanced in
their studies. As the movement had few material or social benefits to
offer, their commitment had idealistic rather than materialistic motives.
Not only was success far from assured, but during the initial years the
survival of the movement itself was in question. By the time of Khomeini's
second arrest and deportation in November 1964 the movement had
lost much of its initial support among the people, who were reluctant
to engage in further protests. Although the arrest of a leading cleric
was a humiliation to the clergy, many in Qom were relieved to be rid of
this troublemaker. Shariatmadari and Golpayegani, who had earlier
warned Khomeini to temper his rhetoric, possibly felt that he had only
received what he had asked for.

    For Montazeri and the other activists, one of the main preoccupations
at this time was to assure that Khomeini's stipends continued to be paid.
Stipends were the main instrument to bind students to a source of
emulation, and if they no longer received this money they turned to
another *marja'-e taqlid* for support. In addition to raising money, the

students tried to keep the memory of Khomeini alive. In 1965, Montazeri and Meshkini organised a meeting in the Feiziyeh to protest against his exile. Later they also tried to persuade Shariatmadari to hold a strike, but he refused.[71] While Khomeini was still in Turkey, Montazeri secretly travelled to Najaf to persuade Ayatollah Mohsen al-Hakim, who was the leading *marja'-e taqlid* in Iraq at the time, to recognise Khomeini as a source of emulation. Although Hakim remained suspicious, Montazeri's initiative possibly helped smooth the way for Khomeini when he was forced to move from Turkey to Najaf in October 1965. After initial difficulties he managed to establish himself as one of the city's leading clerics. Following his move to Najaf, several dozen clerics and students in Qom on 21 November sent an open letter to Prime Minister Amir Abbas Hoveyda, with Montazeri among the first signees. In this letter they protested against the continuing exile of Khomeini but also criticised the lack of justice, the censoring of the press and the illegal arrests, warning that the people would not tolerate the regime's capitulation to the colonialist powers much longer – all points that the secular opposition would have formulated in much the same way.

> Not a day passes without new terrible and troubling reports coming to the ears of the people. The doors of the prisons and torture chambers are open, while the courts are closed to those demanding justice. The nation has no knowledge of the government's daily dealings. Against the will of the police nothing appears in the newspapers. Group by group, the people are condemned to death, exile and long prison sentences of which the people hear no news [...]. This is the meaning of freedom in the democratic state of Iran. It is true that problems also exist in other countries, but there is an obvious difference between governments who fight colonialism for the sake of their people and governments who fight their people for the sake of colonialism. Mr Hoveyda, the Iranian nation cannot sit silent while a marja'-e taqlid and his religious followers are exiled and other national leaders placed under arrest.[72]

After his arrival in Najaf, Khomeini sent Montazeri a letter in which he appointed him as his official representative in Qom in charge of his administrative and religious affairs.[73] He also appointed Motahhari, Beheshti, Mohammad Javad Bahonar, Khamene'i and Rafsanjani as his representatives. In this function they were responsible for the collection of donations, the distribution of stipends and later for helping the families of imprisoned activists. It appears that they acted less on a collective than on an individual basis as it was often difficult to keep in contact, many being in prison or in exile in different and often distant parts of the country.

During the 1960s and 1970s the political clergy was just one opposition group among many, yet it had a number of advantages over its secular rivals. One advantage was that, unlike the leftist parties, the clerics had no difficulty reaching the lower classes and the rural population. They were able to use the vast network of religious schools, seminaries and mosques to disseminate their message – a network that reached down to the most remote of villages. The autonomous structure of the Shi'i clergy, with its own financial resources and a whole network of communication channels, proved well suited for the political and propaganda work of the activists. A second advantage was that the political clergy had at their disposal a language and an imagery familiar to all. In particular, the story of the Battle of Kerbala between the righteous Imam Hussein and the Caliph Yazid offered an imagery that could easily be adapted to the present situation. Every year during the month of Moharram, this legendary fight between good and evil was brought to life by the traditional religious theatre (*tayziyeh*), which was vastly popular among the people. There was no fear of being misunderstood if one denounced the Shah as the new Yazid, as it had become a common rhetoric figure since the Ashura' events of 1963. A third advantage for the political clergy was that, unlike the liberal and leftist groups, they were perceived as defenders of tradition. At a time of rapid social, economic and cultural change, the traditional lifestyle defended by the clergy appealed to many who were perturbed by the modernisation policies of the Shah. His agrarian and economic reforms endangered the livelihood of many peasants, traders, craftsmen and other members of the traditional sectors of society. Many people from rural areas were forced to migrate to the cities to look for work in industry. Only a minority benefited from the reforms, while for most they meant increased insecurity. Adding to this sense of disorientation was the rapid cultural change. The opening of the Iranian economy to foreign investors during the 1960s and 1970s led to the arrival of thousands of Western expatriates. The close cooperation with the USA in political and military affairs brought even more foreign technical and military advisors to the country. Their privileged position caused irritation among Iranians, and their presence brought new cultural influences to the country. Not only were the Islamists alarmed about the loss of influence of Islamic values, but also the nationalists were opposed to what they perceived as a selling-out of Iranian culture.

These aspects partly explain why the political clergy ultimately came to dominate the opposition to the Shah. However, while some scholars argue that no one should have been surprised at the clergy's rise to power, since this was in direct line with the Constitutional Revolution of 1906 and the Islamic uprising of 1963,[74] others maintain that it was neither foreseeable nor inevitable that the clergy would lead what was to become known as the Islamic Revolution.[75] After all, for many years the struggle against the Shah was led by secular groups. Although by the late 1960s the once-dominant Tudeh Party and the Jebh-e Melli had been banned and their members arrested or forced underground,[76] their ideas continued to dominate the political discourse. They enjoyed strong support not only among the urban middle class but also among industrial workers. Notably, in the crucial oil sector the labour movement was deeply rooted and well organised. Although small in number the oil workers were to play a decisive role during the final phase of the revolution when their strikes threatened the regime's main source of revenue. Nationalist and leftist ideas were also dominant in the vocal and highly active student movement as well as among intellectuals. Profiting from the cautious liberalisation during the 1970s, lawyers, journalists, professors and writers set up associations to defend their professional interests and to call for freedom of the press, civil rights and popular participation.[77]

Furthermore, the political clergy were not the only group to lay claim to Islam. Since the 1940s, several lay parties sought to combine leftist and nationalist theories with ideas inspired by Islam. The most influential of these groups was the Nehzat-e Azadi (Freedom Movement). Founded in 1961 by Mehdi Bazargan, Yadollah Sahabi and Ayatollah Mahmud Taleqani, all of whom had for many years been active in the Jebh-e Melli, it was a political party with a religious ideology that advocated a return to the values and principles of Islam as these were considered to be constitutive for the Iranian identity.[78] Although the Nehzat-e Azadi was banned, along with most other parties, and its founding members imprisoned in 1962, its idea of an Islamic but democratic system remained for many among the educated middle class an attractive alternative to the more radical ideas of the political clergy.

During the following years, as all legal political activity was made impossible, a number of more radical and violent groups emerged, the most important of which was the Mojahedin-e Khalq. Founded by young members of the Nehzat-e Azadi in 1965, this radical guerilla group promoted a mixture of Islamist and socialist ideas.[79] Inspired by the military tactics of Che Guevara, it pursued a double strategy of political agitation and terrorist attacks on the regime and its foreign allies. In its ideology, the group was deeply influenced by the Islamist ideologue Ali Shari'ati (1933–77). Born as the son of a politically active former cleric from Mashhad, Shari'ati had, as a student at the Sorbonne, come into contact with the ideas of leftist intellectuals like Frantz Fanon. Combining Shi'i and socialist elements, he sought to transform Islam into a revolutionary ideology capable of mobilising the masses. In 1964, he founded with Motahhari the Hosseiniye Ershad as a progressive religious centre in northern Tehran, and due to his skilled rhetoric and charismatic personality quickly drew large crowds of listeners.[80] Initially Montazeri and other political clerics regarded Shari'ati's efforts to develop a Shi'i liberation theology with sympathy, but his anti-clerical stance in the end led even Motahhari to distance himself from him. Later Motahhari devoted much energy to counter his influence among the students, but his ideas never attracted the same support or influence as Shari'ati's.[81]

As with Shari'ati, the clerics' relationship with the Mojahedin also deteriorated over the years. There were many tactical and ideological differences, and their social background, their intellectual outlook and their view on religion profoundly differed. When in 1975 the majority of the Mojahedin turned their back on Islamism in favour of Marxism the clerics saw this as treason to their cause, and tensions further intensified. The reason for this split was a dispute about the future strategy of the group. By this time the original leadership had been severely reduced by arrests and executions, and it could no longer be denied that it had failed to mobilise the masses.[82] Although it had strong support among university students, its radical ideology, its intellectual discourse and its violent tactics had failed to convince the working class and the rural population. However, the ideological repositioning of the group did not stop its decline and during the following years the Marxist majority was further weakened by internal disputes, while most of the leaders of the Islamist minority were imprisoned in Evin, where they joined the political clerics arrested during the preceding years.

The clerical movement had the advantage that the regime could not close the seminaries or ban prayers, but like all other political groups and parties its members were not safe from arrest. After the repression of the Ashura' protests, almost all members of its inner circle were at one time or another arrested, interrogated and imprisoned. The first wave of repression hit them when on 21 January 1965 Prime Minister Hossein-Ali Manzur was shot on the steps of parliament by a member of the Hey'at-ha-ye motalef-e eslami (Coalition of Islamic Societies). This was an Islamist terrorist group founded by former members of the Fedaiyan-e Eslam after 1963. It was close to the bazaar merchants and well connected to the group around Khomeini. When questioned, the assassin Mohammad Bekhara'i said he had killed Manzur to take revenge for the exile of Khomeini. Due to their close links to the assassins, Rafsanjani, Beheshti, Motahhari and other clerics were arrested after the attack.

One year later, on Nouruz 1966, Montazeri too was arrested in his house in Qom along with his eldest son Mohammad, who had been found distributing tracts. After a brief interrogation he was brought to Qazl Qale prison in Isfahan, where a number of other clerics were already detained.[83] According to his own account, Montazeri was questioned about the organisation of the movement, and when he refused to respond he was whipped and beaten. His son was also badly beaten and burnt so that he suffered severe injuries and damage to his eyes and ears. At times he was tortured in the presence of his father, so as to break the latter's will. The brutality of the interrogations further intensified when, during the search of Azari-Qomi's house, the Savak found the programme on the reform of the seminary which had been written by Mohammad Khamene'i in 1962 and distributed to the members of the group. Upon his arrest, Azari-Qomi gave the Savak the names of all members of the group. Several of them were already in prison, while several others managed to escape. Although Montazeri denied having any knowledge of the programme, he and Rabani-Shirazi were tried by a secret military court and sentenced to three years in prison.[84]

For Montazeri, this first term in prison ended prematurely when in October 1966, after just seven months behind bars, several high-ranking clerics with good relations with the royal court managed to secure his release. However, when, some months later, he returned from a secret trip to Kerbela and Najaf, where he had met Khomeini, he was once again arrested and jailed for three more months. After a brief stay at his home in Qom, Montazeri was then exiled along with other prominent opposition members, as the regime feared that they would use the coronation ceremony of the Shah on 26 October 1967 as an opportunity to stage further protests. In the small town of Masjed-e Soleiman in Khuzestan, where Montazeri was to spend his exile, the governor arranged for him to live in a friend's house. One night his host woke him up because his room had filled with gas from a pipe that had supposedly been repaired during the day. When a few days later his host suffered a heart attack after having received a visit from several officials, Montazeri decided to move to a room in the local mosque. After just 20 days in exile, the officials in Tehran accepted the complaint he had lodged upon his arrest and allowed him to return to his home town of Najafabad.[85]

Yet again, his freedom did not last long. Since he refused to cease his political activities and agitation, the regime sentenced him to three years in custody – later reduced to 18 months – which he passed in Isfahan's Qazr Qale prison. Upon his release in May 1970, he returned to Najafabad, where he introduced a regular Friday prayer, which drew large crowds from the surrounding countryside. He was careful to use simple language that could be understood by the people, and he regularly addressed issues of daily relevance and political interest.[86] At this time Montazeri parted ways with his son Mohammad, who after serving three years in prison had returned to Qom and devoted his time to setting up a network of like-minded students. However, denounced to the Savak in September 1971, Mohammad was forced to flee with the help of smugglers to Pakistan. While for his father the struggle remained a battle against the authoritarian and un-Islamic regime of the Shah, to Mohammad this was only part of the wider struggle of the Third World countries against imperialism and US hegemony. In his quest to establish contacts with other 'freedom movements' he spent the following years veering from Pakistan to Iraq, through the Gulf states and back to Afghanistan, before he finally ended up with Khomeini in Paris.[87]

Meanwhile, Montazeri in Najafabad was confronted with a change in tactics of the Savak, who sought to discredit him as a collaborator by paying him courtesy visits and bringing presents. Its agents tried to persuade him to direct his energy against the Marxists and Baha'i rather than against the regime. When this did not work, they tried to create disunity among the clergy by taking advantage of existing rivalries and disputes. One of these disputes concerned the book *Shahid-e javid* (*The Eternal Martyr*), written by Hojatoleslam Ne'matollah Salehi-Najafabadi in 1969, which offered a radical reinterpretation of the story of Imam Hossein and the Battle of Kerbala. In this book Salehi argued that Imam Hossein had not foreseen his own death, but rather had fought to win. This interpretation of Hossein as an active fighter and not as a passive victim was welcomed by the political clergy, and Montazeri and Meshkini both wrote positive critiques of the book.[88] However, when this became known, they were publicly attacked by the more conservative clerics, who started a fierce campaign. Meshkini was forced to withdraw his critique, but Montazeri refused to change his assessment. In his view the controversy was a plot by the intelligence service to create disunity among the clerics.[89]

After an attack by an Islamist group on a police station, the regime once again stepped up the pressure on the activist clergy. In the summer of 1973, the police rounded up 25 of its leading members in Qom and exiled them for three years to various places within the country. Among those banished were Montazeri, Rabani-Shirazi, Meshkini, Sadeq Khalkhali, Mohammad Yazdi, Mohammad Mo'men and Salehi, most of whom were to play important roles after the revolution. The local governor had left the city on a pretext so as not to sign the orders of exile; consequently, his deputy was forced to sign them.[90] Montazeri was deported to the small desert city of Tabas in Khorasan. On his wish, the governor allowed him to stay in a religious school where he received a small room. It was not long before the local Imam, who for health reasons could not read the morning prayers, asked him to read them in his stead. After a short time, Montazeri also introduced a regular Friday prayer, which quickly drew large crowds from the countryside.

The people of Tabas were generally known to be very religious and respectful of the clergy. As Montazeri remarked, even the policemen were so pious that they turned a blind eye to his political agitation.[91] As an ever-growing number of people came to visit Montazeri in Tabas, the Savak once again arrested him. In the hope that he would find less support there, he was taken to the town of Khalkhal in the Iranian province of Azarbaijan. On the way, according to his own account, he became such good companions with his guards that they stopped by a river to go swimming together. In Khalkhal, however, the situation was different. The population comprised mainly ethnic Azeris who were neither very religious nor very welcoming towards Montazeri. He stayed for four months before being deported to the Sunni town of Saqqez in late autumn 1974.[92]

The period from 1964 to 1973 was the golden age of the Iranian regime, when the economy registered an annual growth of more than 10 per cent. The oil revenues increased from $1.1 billion in 1970 to $17.4 billion in 1974, and brought enormous wealth to the government. Although this wealth was not evenly distributed among social classes and economic sectors, even the traditional economy registered a steady growth.[93] During this time the regime pursued a strategy of political non-intervention, refraining from any interference in the people's affairs as long as they did not openly oppose it. However, things began to change in 1975. Inflation increased and shortages began to occur. At the same time the regime intensified its political reforms, shut down the existing parties and set up as the sole representative of the nation the Hezb-e Rastakhiz (Resurgence Party), which all Iranians were invited to join. However, many were suspicious as the party aimed not only to control the traditional economic sector but also to gain discursive hegemony in the political and religious fields. It called the Shah not only the 'political leader' but also the 'spiritual guide' of the community. The Islamic calender was replaced with one based on the alleged founding date of the Persian monarchy, so that the people suddenly found themselves in the year 2535 instead of the year 1355. The legal age of marriage was raised, a new family code was enforced, the tchador was banned from universities and a 'religion corps' was set up to counter the influence of the clergy. Furthermore, the regime alienated the bazaar merchants by interfering in their structures, imposing new rules and blaming them for the rising inflation.[94]

The clergy was alarmed at these measures, as they threatened its religious and economic position. On 5 July 1975, they organised large demonstrations in Qom and Tehran in commemoration of the Ashura' protests of 1963. These protests led to large-scale riots, which were violently suppressed by the police. In the following weeks the regime once again arrested numerous clerics, among them Montazeri. They raided the house in Saqqez which he had rented for his family, seized all his writings and books and brought him to the notorious Evin prison at the foot of the Elburz Mountains in northern Tehran. After six months without trial he was sentenced by a military court to ten years in prison. In Evin he met numerous members of the Tudeh Party, the Nehzat-e Azadi and the Mojahedin. Initially there were few other clerics in Evin, but over time their number rose to ten – among them Taleqani, Rabani-Shirazi, Rafsanjani, Mohammed Reza Mahdavi-Kani, and Montazeri's son-in-law, Hadi Hashemi. The prisoners organised the cooking, washing and other affairs of everyday life themselves, and could hold meetings as long as they were not political. Thus, Montazeri with Taleqani, whom he admired for his uncompromising piety, held courses on the Qur'an for the other, mostly much younger, clerics. Montazeri also organised a Friday prayer for some weeks.[95]

There were many conflicts with the communists and Mojahedin who were in the same prison block. As neither of these groups respected the religious rules of purity, Montazeri, Taleqani and other clerics refused to have contact with them.[96] At the time, this decision was controversially discussed among the clerics, but in the end the purists prevailed. They were not willing to make compromises on religion for the sake of politics, especially as in their eyes the Mojahedin had become Marxists when they had turned away from their original Islamist ideology in 1975. After the revolution, however, the clerics were accused of having caused a split within the opposition. When in January 1977 the Democrat Jimmy Carter became president of the USA, the Iranian regime came under pressure to allow more political freedom. Consequently, the regime offered to free political prisoners if they promised to abstain from politics and declare their allegiance to the Shah. Although many of the clerics were dispirited by the years in prison and the ideological change on the part of the Mojahedin, according to Montazeri no one from his group accepted the proposition. Nevertheless, as many of the clerics were transferred to other prisons or pardoned, in the end only Montazeri remained with one other cleric in Evin. When Montazeri too was finally released and brought back to Qom on 30 October 1978, the revolution was already in full swing. In total, he had spent more than 12 years in exile or in prison. He had been separated from his family, kept from his studies and had endured many hardships. Although in his memoirs he refers to prison as a class that forced him to confront God and his own self, and which shaped his being and prepared him for life, the hardships he experienced during this time marked him indelibly and made him more sympathetic to the sufferings of other prisoners.

## Conclusion

When Montazeri first entered the seminary, the Iranian clergy kept a careful distance from political affairs. Under pressure from the Shah, they not only withdrew from politics but also largely retreated from society. By the 1940s, the religious field had become closed off from politics as well as from the fields of secular education and modern science. Political questions were not discussed in the seminaries or in the mosques, newspapers were not read, foreign languages were not taught and modern sciences were largely ignored. Although Montazeri had been shaped by the seminaries, he was critical of this system, which in his eyes had become introverted and out of touch with the concerns of the people. Starting in the 1940s, the clergy was faced with a growing number of challenges: on the one hand the increasing influence of the Baha'i religion, communist ideology and Western culture threatened the hegemony of Islam in society; on the other hand the emergence of a number of lay intellectuals challenged the clergy's position as the sole interpreters of religion. While the leading clerics clung to the position of political quietism, which had thus far assured the autonomy of the religious field, a generation of younger clerics advocated a more active engagement in society and politics to counter the loss of influence of religious norms and values. Therefore, the religious field hesitatingly opened up to new ideas and influences: at the seminaries regular exams were introduced, more books were published and a range of magazines and institutions for the propagation of religion were founded. A number of young clerics joined the newly created secular universities to study and teach theology and philosophy, which brought them into contact with new ideas on religion and society. The seminaries in Qom, Isfahan or Mashhad too were increasingly affected by the social and economic changes, and the conflict over the nationalisation of the oil industry led to an unprecedented politicisation of the younger students. At this time, the discourse on religion's relationship with society and politics was as much a discourse on the legitimate interpretation of the scriptures as a discourse over the rules and limits of the discourse itself. Who could take part: could only the clergy participate, or also lay intellectuals such as Kasravi, Safavi, Bazargan and Shari'ati? What could be said: was an activist interpretation of the myth of Kerbala, such as in Salehi's *Shahid-e javid*, legitimate? In what way could it be said: were Khomeini's radical rhetoric or Safavi's militant tactics permissible? And where could it be said: was it to be discussed only in the mosques and seminaries, or also in new institutions such as the Hosseiniye Ershad?

This discourse was conducted as much between clerics and non-clerics as among the clergy itself. The religious field consisted of numerous institutions, groups and individuals, which held often widely diverging opinions on the rules, structures and objectives of the field. The younger generation of politically active students and clerics was highly critical of the traditional clergy, whom they blamed for the current state of religion as much as the regime itself. However, this group of young activist clerics was not one cohesive block, and although they had been influenced by the same events and experiences they did not share the same habitus. While all of them had entered the field of politics during the 1963 protests and shared the experience of exile and prison, some were only young students while others were experienced teachers, and some had remained within the clerical cosmos while others had entered the field of secular education. In Montazeri's case, his primary habitus was still marked by the traditional structures of the religious field as well as his personal experience of material hardship and social marginalisation in his youth. His secondary habitus as an adult was marked by his social and political activities – first against the Baha'i, then against the Shah, and later the long time of exile and prison. In contrast to Motahhari or Beheshti, who had lived in Tehran and Hamburg for many years and who were acquainted with modern society, he was a pure product of the seminaries: his world was the mosques and schools of Qom, Isfahan and Najafabad. By 1978 he was an experienced activist, but above all he was a religious scholar who was more at home in the field of religion than in the field of politics. Nevertheless, when after the revolution he was elected chairman of the Expert Assembly in Tehran, he seized the opportunity, together with Beheshti and others, to ensure the establishment of a system true to the ideal model imagined by Khomeini.

# CHAPTER 2

# THE INVENTION OF A NEW SYSTEM

## The Islamisation of the Political Discourse

I and other political prisoners, who under empty and weak accusations were kept for many years of their life in dark prisons, are indebted to the Muslim nation whose audacious and selfless actions have secured our release. This courageous action will clearly continue until victory is achieved, the country is freed from the foreigners' claws [...] and an Islamic state is established under the leadership of Grand Ayatollah Khomeini.

(Montazeri, in a message to the people of Isfahan on
5 November 1978)[1]

According to the current regime's version of history, the revolution began on 6 January 1978 when an article insulting Khomeini appeared in the newspaper *Etela'at,* sparking violent protests by clerics and students in Qom. However, in reality the first major protests had taken place some months earlier in Tehran on the initiative of secular intellectuals. In spring 1977, 40 writers of the Kanun-e Nevisandegan-e Iran (Association of Iranian Writers), which had been refounded during the time of political liberalisation, had sent an open letter to Prime Minister Hoveyda in which they criticised censorship and called for freedom of opinion. When this letter went unanswered, the association, in cooperation with the Tehran Goethe-Institut, organised ten nights of poetry lectures in October 1977.

As the poets used the occasion to criticise the regime, this cultural event, which was attended by thousands of enthusiastic listeners, turned into a political demonstration of a scale yet unseen by the regime.[2] In the following months student groups, trade unions, political parties and the clerical movement set out to mobilise their supporters and the general populace and to organise sit-ins, strikes and other forms of protests, to which the regime reacted with increasing violence. When Montazeri was released from prison on 31 October 1978, the protests, strikes and demonstrations were at their height. At the end of the month of Ramadan there had been large demonstrations in Tehran, and the regime had imposed martial law. On 8 September, when the protesters in defiance of a curfew had assembled in Jaleh Square in the centre of Tehran, the army had been ordered to shoot. On what became known as Black Friday, several hundred people were reportedly killed – but the protests continued. When in October the oil workers of Abadan joined the movement, it reached a new, truly threatening scale as the regime risked being cut off from its main revenue source.

By this time, the political clergy had come to set the pace and to dominate the discourse of the revolutionary movement. In the preceding decades, the secular parties had recognised the importance of religion but they had refused to accept it as a legitimate part of the political discourse. It was only during the revolution that they accepted the (temporary) Islamisation of the protests in the expectation that they would later regain control of the movement. For the secular parties this had several advantages: the religious rituals in commemoration of the movement's martyrs offered a pretext for new protests, and the religious wording of political slogans enabled the movement to draw on a powerful cultural imagery. Furthermore, by bringing the protests into the field of religion any attack on the protests could be interpreted and sanctioned as an attack on religion. While the secular opposition adapted its rhetoric, the political clergy also modified its discourse and adopted some of the arguments of its secular allies while silently dropping its more radical and controversial demands. Khomeini himself owed his acceptance as the leader of the revolutionary movement precisely to the fact that he had adopted a number of key demands of the democratic and civil rights movement.

In the numerous interviews he gave during his exile in Paris, Khomeini remained deliberately silent on his ideas regarding *velāyat-e faqih*.

Rather than speak of an Islamic state (*hokumat*), he spoke of an Islamic republic (*jomhuri*) and stressed his support for democracy, freedom and the rule of law.[3] Khomeini explained that an Islamic republic was to be no different from any other republic. It was to be a system based both on the principles of Islam and the will of the people. All decisions were to be taken in accordance with religious principles and the will of the majority. Furthermore, it should be based on justice and independence from foreign influence, and it should guarantee freedom of opinion and belief. The clergy should provide advice and guidance and supervise government, but not monopolise politics or exercise power itself. He envisaged for himself a role as spiritual guide and did not plan to hold a political post.[4] Khomeini apparently had recognised that the people would not accept the rule of the clergy, but it is not clear whether at this point he had truly given up the idea of *velāyat-e faqih* (guardianship of the jurist) in favour of *nezarāt-e faqih* (supervision of the jurist). It is quite possible that the shift from *hokumat* to *jomhuri* was only temporary and tactical.[5] In any case, this shift must be understood as a consequence of his move from Najaf to Paris, where he came into contact with more liberal activists.

On 12 October 1978, Khomeini had left Iraq for France under pressure from the Iranian regime. In his new place of exile he was surrounded by people who were quite different from his students in Iran. When Montazeri came to Paris in December, he was annoyed to see that apart from Khomeini's son Ahmad and his son-in-law Eshraqi, his closest assistants were Ebrahim Yazdi, Abolhassan Banisadr, Sadeq Qotbzadeh and Hassan Habibi. All four of them were activists of the Iranian student movement who had studied and lived in the West for many years and who were of a more secular, moderate and leftist orientation than the clerical leaders in Iran. The most important and influential figure in this small cosmos was Yazdi, who, to Montazeri's constant irritation, acted as Khomeini's speaker and interpreter and was present at all meetings.[6] Khomeini, at this time already aged 76, was a frail old man who needed the help of men like Yazdi, who knew the workings of politics and society in France and who spoke the language, to communicate with Western officials and journalists who came to visit him in great numbers. These assistants had considerable influence at the time – though their belief that they would also be able to control Khomeini in Iran ultimately proved to be an illusion.

Also present in Paris was Montazeri's own son Mohammad, whom he had not seen since he had illegally left the country for Pakistan in 1971. When Montazeri arrived with his wife and one daughter at the airport on 19 December, Mohammad was among those to receive him. Montazeri stayed one week in Paris to discuss with Khomeini the situation in Iran and their future strategy. Although it was the first time that Montazeri had visited a European country he was unimpressed. In his memoirs he noted that, apart from the metro, Tehran at this time was not much different from Paris.[7] When Khomeini asked him to persuade Karim Sanjabi to join his future cabinet as Minister of Foreign Affairs, Montazeri with his son Mohammad returned to Iran via Syria and Iraq. On his return, the success of the revolution was imminent and several cities were under the control of the spontaneously established revolutionary committees. On his way from the Iraqi border to the capital, Montazeri's convoy attracted large crowds of people who urged him to hold speeches and to tell them about the events in Paris. When he later continued to Isfahan he was greeted with even more enthusiasm. Having been received by the city's clerics outside the town, Montazeri gave a speech from the balcony of Ali Qapur Palace to the crowd assembled on the central Meydan-e Imam before continuing to his home town of Najafabad.

Back in Tehran, Montazeri and Beheshti organised a sit-in on the university campus to exert pressure on the government to open the airport for the return of Khomeini. Since 4 January 1979, the government was led by Shapour Bakhtiar, a former member of the Jebh-e Melli. Although he acquiesced to many of the demands of the opposition and freed political prisoners, relaxed martial law, lifted censorship and called for a constitutional assembly to decide on the future of the monarchy, most opposition groups refused to cooperate with him. When the Shah left the country on 16 January 1979, Bakhtiar proposed to directly negotiate with Khomeini in Paris. Apparently, he still hoped that Khomeini would return as a religious and not as a political leader. According to Montazeri, Yazdi agreed to this, hoping to preserve power for his own group. However, when contacted in Paris Khomeini confirmed that he would not receive Bakhtiar as long as he was still in office.[8] Eventually the government was forced to open the airport, and on 1 February Khomeini returned in triumph to Tehran. Although upon his return Khomeini once more emphasised that he would be content to act as his nation's guide, the following months showed that he was not willing to leave power to others. Nevertheless, this does not mean that on his return he already held a concrete plan for government. Rather, the debate over the constitution showed that neither he nor his movement had a clear strategy or a clear vision of what form the future system should take.

## The Moderates' Draft Constitution

Government and legislation must be given to the just jurists aware of the affairs of their time. The executive too should be under their supervision and command: in reality it acts as their delegate and has no autonomy. Judging too is the right of the jurist or of the person appointed by him. Hence the three powers are not separate but interconnected.

(Montazeri, in his message on the draft constitution)[9]

While still in Paris, Khomeini had asked Hassan Habibi, Ahmad Sadr Seyyed Javadi, Abbas Minachi and Nasr Katouzian to work out a constitution for an Islamic republic. Habibi had earlier begun to work on a draft that was based on the model of the French constitution, but the result was judged unsatisfactory. In the autumn of 1978 Javadi, Minachi and Katouzian began their work on the text in a series of secret meetings in Tehran, with Habibi serving as their link to Khomeini in Paris. All members of the commission were from Bazargan's Nehzad-e Azadi and were of liberal or leftist orientation. Based on constitutions from European and Islamic countries, they worked out a political system based on the norms and values of Islam but which also guaranteed civil and human rights. Although its institutional structure closely resembled a Western democracy with a popularly elected president at its head, it differed in one important aspect from this system as it submitted laws passed by parliament to the approval of a so-called Guardian Council. The idea for this council, which was to be composed of five *mojtaheds* (religious jurists) appointed by the *marāje'-ye taqlid* and ten lay experts chosen by parliament and the judiciary, was taken from the Iranian constitution of 1906.[10] However, contrary to its predecessor it was given the right to veto any proposal judged contrary to the constitution or the Islamic laws. Furthermore, its five clerical members were given the power to override the opinion of the ten lay members. Although the council was to examine laws only if asked to do so by the president, the chairman of the supreme court, or one of the *marāje'-ye taqlid*, it effectively allowed the clergy to block laws judged contrary to Islam.[11] In February 1979, this draft was submitted to Khomeini for approval and, after detailed scrutiny, was returned with a number of comments for further revision. During the following months the draft was amended by different commissions before it was again presented to Khomeini in early June. Although it still lacked any reference to *velāyat-e faqih* and did not provide for the position of a *vali-ye faqih* (ruling jurist),[12] Khomeini did not raise any objections. However, it appears that this time he did not read the draft in detail and hence did not immediately notice that in some aspects it significantly differed from the February version. The most notable change concerned the Guardian Council, which in the revised text had lost its right of veto and could no longer reject laws but only send them back for further revision. Furthermore, the number of its members was altered to five *mojtaheds* and six lay experts and the preponderance of the clerics was reduced.[13] When the interim government officially presented the draft to the public on 14 June, Khomeini initially expressed his support for the text. However, just days later he began to criticise the draft and called on the clergy to stand up against secular intellectuals and to make their voices heard in the debate on the constitution:

> It is those knowledgeable in Islam who may express an opinion on the law of Islam. The constitution of the Islamic Republic means the constitution of Islam. Don't sit back while foreignised intellectuals, who have no faith in Islam, give their views and write the things they write. Pick up your pens and in the mosques, from the altars, in the streets and bazaars, speak of the things that in your view should be included in the constitution.[14]

This change of mind, which finally led Khomeini to call for a complete revision of the draft in order to assure that the new system be entirely based on Islam, has long puzzled scholars. However, it makes sense if one assumes that he had approved the June version believing that it resembled the February version in that it gave the clergy the right to reject legislation deemed to infringe on Islamic principles. He possibly thought that this provision was sufficient to assure the supervision of the clergy. Once he recognised that this right was no longer guaranteed, he changed his stance towards the draft.[15] Nevertheless, neither then nor during the following weeks did he mention *velāyat-e faqih* – a silence that remains difficult to explain. Saffari speculated that Khomeini was already so sure of his political position that he did not consider it necessary to be officially enshrined in the constitution.[16] Kadivar surmised that Khomeini, having recognised that the people were not ready for the rule of the jurist, had accepted that instead of guardianship (*velāyat*) he would only have supervision (*nezarāt*), possibly hoping to later strengthen his power.[17] Montazeri claimed that Khomeini did not want to interfere with the work of the Expert Assembly, but such restraint hardly seems consistent with his character.[18]

Possibly Khomeini at this point was simply still unsure as to how far he could go, what form the new system should take and what role he and the rest of the clergy should play. The developments in the months before and after the revolution indicated that he did not have a clear plan but rather reacted to events, repeatedly changing his stance. While still in Paris he had said that he would be 'content to be my nation's guide'[19] and after his return to Iran initially truly seemed willing to leave everyday politics to lay politicians and limit himself to a role of guidance without actually wielding power. Thus, in February he appointed the widely respected Bazargan as president of the interim government, and in March withdrew to his house in Qom. However, he continued to play a central role in politics, and politicians continued to consult the 'Imam'[20] in Qom before any important decision was taken. He also began to build up a parallel structure of revolutionary institutions under his and the clergy's control. This led to a double structure of power in the political and military field, which was to remain characteristic of the Islamic republic. Thus, shortly after appointing Bazargan as president, he formed a Revolutionary Council presided over by Beheshti which quickly became a rival centre of power to the interim government and at times eclipsed it completely. The 11-member council was initially composed of Khamene'i, Rafsanjani, Abdolkarim Musavi-Ardebili and Mahdavi-Kani as well as Bazargan and the group from Paris, i.e. Banisadr, Yazdi, Qotbzadeh, Habibi and Sahabi. Taleqani was also a member but did not often take part in its meetings, while Montazeri refused an appointment because he wanted to stay in Qom and therefore only occasionally came to the meetings.[21] The Revolutionary Council was closely connected to the

Islamic Republican Party (IRP), which had been founded immediately after the victory of the revolution. Although it was designed as the platform of all parties and groups engaged in the revolutionary movement, it quickly came under the control of Beheshti and Rafsanjani, who used it as an instrument to counter the influence of the secular groups allied to Bazargan and Banisadr. Despite lacking a political programme and a coherent structure, it played an important role in the fight over discursive hegemony and physical dominance on the streets.[22]

While Khomeini at first felt compelled to compromise with the liberal and secular factions in favour of a truly democratic and republican system, after the overwhelming success of the referendum on the Islamic Republic on 30 March 1979[23] he began to intervene more openly in political matters and to press for the further Islamisation of politics. When the draft constitution was presented in June, he was so sure of his power that in spite of the protests of the nationalist and leftist groups he rejected their demand for the election of a large constituent assembly, arguing that it would take too long to convene and would need too much time to discuss the constitution. Instead he approved the formation of a smaller assembly of experts to rapidly revise and ratify the text. As the opposition pushed for a thoroughly secular constitution, he declared that the legitimacy of any argument in the political discourse depended on its conformity to Islam, and that he expected the constitution to be entirely based on Islam. Yet, neither then nor later did he demand the inclusion of *velāyat-e faqih* in the document.

Initially, Montazeri did not mention the doctrine either. In an interview with *Etela'at* on 16 June, he declared that Khomeini would certainly not agree to run for the presidency, but he did not bring up the idea of giving him the post of *vali-ye faqih*. Instead, he said he was confident that the recently published draft would not need to be much revised. Apart from insisting that the constitution be based on the principles of Islam, he had no specific demand.[24] In a message published on 24 June in *Keyhan* Montazeri defended the article, defining Islam of the Ja'fari law school as the official religion of state against the criticism of the Sunnis, and demanded that candidates for the presidency or parliament be practising and pious Muslims of the Ja'fari school with knowledge of Islamic norms.[25] However, he still did not mention the guardianship of the jurist. It was only on 10 July that he publicly called for the implementation of *velāyat-e faqih* in a long text that, along with his earlier message, was published as *Majmu'e do payam* (*Collection of two messages*). Man is born free, Montazeri wrote in this text. He owes obedience only to God and only God's legitimate representative may give him orders. According to the belief of the Shia, he wrote, government belongs to the Prophet, to the Imams and in the time of occultation to the just jurists. These should not only supervise the executive but also the judiciary and the legislature, so that all three powers are under their control:

> Government and legislation must be given to the just jurists aware of the affairs of their time. The executive too should be under their supervision and command: in reality it acts as their delegate and has no autonomy. Judging too is the right of the jurist or of the person appointed by him. Hence the three powers are not separate but interconnected.[26]

Should the control and coordination of the three powers be given to the president, as provided for in the draft, he should either himself be a jurist or he should be appointed by one, and act under his supervision. The best scenario however, would be that the jurist appoints a leadership council.

> Ideally, the just jurist aware of the affairs of his time will give the government of the country to a council of three to five persons who under his supervision exercise their duty. In this way the country will be better protected from oppression and dictatorship. Conferring politics to a president without taking into account the [concept of] guardianship and the government of the just jurist would make it a Western government incompatible with Islam.[27]

The president should not only be Iranian and Muslim, but a mature, pious and just man of Shi'i creed known for his ethical conduct, Montazeri declared. The same should be the case for the other leading posts. In his view women were generally not suited for the executive or the judiciary, because they were by nature of tender and delicate spirit and less given to thinking than men. Montazeri declared that God had given them the responsibility for the family; giving them additional duties in the judiciary or the executive would be against their nature and not in their own interest. He demanded that the constitution not simply state that men and women are equal, but that they are equal in the limits set by Islam in accordance with their natural dispositions. It should not simply state that politicians follow Islamic ethics and beliefs, but Islamic ethics, beliefs and *laws*. Furthermore, it should not state that the basis of government is the vote of the people, but the vote of the people in accordance with Islamic laws. Finally, he objected that in the Guardian Council the clerics were to be in the minority and that the council was not to be given a veto power against laws judged contrary to Islam. It appears that Montazeri was convinced that if power was not exercised by 'just jurists' and not restricted by Islamic law, it would lead to abuse, oppression and the violation of the sacred order of society. In his view, Islam was the guarantor of justice and clerics were immune to the corrupting effect of power. Montazeri wanted Islam to be not only a limitation of politics but its very basis. To assure the Islamic character of the State, he wanted to place 'just jurists' not only in the Guardian Council, but in all positions of power. However, he did not explain how to discern these 'just jurists' nor what their relation to the *marāj'e-ye taqlid* should be.

In his memoirs Montazeri claimed that at this time *velāyat-e faqih* was much discussed by the people, since many had read Khomeini's writings and were convinced that a cleric was more qualified to lead the country than a lay politician.[28] While it is true that along with Montazeri several clerics began to publicly demand the inclusion of *velāyat-e faqih* in the constitution,[29] it is doubtful that apart from Khomeini's close supporters many had read his *Velayat-e faqih*. It also appears highly unlikely that at this time a majority favoured a cleric assuming political leadership. The overwhelming support expressed in the referendum for an 'Islamic republic' was more a vote against the old regime than a vote for an Islamic state on the model of *velāyat-e faqih*. By the time of the debate on the constitution the initial enthusiasm at the fall of the Shah had given way to a feeling of fear and insecurity as a wave of arrests swept the country. Thousands of functionaries of the old regime were imprisoned and hundreds executed after brief trials by the hastily convened Revolutionary Courts.[30] Threatened with persecution, thousands of members of the political, military and intellectual elite fled the country. When the arbitrary and unlawful detention of real or suspected opponents continued, they were joined by large parts of the modernised middle class.

As the clergy entered the political field and seized not only the posts but also the property of the former elite, their reputation started to wane. Rather than support a clerical government, the people were increasingly concerned that the clerics were trying to monopolise power. This concern was further sustained by the elections to the Expert Assembly on 3 August, which ended with the triumphant victory of the political clergy. While the secular opposition remained fragmented, the IRP succeeded in uniting the political clergy on its list and with the support of the revolutionary militias managed to dominate the campaign. While some of the secular opposition candidates retired in protest at the pressures and manipulations of the IRP, it skilfully used the mosques to mobilise the people. Although the legitimacy of the assembly was weakened by the low turnout, especially among ethnic minorities like the Kurds, the result of the election was fully in favour of the political clergy: with 55 delegates it held more than two-thirds of the 73 seats.[31] Besides Montazeri, who upon the publication of his candidacy just one day before the election was elected for a constituency in Tehran, many prominent clerics were present. Amongst them were Taleqani, Beheshti, Rabani-Shirazi, Meshkini, Ahmad Khomeini, Bahonar and Abol Hossein Dastgheib. Apart from Banisadr, Javadi, Ezatollah Sahabi, Hamidollah Mir Moradzehi and Rahmatollah Moqaddam Moraghe'i only a few moderates secured a seat. The leader of the Democratic Party of Iranian Kurdistan, Abdolrahman Qasemlu, was elected but could not take part because he was threatened with arrest in Tehran.

## The Debate in the Constitutional Assembly

> This [the conditionality of freedom] is the story of all societies in which there is a specific commitment to an ideology, where public ballot is not the sole arbiter of the form of government. The point is not which dress the leader should wear, ruhani or otherwise, what is at stake is our creed. Our people are sensitive about the protection of our religion, not about the garment of its guardians.
> (Beheshti, in his speech in defence of *velāyat-e faqih*)[32]

When the Expert Assembly first convened on 19 August 1979, the opening session was overshadowed by the recent outbreak of armed conflict in Iranian Kurdistan. As Kurdish guerrillas and Islamic militias clashed in fierce fighting, tension increased in the capital and the political discourse became ever more polarised. In a speech to the delegates, who on the eve of the opening session had come to visit him in Qom, Khomeini made clear that he was not going to tolerate any further opposition. Explicitly naming the Democratic Party of Iranian Kurdistan, which led the revolt, Khomeini called on the government to intervene against all parties, politicians and newspapers, who misused the new freedom to obstruct the government's policies. Nobody, so Khomeini declared, could claim to represent the people while working against Islam and the Islamic Republic, as the people had clearly and freely expressed their support in the referendum for both religion and the new regime. Before the revolution, he declared, he had wanted the press and the parties to be free, but now he saw that these freedoms were misused by divisive and destructive elements. Nobody could pretend that he had not been willing to give freedom of speech and freedom of assembly, he said, but to prevent chaos and bloodshed he was now obliged to intervene and withdraw these rights:

> We must prevent rebellion and are obliged by Islam to defend the interests of the Muslim people [. . .]. Therefore, with great regret, we can no longer accord those freedoms we have so far accorded and we cannot allow these parties which have spread corruption and chaos to continue their work [. . .]. We have all made mistakes. We thought we were dealing with human beings and hence treated them with humanity. However, it has now become clear that we were not dealing with humans but with wild animals. One cannot treat wild animals with moderation and we will not do so any longer.[33]

The next morning, at the opening of the Expert Assembly, Rafsanjani read out a message by Khomeini to the delegates, in which he declared that they were not bound to the text of the draft, because the primary criteria for the constitution was its conformity with Islam. He admonished the delegates to respect the will of the people, who in the revolution had fought for Islam and in the referendum had voted for an Islamic republic, to then continue:

On account of this [the people's vote for an Islamic republic] the constitution and the other laws of this republic must be based on Islam to one hundred per cent [. . .]. Therefore, any vote or project presented by one or more delegates to the assembly, which is against Islam, is against the nation and the Islamic republic. The mandate of any delegate elected to the assembly is confined to [the erection of] the Islamic republic. The exposition or support of any proposal contrary to Islam or the republican system is outside the limits of the mandate.[34]

He forbade all non-clerical deputies from intervening in matters related to religious law since they did not have the expertise required for such matters. Should any of the delegates be under the influence of Western or Eastern powers or ideas, they should not seek to introduce these ideas in the constitution. Should the clerical deputies find passages in the draft contrary to Islam they should publicly denounce them and not let themselves be intimidated by the Westernised intellectuals who dominated the press. In Khomeini's view the delegates were not bound to the text of the draft, but they were also not free to discuss any alternative.

The moderates would have preferred Taleqani and Banisadr to head the assembly, but in a secret vote Montazeri and Beheshti were elected as chairman and vice-chairman. The interim government pressed Montazeri to ratify the draft in one month, but he insisted that the delegates would need more time for their discussions. During most sessions Montazeri left the chair of the assembly to Beheshti, whose greater tactical and political skills he willingly acknowledged.[35] It was also Beheshti who wrote the articles on *velāyat-e faqih*, who gave the speech in their defence and who played a crucial role in organising support for the concept in the assembly, but it was Montazeri who was its most senior clerical defendant. When the assembly took up its work on 19 August, the sections of the draft constitution were divided among seven committees and the delegates assigned according to their abilities. The sessions of the assembly were held in the building of the former parliament, and it had been planned that the delegates would be brought to a hotel for lunch and dinner. However, on the first day, Montazeri spread out his cloak on the floor and declared he would stay there and eat some bread and cheese. After a few days all delegates followed his example. This demonstrative show of modesty was in line with the ascetic lifestyle practised by Khomeini but also typical of Montazeri himself.[36] The proposed articles were discussed in the committees, before a revised version was drafted which was then proposed to the full assembly for further debate and the final vote. Beheshti headed the committee on the goals of the constitution, in which crucial questions were discussed. Among the other members of the committee were Farsi, Meshkini, Dastgheib, Rabani-Shirazi and Hassan Ayat, the IRP ideologue, while the only moderate present was Javadi, who had been in the original drafting commission.[37]

As no minutes of the committee's debates exist, the individual positions of its members are unknown. Considering that they agreed in just two weeks on Article 5, pertaining to the position of the *faqih*, it can be assumed that its critics were quickly silenced. However, when in early September the article was proposed to the full assembly it led to a controversial debate, and many delegates objected to the powers to be given to the *faqih*. In the face of this opposition Montazeri warned: 'Let the gentlemen be sure, that we will never endorse a constitution that does not include the issue of *velāyat-e faqih* and laws based on the book and the sunna. The Iranian people have elected the olamā so that they may have an Islamic constitution.'[38] Remarkably, during the entire debate on the topic Khomeini's book *Velayat-e faqih* played practically no role. Only once during the 67 sessions of the assembly did a delegate mention it, referring to it as the book of a certain Kashef al-Ghata – he apparently ignored the fact that this was the pseudonym employed by Khomeini.[39] Curiously, Montazeri and Beheshti also did not refer to Khomeini's text, but argued that, as in the Soviet Union, where an experienced communist was placed at the head of the system to ensure the enforcement of communist ideology, an experienced jurist should be placed at the head of the Islamic system to ensure the enforcement of Islamic law.[40]

The concept's most vocal critics were the liberals Moradzehi, Moraghe'i and Sahabi. They pointed out that the draft had been approved by Khomeini and the other senior clerics despite the fact that it did not provide for the position of the *faqih*. They also warned that if the *faqih* was placed at the head of the State, the post of president would become superfluous. Banisadr warned that the *faqih* must also have knowledge of social, economic and cultural matters, implying that a religious scholar might not be entirely fit to rule the country. However, he did not openly oppose the doctrine and at the time of the final vote on Article 5 remained absent. Taleqani too did not openly speak out against *velāyat-e faqih*, although he feared that under its guise a new dictatorship was being set up, which risked being even more totalitarian than the monarchy as it laid claim to a divine legitimacy. He favoured a popularly elected government under the guidance of a clerical council, as had been set out in the draft. In spite of his immense popularity, which placed him second only to Khomeini, Taleqani's power was limited, and after the arrest of his sons as members of a leftist guerilla group in April he feared being attacked or imprisoned himself.[41] On 9 September, just days before the final vote on Article 5, Taleqani died of a heart attack. With his death the supporters of a democratic system lost their most prominent and most popular representative in the assembly.

As hundreds of thousands attended Taleqani's funeral, public life in Tehran came to a standstill. However, three days after his death Article 5 was put to the vote. In the final debate Moraghe'i, as the representative of the opponents, argued that even though *velāyat-e faqih* had not been included in the draft it had been approved by Khomeini, the provisional government, the Revolutionary Council as well as the *marāje'-ye taqlid*. He argued that 'Islam must command but Islam cannot be dominated by one group [the olamā].' He cautioned that 'the struggle was started by all the Muslim people, but now after our triumph a few want to dispose of their partners'.[42] In his reply, Beheshti argued that only a *faqih* could assure an Islamic social order. Even though at the time no allusion had been made to the concept, Beheshti claimed that the referendum on the Islamic republic had been the expression of the people's wish for establishing *velāyat-e faqih*. Nothing else could assure the Islamic character of the system.[43] However, Beheshti also tried to allay the fear that *velāyat-e faqih* meant the imposition of clerical dictatorship:

> Does Article 5 negate the significance of the public ballot? Does Article 5 undermine basic liberties? Does Article 5 relegate all power to a particular group or social class? Does it suggest that the president and prime minister from now on ought to be turban-wearing clerics? Never. I want you to pay closer attention to this article and show me where does it suggest any of these?[44]

Interestingly, Beheshti pointed out to his critics that in the Islamic Republic, just as in other ideological systems such as Maoist China or Marxist Bulgaria, freedom is conditioned by the particular ideology of the State and decisions must be made in accordance with this ideology:

> This [the conditionality of freedom] is the story of all societies in which there is a specific commitment to an ideology, where public ballot is not the sole arbiter of the form of government. The point is not which dress the leader should wear, ruhani or otherwise, what is at stake is our creed. Our people are sensitive about the protection of our religion, not about the garment of its guardians.[45]

After Beheshti's reply others called for further debate, but despite the protests of the moderates Beheshti, as the chairman of the session, called on the assembly to vote on Article 5. The article passed with eight votes against and four abstentions. It read as follows:

> During the occultation of the Lord of the Age [...], the governance (velāyat-e amr) and leadership (imamat) of the community of believers devolve upon the just and pious faqih, who is acquainted with the circumstances of his age; courageous, resourceful and possessed of administrative ability; and recognised and accepted as leader by the majority of the people. In the event that no faqih should be so recognised by the majority, the leader or the Leadership Council, composed of foqahā possessing the aforementioned qualifications, will assume these responsibilities in accordance with Article 107.[46]

When on 9 October the other articles on the faqih's position were discussed, Hojatoleslam Mohammad Hojati-Kermani objected that Article 107, on the faqih's mode of designation, was vague and might give rise to abuse. Furthermore, he asked, 'what is the relationship between the marāje'-ye taqlid, who may be more learned and command a greater number of followers than the elected supreme leader who may be opposed by those marāje'.[47] This question, which was to become of central importance after Khomeini's death, was dismissed by Meshkini, who said that 'God willing, in the future the title of marja' and the supreme leaders will become one'.[48] The article was passed with three votes against and six abstentions. It read as follows:

> Whenever one of the foqahā possessing the qualifications specified in Article 5 of the Constitution is recognised and accepted as marja' and leader by a decisive majority of the people – as has been the case with the exalted *marja'-e taqlid* and leader of the revolution, Imam Khomeini – he is to exercise governance and all the responsibilities arising there from. If such should be the case, experts elected by the people will review and consult among themselves concerning all persons qualified to act as *marja'* and leader. If they discern outstanding capacity for leadership in a certain *marja'* they will present him to the people as their leader; if not, they will appoint either three or five *marjas* possessing the necessary qualifications for leadership and present them as members of the Leadership Council.[49]

The question of the *faqih*'s powers once more caused much debate. According to Article 110, the *faqih* appoints the six jurists of the Guardian Council, the chief of the judiciary, the chief of the general staff, the commander of the Revolutionary Guards (Sepah-e Pasdaran) and several other senior officers of the armed forces, over which he has supreme command. He has the right to confirm the elected president and to dismiss him should he be found guilty by the Supreme Court of having failed to fulfil his legal duties or should the parliament withdraw its confidence. Furthermore, he has the right to pardon prisoners recommended by the Supreme Court. Several clerics – among them Ahmad Khomeini, Ruhollah Khomeini's second son[50] – cautioned against giving military command to the *faqih* instead of the president. Ayatollah Naser Makarem-Shirazi warned that this would further confirm the suspicion that the clergy was trying to create a new dictatorship:

> [*Velāyat-e faqih*] in its current form is unrealistic and unattainable in the contemporary world [...]. Our enemies inside and outside of the country are going to accuse us of despotism [...]. Do not allow our enemies to say that a bunch of *mullahs* sat there and wrote a constitution to justify their own rule [...]. By consigning all the power to the faqih, do not turn the sovereignty of the

people into a lion without a head, tail and body. For God's sake, do not do this.[51]

Taking up this line Hojati-Kermani warned that 'rumours concerning the despotism of the clergy have been spread throughout the country. Tomorrow the mass of the homeless, the unemployed, the hungry and the discontent will join with the disgruntled intellectuals'.[52] Montazeri however, in a sharp reply, reproached his opponents for raising the fear of clerical despotism and accused them of being overly concerned with the reactions of the West:

> I ask these gentlemen not to extol how things are done in the West, to concern themselves with what goes on in the world, and to worry that, if we behave in a particular way, they would ridicule us. We are rational human beings and our nation is conscious of its own decisions. Our nation has chosen the Islamic republic. It is irrelevant whether [foreigners] like it or not [...]. If we cared for what the world thought, Mohammad Reza Pahlavi would still be ruling over us [...]. *Gharbzadegi* is not limited to the way we dress or how we decorate our home, its most important manifestation is the loss of confidence and self-respect. One of the signs of our *gharbzadegi* is that we listen to the noises they make in Europe and America and look for their approval for actions we take in our own land. We are Muslims and ought to believe in ourselves and be mindful of our religious responsibilities.[53]

Giving military command to the *faqih* instead of the president did not, in Montazeri's view, lead to despotism, but was precisely a protection against tyranny. In his view, the *faqih* as a just and pious person is immune to the temptations of power while a president might misuse his powers. In the debate on this article Montazeri also declared that in his view the legitimacy of politics depends on the *faqih's* approval. 'In order to be Islamic, the government must be based on a leader appointed by God or his intermediary. The commands of a president who has not been approved by the *vali-ye faqih*, even if the entire population has voted for him, has no binding value,' Montazeri said. In his view, approval by the *faqih* makes the difference between a religious and a worldly government. Without his approval it remains a despotic regime, even if it has the approval of the people.[54] This passage clearly showed that at this time Montazeri believed that the *faqih* is the primary source of political legitimacy. Contrary to his later view he did not believe that the *faqih* is elected by the people, but appointed by God.

## The Public Controversy about *Velāyat-e Faqih*

Everyone shall be given responsibility according to his own specialisation. [However,] it is not enough that the approved laws do not contradict Islam, rather they also have to be executed by the *faqih* or one of his representatives [...]. If we want to set up the Islamic republic according to the principles of Islam it should be placed under the control of an Islamic expert.

(Montazeri, in Friday prayers on 22 September 1979)[55]

While only few delegates dared openly voice their opposition to *velāyat-e faqih* inside the Expert Assembly, public criticism of the concept was widespread. Both religious and secular groups protested that they had not made the revolution to then lay power in the hands of a cleric. The secular opposition was led by the newly established National Democratic Front, while the main party of the religious opposition was the recently founded Muslim People's Republican Party. Both parties had openly opposed *velāyat-e faqih* since the beginning of the debate, and were therefore at the forefront of the protests. The National Democratic Front had been founded in March 1979 as the platform of the secular nationalist forces. Its supporters were alarmed at the direction the revolution was taking, and sought to counter the increasing monopolisation of power by the clergy. On 22 June, it organised a large demonstration in support of a constitutional assembly and later called for a boycott of the elections to the Expert Assembly. When in August the liberal *Ayandegan* was closed down for its criticism of *velāyat-e faqih*, the party organised a massive demonstration to protest against both the closure of the newspaper and the opening of the Expert Assembly.[56]

The Muslim People's Republican Party also openly opposed the rule of the clergy. Founded in March 1979 with the support of Shariatmadari, it was the platform of the Islamic moderates. In contrast to other leading clerics, Shariatmadari had never made a secret of his opposition to *velāyat-e faqih*. This doctrine, he argued, was contrary to Islam as it relied on an erroneous interpretation of the scriptures and it was undemocratic as it denied the people's sovereignty.[57] Like other moderate clerics he demanded that, with the exception of the articles on the monarchy, the 1906 constitution should temporarily be reinstated. Grand Ayatollah Hassan Tabatabai-Qomi, who was the second influential clerical opponent of *velāyat-e faqih*, also warned against giving power to a single *faqih*. This, he pointed out, was incompatible with the structure of the religious field which was traditionally characterised by the plurality of religious opinions. Unless the *marāje'-ye taqlid* were willing to submit to the religious rulings of the *vali-ye faqih*, they would come into conflict with the *faqih*, he warned: 'Either his rulings are forced on the followers of other *marāje'-ye taqlid*, or they are not. If they are then that is dictatorship, and if not then there is anarchy.'[58]

Faced with the accusation that *velāyat-e faqih* was nothing but a new form of dictatorship, Montazeri repeatedly defended the doctrine in public. Having been appointed Tehran's Friday prayer leader after the death of Taleqani, he conducted the prayers in the cemetery of Behesht-e zahra on 15 September – two days after the article on *velāyat-e faqih* had been voted upon in the Expert Assembly.[59] In his sermon, which was attended by several hundred thousand people, he argued that the people had voted not for a democratic republic but for an Islamic republic, which meant that the people could elect their government but that this government had to be based on Islam. He claimed that placing the State in the hands of a single *faqih* would not lead to dictatorship, as the *faqih* was bound to the laws of Islam and hence not free to do as he pleased. In contrast to the democracies of the West, in which the majority determines the policies of the State, the Iranian people, by their vote for the Islamic republic, had chosen a system based on the 'ideology' of Islam, Montazeri argued. It was only natural that in such an ideological system an expert of this 'ideology' be placed at the head of the State. Similarly to Lenin in the Soviet Union and Mao in Communist China, the *faqih* in the Islamic republic would guarantee that the system be set up according to the principles of the dominant ideology. In his sermon the following Friday, Montazeri affirmed that the *faqih* should not only supervise but also control the State:

Of course this does not mean that all work should be in his hands.
Everyone shall be given responsibility according to his own
specialisation. [However,] it is not enough that the approved laws
do not contradict Islam, rather they have also to be executed by the
faqih or one of his representatives [...]. If we want to set up the
Islamic republic according to the principles of Islam, it should be
placed under the control of an Islamic expert.[60]

As criticism continued that the clergy was trying to monopolise
power, Montazeri somewhat surprisingly affirmed that the leading
ideologue must not necessarily be a cleric as long as he is an expert of
Islam. In his sermon on 30 November, he emphasised that the *faqih* is
equal to other citizens before the law. Just like the president he is elected
by the people (albeit indirectly), and should he not fulfil his obligations
he could be replaced by the people. He also once more explained that
the Expert Assembly had given the supervision of the three powers
and other key functions to the *faqih* to prevent their misuse by the
president.[61] However, such affirmations could hardly allay the fears
of the moderates, who watched with growing concern as the Expert
Assembly turned the democratic system laid out in the draft into an
authoritarian theocracy. After several months of silence Bazargan
turned to Khomeini in October, asking him to dissolve the Expert
Assembly as it had exceeded the powers it had originally been given, i.e. to
revise and ratify the draft of the constitution.[62] However, Khomeini
rejected his appeal. When on 4 November 1979, students of the 'Line of
the Imam' occupied the US Embassy in Tehran, the simmering conflict
between moderates and radicals came to a head. While Khomeini initially
appeared unsure how to react, after two days of silence he endorsed the
occupation and sent Hojatoleslam Mohammad Khoa'iniha as his
representative to bring the students under his control. When Bazargan
realised that he was unable to resolve the issue he offered his resignation,
which was duly accepted on 6 November. Until elections could be held,
Banisadr was appointed as president and the Revolutionary Council placed
in charge of the executive.

This was the situation when on 11 November, the constitution was
officially presented to the public. Although Khomeini was reportedly
dissatisfied with the semi-democratic structure of the new system, he
approved the text and presented it to a popular referendum. Many

moderate and liberal forces were alarmed by the powers reserved for the clergy, and the Muslim People's Republican Party called for a boycott of the referendum. When the party's spiritual leader Shariatmadari was attacked in his house in Qom by revolutionary militias, the conflict turned violent. In protest against the attack on their leader and against the constitution, large demonstrations were staged in Qom and Tabriz where Shariatmadari, who was of Azeri origin, had many followers. Khomeini set him an ultimatum of 6 December to dissolve his party, but the demonstrations continued. It was only after several days of violent clashes that Shariatmadari finally backed down. In the ensuing weeks and months many of his supporters were arrested, his party was dissolved and he was placed under house arrest.[63]

In the end, all protests were to no avail. In the referendum on 2 and 3 December, the constitution was approved – officially with an overwhelming majority. Thus, for the first time in Islamic history, a cleric assumed supreme power. However, the constitution established not only the post of ruling jurist but also a democratically elected president and parliament. It not only stipulated that all laws must be based on Islam, but also that political decisions must be taken in accordance with public opinion as expressed by the means of elections. Clearly, it was not a coherent system but an inadequate compromise between differing views, concepts and interests. It was an attempt to satisfy the different ends of the political spectrum, but in the end the introduction of *velāyat-e faqih* into a republican system led to irresolvable contradictions that continue to haunt Iran to this day.

## Conclusion

It is not entirely clear what Montazeri's intention was when he pressed for the inclusion of *velāyat-e faqih* in the constitution. His statements before and during the debate in the Expert Assembly indicate that he believed that giving power to a just jurist was the best way to assure the Islamic character of the State and to prevent the recurrence of despotism. An analysis of his speeches, sermons and statements from June to December 1979 shows that he had no ready-made vision of *velāyat-e faqih*, but that his views changed considerably in the course of the debate. It is remarkable that he did not mention Khomeini's book *Velayat-e faqih*, but rather pointed to the Soviet Union to justify the need for placing an expert of ideology at the head of the State. During the debate in the Expert Assembly he argued that the *faqih* was appointed by God to govern the people. Although this position was based on Borujerdi's idea of the collective guardianship of the jurists over the people, Montazeri unlike his teacher believed that this guardianship should be exercised by a single *faqih*. He asserted that all three powers should be bound to his orders. Without his approval the democratically elected president and parliament should have no legitimacy and no autonomy. He was clearly more concerned with safeguarding the Islamic character of the State than with assuring the participation of the people. It appears that if he had had his way the constitution would have contained even fewer democratic elements.

However, in the face of broad public opposition his argument changed. During his sermons he emphatically, though not very convincingly, argued that placing a just jurist at the head of the State is the best protection against despotism. In his later sermons he also emphasised that the *faqih* is elected by the people and can be replaced by them if he does not fulfil his obligations or if he becomes too old. Whether this was a genuine change of heart or only a tactical concession to allay the concerns of the critics remains unclear. In *Enteqad az khod (Self-Criticism)*, Montazeri confirmed that in 1979 he still believed that the *faqih* is appointed by God. According to his account it was only in 1985 that he began to reconsider his stance on *velāyat-e faqih* and to develop a more democratic reading of the concept in order to resolve the contradictions of the constitution. He acknowledged that during the preceding centuries the Shi'i clergy, because of its belief in the illegitimacy of government during the time of occultation, had paid too little attention to political and social matters and had failed to develop a distinct political theory. He also acknowledged that during their struggle against the Shah he and the other clerics had given little thought to the time after the overthrow of the regime. Khomeini himself had deferred the question of the future system to the time after the victory of the revolution. Furthermore, the revolutionaries had neglected to train functionaries capable of filling the diverse functions necessary for administering a modern state and society. In hindsight, Montazeri wrote, many errors could have been avoided had they had more knowledge of the functioning of political systems and paid greater attention to the constitutions of other states.[64]

# CHAPTER 3

# THE DIFFICULT CONSOLIDATION OF THE REGIME

## Revolutionary Idealism and Political Realities

Is our duty [as parliamentarians] to uphold Islam and the undisputed formulations of *feqh*, or to protect the weak and to do what is best for them? Included amongst the undisputed ordinances relating to the questions of renting, is the recognition of an owner's right to own and dispose of his property as he wishes. If it is necessary to protect the weak, a different way must be found.

(Mohammad Khamene'i, in the debate on the new rent law in April 1982)[1]

The revolutionary regime set out not only to change the structures of power in Iran, but also to create an entirely new state and society. This state was meant to be truly independent of foreign interference and to bring into existence a realm of justice as embodied in the laws of Islam. The revolutionary clerics saw it as their mission not only to free Iran, but also to deliver the other disinherited people of the world. As they considered Islam the basis of political decisions, they saw it as their duty as the guardians of the scriptures to determine the policies of the State. Drawing on their religious authority, thousands of clerics swept to positions of power. They not only took over existing posts, but also created new institutions and functions. Although not all of the revolutionary councils, militias and foundations were created on their initiative or initially served their interests, in the end all came to be dominated by the clerics. However, it soon became apparent that their lofty objectives were far removed from reality. It not only proved more difficult than expected to bring the laws into line with Islam, but it also soon appeared that they lacked the experience to accomplish their task. Hardly any of the clerics had practical political experience, and only a few were acquainted with government structures or legislative proceedings. Even in the judiciary, which the clergy had long considered its core field of competence, there were nowhere near the required numbers of trained jurists. This lack of qualified personal led to numerous abuses in the courts, which tarnished the reputation of the clergy.

In the security forces, which had to be entirely rebuilt after the revolution, the situation was no better. Until the government could resume control, the vacuum was filled by spontaneously created groups and militias that lacked discipline, experience and clear structures. Many of them stood under local command, acted on their own accord and refused to submit to the government. Numerous people took advantage of the chaos to pursue their own interests and to settle old scores. Arbitrary detentions, summary executions and illegal confiscations were the result. After the occupation of the US Embassy in November 1979, the conflict between moderates and radicals over the course of the revolution took an increasingly violent turn. In spite of the invasion by Iraqi forces in September 1980, the fight for discursive hegemony and physical control of the streets continued unabated. Although President Banisadr had the support of leftist and liberal groups as well as large parts of the population, he increasingly lost the confidence of Khomeini. Appointed supreme commander of the armed forces in February 1981, Banisadr spent ever more time at the front and was for long periods absent from the capital.

In April and May 1981, Banisadr's and Bazargan's newspapers were shut down, depriving them of an important means to influence the discourse. In June 1981, seeking to turn the balance in his favour, Banisadr tried to replace the Islamic radical Mohammad Ali Raja'i at the head of government with Massud Rajavi, the leader of the Mojahedin-e Khalq. As the IRP scheduled a vote of no confidence against Banisadr, the Mojahedin staged a huge demonstration in Tehran which led to violent clashes.[2] The following day Banisadr was impeached as president, and hundreds of his supporters arrested. With their last hope for power shattered, the Mojahedin turned against the regime. On 28 June, a massive explosion attributed to the Mojahedin shattered the IRP headquarters in Tehran, killing 72 members of the political elite including Beheshti and Montazeri's eldest son Mohammad. On 30 August, a second bomb killed Raja'i and Bahonar, who had recently been elected president and prime minister respectively. With the country on the brink of civil war, the regime unleashed an unprecedented wave of repression against the opposition.[3] Many of those detained during the following months were mere sympathisers, whose only offence was often the possession of leftist newspapers. Often from the urban middle class, these young men and women were detained without knowledge of their charges and systematically mistreated and tortured. During interrogations they were forced to make confessions, which were broadcast in the media, to humiliate the accused and to express symbolic submission to the regime and the public recognition of its superiority.[4] In the face of the repression, thousands from the urban middle classes fled the country. This was clearly not the Islamic utopia promised to the people.

Furthermore, it soon proved that Islamic laws were not as easily applied as the clergy had imagined and as it had led the people to believe. According to Islamist ideology, the shari'a constitutes a complete system of rules and regulations for the social, political and economic order that can be directly applied to society. The legislature merely works out the practical details for the application of existing religious laws, and does not have the right to decree new ones. This belief finds its expression in Article 4 of the constitution, which states that 'all laws and regulations must be based on Islam' and that 'the Guardian Council are judges in this matter'. However, the authors of the constitution were aware that the laws of the shari'a were not sufficient to govern a modern society and that laws on science, technology and many other matters could not simply be derived from the shari'a. Therefore, Article 71 stated that the majles (parliament) can 'establish laws in all matters within the limits of the competence of the constitution', which suggests that its rights are not restricted to working out the details of the laws of the shari'a but also to enacting new laws. Nevertheless, the question as to what extent parliament could depart from the shari'a became the object of an intense debate.[5]

It soon became clear that not only was the shari'a unable to respond to all requirements of the contemporary world but also that the religiously permissible was not always the politically desirable, as the laws of religion in many cases contradicted the objectives of the revolution and the interests of the State. The ensuing debates also showed that there was not just one but several competing interpretations of Islam. The clerics who had been elected in great numbers to the first majles soon split up along lines which were more defined by political than religious criteria, while a more general rift emerged between parliament and the Guardian Council. While the majles was guided more by political necessities, the Guardian Council acted primarily according to religious requirements. Although it could not reject laws altogether it could send them back for amendment if it perceived them to be in conflict with Islam. On the grounds that Islam forbids political intervention in the economy, the council opposed many of the key reforms of the Islamic left, which sought to improve the situation of workers, peasants and the poor. Even the agrarian reform, which was of great political and symbolic importance, was blocked by the council as it was perceived to violate the property rights enshrined in Islam.

In these conflicts Montazeri did not have a coherent position. Although he generally believed that the free play of offer and demand is best able to set prices and wages, he repeatedly sided with the Islamic left, which favoured more redistributive policies and a more interventionist approach. In the important question of agrarian reform he approved the distribution of fallow estates among the landless, but opposed the expropriation and partition of other estates. Rather than split up large properties he favoured farmer cooperatives for cultivating the land.[6] Although he was critical of the legal tricks used by parliament to make laws pass the Guardian Council, he was also conscious that it was necessary to find a solution to avoid a blockade of the legislative process. Therefore, he declared that, according to the Qur'anic injunction 'regulate your affairs', the State has the right to pass laws on matters not defined by the shari'a. If a law is accepted by both the majles and the Guardian Council, he declared, it should have the same validity as a law of Islam.[7] Despite such rulings, many of the conflicts between the different legislative and executive institutions of the regime could only be resolved by the personal intervention of Khomeini, who thus obtained a decisive position in politics. As the key arbitrator he had the last word in all matters.

Although he often remained deliberatively vague, leaving matters to others to decide, once he did take a decision it was impossible to ignore or circumvent. While he was careful to guard his impartiality, he was generally more in favour of the Islamic left. Over the years, he also increasingly gave priority to the interests of the State over the requirements of religion.

On 2 January 1988, in a highly controversial statement he declared that, if it were in the interest of the State, the *faqih* had the right to overrule all religious regulations including the most basic principles of Islam.[8] In a letter to President Khamene'i he wrote that the interest of the Islamic state is above the requirements of Islamic law. Arguing that government is one of 'the most important divine injunctions' and 'part of the absolute vice-regency of the prophet', Khomeini asserted that upholding government takes precedence over all other orders. If it were in the interest of the State, he argued, the ruling jurist has the right to overrule even such basic principles of Islam as fasting, praying and performing the hajj: 'The government is empowered to unilaterally revoke any lawful agreement if the agreement contravenes the interests of the country. It can prevent any matter, whether religious or secular, if it is against the interests of Islam.'[9] With this declaration, Khomeini strengthened the proponents of a more pragmatic reading of religion, but weakened their claim to religious legitimacy. More generally he raised the question of how far a state can claim to be Islamic if it ignores the most basic rules of Islam.

## Montazeri's Reluctant Rise to Power

In the presence of the honoured excellencies of the clergy and the blessed *maráje'-ye taqlid*, it was neither right nor honourable that under the present circumstances you should discuss my person. I am full of hope [...] that God will grant long life and good health to the leader of the revolution so that there is no further need for a designation [of a successor].

(Montazeri, in his letter of protest against his election as deputy leader)[10]

After the end of the work on the constitution Montazeri had withdrawn to his studies in Qom and, during the following years, refused to accept any state function. However, if he preferred to keep his distance from the turbulent world of politics in Tehran this did not mean that he did not intervene in the political field. Over the years he built up a network of representatives in the mosques, seminaries and universities as well as in the courts, prisons and the military, through which he exerted considerable influence. Moreover, he set up a number of cultural, political and also military institutions, many of which had the objective of promoting the export of the revolution, which was a question of much importance to him. In addition, Khomeini repeatedly delegated jurisprudential questions for him to decide and asked him to assist him in key tasks such as the choice of Friday prayer leaders, the appointment of judges and the supervision of prisons. Thus, shortly after the revolution, Khomeini asked Montazeri to choose prayer leaders for the major cities. These posts were key positions in the religious and political field as the weekly prayer meetings were one of the regime's central means of propaganda. As the *faqih's* representatives in the provinces, the leaders also had the task of controlling the governors appointed by the Interior Minister. Their function was of such importance that on Montazeri's initiative a special school was set up in Qom to assure their training.[11]

The second task Khomeini delegated to Montazeri, together with Meshkini, was to appoint new judges and to organise and supervise their training. This was urgent, as the hastily established Revolutionary Courts under the supervision of Sadeq Khalkhali, who was called the 'hanging judge' for the numerous death sentences he pronounced against members of the former elite,[12] were not able to handle the wave of arrests which swept the country after the victory of the revolution. As Montazeri remarked in his memoirs, the clergy were not prepared to assume the functions they had called for prior to the revolution, and instead of the required 1,000 *mojtaheds* hardly ten suitable clerics could be found throughout the country.[13] Due to the lack of trained personnel the situation remained chaotic and characterised by arbitrary arrests, unlawful detentions and summary trials. Unlike other clerics, Montazeri did not publicly protest against the excesses of the militias and the courts, but he too was concerned. In February 1980, he issued a decree to the courts in which he laid down basic rules for trials. After the crackdown on the Mojahedin-e Khalq in the summer and autumn of 1981, he set up a court of appeal in Qom to which all death sentences had to be sent for review.

The third task Khomeini delegated to Montazeri in 1983 was the supervision of the detention system. Due to the arrests of thousands of real or presumed members of the royalist, democratic and leftist opposition parties, the prisons were severely overcrowded. During interrogations torture was widespread and unlawful executions were not uncommon. Montazeri, who himself had spent many years in prison, sympathised with the prisoners and was genuinely shocked at their treatment, which was often far worse than under the regime of the Shah. In 1983, Montazeri, on his own request, was given the right to pardon prisoners. He appointed a commission composed of four clerics. This commission sent its representatives to the prisons to propose the names of prisoners for amnesty. These names were then sent to Montazeri who, after approval by the intelligence service, pardoned them in the name of the *faqih*.[14] By 1986 the situation had considerably improved, but when Montazeri was sidelined the following year the hardliners rapidly regained control over the prisons.

Apart from these political functions and initiatives, Montazeri was also active in the religious field. On his initiative, a board of governors was formed for the supervision of the seminaries in Qom, to which the two highest-ranking clerics, Khomeini and Golpayegani, both sent three representatives. He also founded a number of religious schools, seminaries and universities in Qom, Tehran and other cities, which were meant to combine the traditional theological disciplines with more modern subjects. The most prominent of the institutions founded by Montazeri was the Imam Sadeq University in Tehran. Its graduates were mainly destined for work in the embassies and for cultural and missionary activities abroad. Montazeri had for many years complained that there were not enough missionaries to be sent abroad because too few Iranian clerics spoke foreign languages. To remedy this situation, the new university not only taught religious studies but also political sciences and foreign languages.[15]

Many of these political and religious initiatives were not uncontroversial. Montazeri's fervent support for the export of the revolution proved a notable point of contention with other factions of the regime. However, personal reasons also lay behind the fact that parts of the clerical and political elite disapproved of his gradual rise to power. Montazeri was certainly respected for his suffering, his courage and his perseverance during the struggle against the Shah, but many did not think him entirely suited to politics and did not take him quite seriously. Despite his radical stance in foreign policy and his unyielding defence of *velāyat-e faqih*, Montazeri was known to be affable, amenable and good humoured. His thick Isfahani accent, his simple manners and his peasant features were the object of numerous popular jokes. Even many allies regarded him as not quite suited to the tactical games of politics, while his opponents scorned him as naive and simple-minded. With his short build and his high-pitched voice he was indeed neither a very charismatic figure nor a very impressive orator. He himself recognised this when he left the chair of the Expert Assembly to Beheshti and the post of Tehran's Friday prayer leader to Khamene'i[16] and withdrew to his religious studies in Qom once the work on the constitution was completed. That Montazeri nevertheless emerged over the years as the second most senior cleric of the regime was no accident. Even those who doubted his political abilities were obliged to recognise his religious erudition, his steadfastness and his commitment to the revolution. Furthermore, other clerics such as Motahhari, Taleqani and Beheshti who by their religious authority, their personal charisma and their political abilities could have disputed him his place were all dead by 1981. Others like Khamene'i, Rafsanjani or Meshkini were certainly able politicians, but none of them had attained the religious authority of Montazeri.

When, in the light of Khomeini's old age and failing health, it was decided to chose a successor in 1983, Montazeri was therefore among the first to be discussed. The constitution actually did not provide for the designation of a successor during the lifetime of the leader, but given the fragile state of the system it was feared that the leader's death would trigger a serious crisis if the question of succession remained unresolved. In July 1983, the Expert Council therefore assembled under the presidency of Meshkini to discuss the question of succession. Of the debate, no details were made public and it remains unknown which candidates were discussed. However, the fact that it took two years to come to an agreement indicates that the discussions were difficult. As the position of the *faqih* had been more or less explicitly designed for Khomeini, it was difficult to find a person who had the necessary political and religious authority required by the post, let alone the personal charisma. According to the constitution, the *faqih* should be a pious and just *marja'-e taqlid* with outstanding administrative and political abilities recognised by the majority of the people as their legitimate leader. A number of clerics had the necessary political authority, but few had also the required religious authority.

It was only on 16 July 1985 that the council finally arrived at a decision. In a brief statement, which initially was not made public, it asserted that the majority of the people had accepted Montazeri as the legitimate successor to the leader and that the council recognised the people's choice.[17] This procedure recalled the designation of the *marāje'-ye taqlid*, who are also not elected but who hold their position by virtue of their authority among the people. In this way the experts clad their choice in the mantel of popular legitimacy. When Montazeri first heard of the decision in September, he sent a letter to Meshkini asking for an explanation and expressing his general opposition to the designation of a successor during Khomeini's lifetime. He not only considered such a step an insult to Khomeini but also feared that the lack of transparency would damage the reputation of the clergy and the system. Furthermore, he rightly perceived it to be unconstitutional since the constitution did not provide for the position of deputy leader. In his letter to Meshkini of 21 September 1985 he wrote:

According to what I am told, some months ago a session was called to discuss the conditions for the designation of a future leader according to Article 107 of the constitution. In this context also my name was mentioned though a definite decision was adjourned until a future session. I would like to express my respect to the honoured members of the Expert Council [...] but, in the presence of the honoured excellencies of the clergy and the blessed *marāje'-ye taqlid*, it was neither right nor honourable that under the present circumstances you should discuss my person. I am full of hope, and pray to the Almighty that, until the reappearance of the Lord of the Age, he will grant long life and good health to the leader of the revolution so that there is no further need for a designation {of a successor} [...]. Furthermore, the designation of a person, including myself, is perceived as an insult to his excellency [Khomeini] [...]. Of course, nothing forbids that one discuss this question in general terms. However, the discussion of an individual person is clearly not appropriate.[18]

In his memoirs, Montazeri claimed that he had not been asked whether he was willing to assume the position and hinted that Khomeini too may not have been consulted.[19] Khomeini himself later claimed that he had not given his consent to Montazeri's designation. However, as many of the experts were their close associates it is highly improbable that they should not have known of the discussion. It is possible that Montazeri did not aspire to the position of leader and was not actively involved in his designation, but it appears unlikely that the council's members should not have consulted him in this question. It can therefore be assumed that his initial protest was more out of opposition to the procedure than to the decision itself.

Originally, the Expert Council had planned to keep the decision secret, but when, in November 1985, the Friday prayer leader of Qazvin mentioned Montazeri's designation during prayers, Rafsanjani, as the council's deputy chairman, was obliged to officially announce the decision. This aroused a storm of protest among parts of the public and the clergy who questioned both the suitability of the candidate and the legality of such a procedure. Grand Ayatollah Sadeq Ruhani discussed the question during two days in his seminary, whereupon his house was attacked, his seminary closed and he himself placed under house arrest.[20] Montazeri's designation was also opposed by other *marāje'-ye taqlid*. Their opposition was partly due to the fact that he was not generally recognised as *marja'-e taqlid* in 1985, since at this time he had published his religious treatise (*resāle-ye amali-ye*) but he had spent less than the required time as a teacher in Qom.[21] That in the course of his designation as deputy leader he was elevated to the rank of *marja'* was considered premature by many traditional clerics and viewed as an illegitimate interference by the State in the religious field. In the face of the protest Montazeri initially refused to accept the post, but eventually gave in. Henceforth, his pictures were placed next to Khomeini's, and he was officially addressed as deputy leader and as *marja'-e taqlid*. While it is fairly clear that Montazeri's designation as deputy leader could not have happened without the prior consent of Khomeini, it is not clear who his supporters were in the Expert Council. Montazeri himself believed that Rafsanjani and Khamene'i strongly supported his designation. Both men had been his students and his close associates in the opposition to the Shah. However, by 1985 there were numerous points of conflict and Montazeri maintained a careful distance towards the IRP, which was their centre of power. Possibly they believed that Montazeri would be easy to control as ruling jurist. When in the following years they realised that this was not the case, they were among the first to push for his dismissal.

## Montazeri's Growing Unease

Do you know that in the prisons of the Islamic republic crimes are being committed in the name of Islam which never occurred under the regime of the Shah? Do you know that during interrogations many die under torture? [. . .] Do you know that in several prisons young women are being raped? Do you know that prisoners are even deprived of the light of day for months?
(Montazeri, in his letter to Khomeini of 9 October 1986)[22]

After the revolution, Montazeri had played a central role in instituting an authoritarian system based on a totalitarian vision of Islam that reserved many of the political posts for the clergy and concentrated much of the power in the hands of the ruling jurist. In the first few years of that system, he had supported the elimination of the armed resistance and the repression of the liberal opposition as a necessary step for the consolidation of the revolution and the preservation of the regime. Contrary to other clerics, he had remained silent when the regime restricted political freedom and excluded dissident groups from the political field and the public discourse. However, if Montazeri accepted the detention and execution of political opponents as a necessary consequence of the revolution, he was concerned about the arbitrary and abusive use of power against ordinary people. Not only was he worried about the effects these excesses would have on the revolution's reputation, as well as on the image of Islam, the clergy and the country, but he was genuinely shocked when he learnt of the unlawful detention and execution of innocent people. As he himself had spent long years in prison and suffered intimidation, insult and torture, he was sensitive to the situation of prisoners.

Montazeri certainly did not question the system, but he was critical of the methods employed by it and sought to improve the functioning of the regime. In private letters and meetings with Khomeini and other

leaders, Montazeri addressed the problems that were related to him by
the people. Unlike other members of the leadership, he saw it as his duty
to personally read and respond to the letters sent to him by ordinary
citizens as well as members of parliament, government officials and
military commanders.[23] These people turned to him so that he might
convey their criticism to Khomeini, who had become increasingly
isolated from the public. During the first few years after the revolution,
visitors had often been surprised how well informed Khomeini was. He
closely followed current events and political debates through foreign
radio stations and Iranian newspapers. During the months in Qom he
held daily public meetings to receive petitioners and deliver sermons.
However, when in autumn 1979, on the recommendation of his doctors,
he took up residence in the cooler and healthier climate of the small
village of Jamaran in the north of Tehran, Khomeini became increasingly
removed from the public. Ordinary citizens and officials were only
rarely able to speak to him in person. His son Ahmad systematically
shielded him in his small house from unwelcome news and visitors, thus
assuring his control over the ageing leader.[24] Furthermore, Khomeini
was known for his unwillingness to listen to criticism or to accept
opposing views. Whenever he was not willing to further argue about
a question, he abruptly ended the discussion.[25] Due to his choleric
character, few officials dared openly address questions which might
anger him. His household was careful to prevent negative news from
reaching him, and reputedly admonished visitors not to raise questions
that might upset the leader. Montazeri claimed that he was one of the
few who did not let himself be intimidated and who continued to speak
his mind in front of Khomeini.

In a letter to Khomeini of 9 October 1986 during the controversy
about Mehdi Hashemi Montazeri criticised the increasing isolation of
the leader: 'Regularly members of government and administration
of high and low rank come to seek my advice and guidance and to hear
my opinion on their problems [...]. All have said, that since it is
impossible to meet the Imam and bring this problem to his
knowledge, we tell you about it and ask you for support.' He
admonished Khomeini to listen to all parties involved in a problem
and not to be misled by the partisan reports given to him by members
of his office: 'The leadership always pursues its own projects and, in the
interest of these projects, only tells you what is good and remains silent

on what is bad. It is necessary that you permit ordinary men from among the people to speak to you, free of fear, in all clarity and honesty, of the situation in the country.'[26] Montazeri criticised the failings of the system because he perceived this to be his duty. In what closely corresponded to the traditional self-perception of the clergy as a critical corrective to the State, he saw himself as the voice of the voiceless and the advocate of the people.

For many years he hesitated to make his criticism public, but behind the scenes pressed for improvements. The detention system, the security forces and the judiciary were of special concern to him. In the face of numerous abuses in the courts, Montazeri and Meshkini in late February 1980 issued an 11-point decree in which they set out basic rules for the courts. This document, which was distributed to all courts, demanded that verdicts should not be based on emotions or rumours, that the accused should be treated with humanity and that, when in doubt, the court should decide in favour of the accused and set him/her free. In addition, the police and the Pasdaran were asked to not interfere in the affairs of the judiciary and to not detain any person without the prior order of a judge. Finally the decree set out that only property obtained by illegal means should be confiscated.[27] However, these rules were only partly applied by the courts and the repression continued largely unabated. In the face of the wave of arbitrary arrests and summary trials that followed the crackdown on the Mojahedin-e Khalq in the summer of 1981, several prominent clerics such as Shariatmadari, Reza Zanjani, Hassan Tabatabai-Qomi and Mohammad Shirazi publicly voiced their protest. Sheikh Ali Teherani even sent an open letter to Khomeini in which he condemned the judiciary's actions as un-Islamic.[28] Montazeri at this time remained silent, but he too was alarmed. In his memoirs, he recalled a court verdict on which the judge had simply written 'condemned to death,' without specifying why or for what cause. In a letter to Khomeini of 27 September 1981, he addressed the situation in the courts and prisons which witnesses described as highly alarming:

Irregular executions, sometimes without the prior order or knowledge of a shari'a judge and sometimes against his will, are frequent. The lack of cooperation between the courts and the executioners, the influence of emotions and anger on the executioners, and the execution of thirteen or fourteen-year-old-girls, who have neither held any weapon nor taken part in any protest but have just made some critical remark, are alarming and brutal [. . .]. The number of prisoners is such that five people have to share a solitary cell under inhumane conditions so that it is even impossible to perform the prayers. According to the report of a shari'a judge, the chaos among some of the interrogators is highly alarming.[29]

In his letter to Khomeini of 9 October 1986, Montazeri gave a detailed description of the situation in the prisons in words that betray his indignation at the conditions the detainees had to endure:

Do you know that in the prisons of the Islamic Republic crimes are being committed in the name of Islam that never occurred under the regime of the Shah? Do you know that during interrogations many die under torture? [. . .] Do you know that in several prisons of the Islamic Republic young women are being raped? Do you know that during interrogations of young women the use of dishonouring words is common? Do you know how many prisoners have as a consequence of irregular interrogations become blind, deaf or paralysed, and suffer from chronic pain without anyone coming to their aid? Do you know that in several prisons the prisoners are even kept from performing the ablutions and prayers? Do you know that in several prisons the prisoners are even deprived of the light of day for months?[30]

By 1982, the excesses in prisons and courts had worsened to such an extent that Khomeini issued an eight-point decree on 15 December, in which he called upon the judiciary and the executive to respect the citizen's rights and property and to abstain from any further illegal detentions, executions and confiscations. Although this did not put a stop to the detentions and executions, it did signal the end of the worst phase of terror.

For several years after the revolution each prison was controlled by a different security organisation, and only in 1985, on Montazeri's initiative, was a central organisation put in charge of the detention system. Until then, Tehran's Evin prison was controlled by Asadollah Lajevardi, who had himself been imprisoned there before the revolution and who was known for his brutality. The revolutionary prosecutor at the time, Musavi-Ardebili, was so alarmed at the situation in Evin that he asked Khomeini to replace Lajevardi. However, Lajevardi was not under the control of the chief justice but operated at the behest of the leader's office, and Ahmad Khomeini repeatedly intervened with his father to prevent his dismissal.[31] It was only in 1985 that he was finally removed on Montazeri's order.[32] Outraged by two executions in Najafabad, Montazeri with the permission of Khomeini set up a court of appeal in Qom, to which all death sentences had to be sent for confirmation. One case concerned a friend of his son Mohammad who had participated in the revolution, the other a girl of sixteen from a pious family. Even though she was not active in politics she had been condemned to death for having expressed her sympathy for Massud Rajavi. Montazeri intervened with Khomeini, but the same evening he was informed that the death sentences had been carried out. As he bitterly remarked, even under the Shah it had been possible to file an appeal.[33] Initially the head of the judiciary, Musavi-Ardebili, rejected the court of appeal with the argument that in Islam no judge has the right to abrogate the ruling of another judge. Montazeri, however, argued that this was only valid for *mojtaheds*, not for the poorly trained judges employed in most courts. When Musavi-Ardebili learnt of the case of a man who had been executed for having criticised the government in his diary, he also gave his consent.[34] According to Montazeri, the court of appeal abrogated more than 6,000 death sentences in the first three years of its existence. In 1985, it was also charged with reviewing the confiscation of property, as complaints about the illegal seizure of estates and other properties by corrupt officials were common. The main beneficiaries of these confiscations were the religious foundations. They had been founded to help the destitute and deprived, but had rapidly turned into immensely wealthy companies. Although the powerful directors of the foundations complained about this directive, it was approved by Khomeini.[35]

The creation of an amnesty commission in 1983 also had its origin in the shocking situation in the prisons. Montazeri had learnt of the case of a young women who had been imprisoned on political charges and had gone insane in custody. He complained to Khomeini that it was dishonourable to Islam that the judiciary detained insane people. Thereupon, Khomeini asked him to form a commission to review the sentences and to recommend prisoners for amnesty. Ever since the first wave of arrests, Iran's prisons, although expanded after the revolution, were severely overcrowded. Prisoners who had served their sentences but refused to repent (*mellikesh*), as well as those who had confessed under torture but were used by the wardens as informants and collaborators (*tavvab*), remained behind bars. To reduce the overpopulation of the prisons Montazeri instructed the courts to deliver less severe sentences, and ordered the conditions of repentance to be eased so that more prisoners could benefit from them.[36] In the first three years after its creation the amnesty commission pardoned and freed 5,000 prisoners, according to Montazeri.[37] From the time when he assumed control of the prisons, the situation considerably improved. His tenure as the head of the detention system did not bring a complete end to terror, but it did bring a certain return to the rule of law. There was a sharp decrease in executions – notably for women, who were exempted from capital punishment – numerous prisoners were released and general detention conditions improved. The use of torture as a form of punishment was reduced, and compulsory classes in ideology abolished. Several former prisoners confirm that conditions improved as a consequence of Montazeri's policies.[38] In his letter to Khomeini of 9 October 1986, Montazeri recalled the situation before he took control:

> Nutrition, hygiene and healthcare were very bad, the opportunities for education were practically non-existent, the prison administrators were inexperienced and brutal people who knew no other means than insult and violence. Prisons were on the brink of collapse [...]. Prisoners are also humans who want bread, life and dignity, but through our narrow-mindedness they are alienated and forcefully pushed into the arms of the opposition.[39]

While initially Montazeri had mainly sought to correct the misconduct of individual officials and institutions, over the years he began to contemplate a more general reform of the system. In the face of the manifest failure of the regime to realise the promised realm of justice and freedom, he began to have second thoughts on the political structures he had helped to create. Khomeini's all too often arbitrary and authoritarian conduct led him to question the wisdom of placing unrestricted powers in the hands of an individual who was manifestly both human and fallible. In 1985, he began a series of lectures on *velāyat-e faqih* in which he arrived at an interpretation of the doctrine that considerably differed both from his earlier views and from the official reading.

## Reinterpreting *Velāyat-e Faqih*

When the people give the authority of government into the possession of a person, the people itself will naturally be his defending and executing force and by consequence the government will be fortified and the system will be strengthened [. . .]. And in the case that the elected ruler does not fulfil the conditions of leadership or that he violates his duties, the people can depose him.

(Montazeri, in *Mabani-ye feqhi-ye hokumat-e eslami*)[40]

By the time of his election as deputy leader, Montazeri was deeply immersed in the world of politics. The consultative and supervisory duties delegated to him by Khomeini in the legislative, justice and detention system brought him into almost daily contact with politics and politicians. Nevertheless, unlike fellow clerics such as Rafsanjani or Khamene'i, he did not become a politician himself. Montazeri was well acquainted with the rules of the political field, but he never fully adapted to its logic. He held considerable power, but he did not entirely succumb to its attraction and remained at a critical distance to the centres of power in Tehran. Once the work on the constitution was completed, Montazeri withdrew to his calling as a scholar and teacher in Qom. He clearly felt more at home in the world of the seminaries than in Tehran. While he readily acted as an advisor to the State, he was less willing to assume executive duties. True to the traditional posture of the clergy, he saw his task primarily as a critical corrective to the State. Even though his own allies were now in power, his relationship with the State remained marked by cautious distance, ever more so when he saw the new rulers repeat many errors of the old regime. Montazeri was certainly conscious of the needs and exigencies of politics, but political expediency was not everything to him. He was a man of profound piety with a strong sense of ethical propriety, who took his religious duties very seriously. More than once he gave priority to the rules of religion to the detriment of his movement. Thus, during his time in prison, he opposed living with the members of the Mojahedin-e Khalq and sharing the cooking equipment with them because they did not adhere to the religious rules of hygiene, which to him were of supreme importance. Even though this robbed his group of a valuable political ally, he was not willing to compromise his religious beliefs.

Yet, if the ethical principles of Islam were his basic guide and reference, Montazeri was ready to develop a progressive reading of the scriptures if the political situation demanded it. Contrary to the orthodox clergy he did not advocate a purely literal reading of the scriptures or a purely legalistic line of argumentation, but was aware of the need to adapt religion to the changing conditions of the world. Like his mentor Khomeini, this repeatedly led him in social and political matters to come up with highly innovative interpretations of the scriptures. Certainly, Montazeri was no modernist. Unlike fellow clerics such as Motahhari or Beheshti, he had spent most of his life in the world of the seminaries and knew little of Western society and modern science. His understanding of religion and his approach to the scriptures remained shaped by traditional hermeneutics, which required a *mojtahed* to carefully study the sayings of the Prophet and the Imams and to consult the opinions of past scholars before arriving at his own conclusion. An expert of the Nahj al-balaqah – containing the sermons, letters and narrations of Imam Ali – Montazeri frequently referred to his example in religious and political matters to sustain his arguments. Unlike religious intellectuals such as Abdolkarim Soroush or Mohammad Mojtahed Shabestari, who in the 1980s began to develop a new reading of the scriptures inspired by Christian theology and Western philosophy, Montazeri was little interested in theoretical innovations and not ready to break with the venerable traditions of Shi'ism. Yet, he agreed with them that it was not only permissible but necessary to interpret the shari'a according to changing conditions of time and place. Moreover, he was aware that to correctly understand the sayings of the Prophet or the fatwas of past scholars it was necessary to bear in mind their original context. Strongly influenced by his teachers – Khomeini, Borujerdi and the philosopher Allameh Tabataba'i – he also accorded great importance to the use of reason.[41] Even though his world remained the world of the seminaries and his moral views remained conservative, his years in prison had brought him into contact with different political groups and opened his eyes to new social realities. This did not mean that he approved of the liberal values of the modern middle class or the secular theories of the left, but he recognised the importance of social justice as a guiding principle for Islamic political theory. Moreover, like many clerics of his generation, he was aware that the world was rapidly changing and that it was necessary to develop a new reading of religion to maintain its relevance to society and to find a new language for the message of Islam in order to reach the secularly educated youth.

This effort to find an answer to the challenges of modernity was particularly apparent in his book *Az aqaz ta anjam: Dar Goftogu-ye do daneshju* (*From Beginning to End: Conversation of Two Students*), which he had written during his time in prison for his son Mohammad. In this book he related a fictional dialogue between Nasser, an eloquent student of theology, and his friend Mansur, a student of science, who does not believe in God and holds a purely positivist view of the world.[42] Strolling around the gardens outside town on a beautiful spring afternoon, the two friends engage in a discussion about the origins of the material world, which rapidly leads them to the central questions of religion. While Mansur argues that science suffices to explain the workings of the world, his friend maintains that religion alone can elucidate the mysteries of the universe and give meaning to human life. Like Nasser, who in a clear and simple language lays out the basic ethical principles of Islam to his sceptical friend, Montazeri in his lectures, speeches and writings sought to present the message of Islam in an accessible and rationally persuasive manner. Montazeri was certainly not always as successful as Nasser, who in the end convinces Mansur of the beauty and superiority of Islam. Nevertheless, he soon gained a reputation for his progressive reading of the scriptures and his lectures were popular with students and other scholars who not only sought a response to the challenges of modernity but also a way to address the religious and ethical questions raised by the involvement of the clergy in the political, military and economic administration of the State.

In 1985, shortly before his election as deputy leader, Montazeri began a lecture series on the theoretical foundations and practical implications of *velāyat-e faqih*. Over the course of four years he discussed the reasons for the establishment of an Islamic government and what this meant in practice. The lectures were published in an edited, extended and annotated form in Arabic in 1988. In the following years, the book was translated to Persian and published in five volumes under the title

*Mabani feqhi-ye hokumat-e eslami* (*The Jurisprudential Foundations of Islamic Government*). The book was not a coherent, well-structured analysis, but an often rambling, repetitive and redundant text without a stringent approach or line of argumentation. At times Montazeri cited dozens of passages from the scriptures and other scholars to sustain his arguments, only to then drop all reference to the texts and adopt a purely rational argument. At times his position remained undecided or even contradictory, and he appeared hesitant to think things through to their logical conclusion. However, in spite of these ambivalences, the lectures were of considerable importance. As they were held at a time when Montazeri was the designated successor to the leader, they were in a way his political programme for the future. Far from being an abstract academic exercise, they laid out how Montazeri envisioned his duties as *vali-ye faqih*. And although his political theory appeared in several points somewhat raw, his intention was clear – to increase the people's control over the government. In a radical departure from his former ideas, he insisted that the *faqih* is not appointed by God but elected by the people and that his powers should be limited to ensure the respect of the people's rights. In his view the *faqih's* election establishes a contract with the people that binds him to respect their will. This was a religious innovation of far-reaching political consequences.

In the introduction to the book, Montazeri described man as a social being who seeks life in society. As communal life always results in conflict of interests and opinions, society needs a system of rules to prevent chaos and conflict. Much like Aristotle, Montesquieu or Rousseau, Montazeri discussed different forms of government but rejected them all. Some scholars, he wrote, consider democracy the best form of government, because both its source and objective are the people. However, the people are not always rational but are susceptible to passions and propaganda and easily come under the influence of others.[43] Islamic government, he explained, differs in two important aspects from other systems, especially Western democracy. Firstly, only the most wise, most just and most pious, aware of the concerns of the people and the problems of their times, are chosen as rulers, in order to ensure that the people are governed with justice, equity and respect for the rights of all – Muslims and non-Muslims alike. Secondly, in the Islamic state, unlike in a democracy, the people and all three branches of the State are bound to the rules and principles of Islam and must not deviate from them. It is a theocracy, in the sense of the rule of God's law over the people.

The absolute right to rule belongs to God, Montazeri wrote, but God has made man his representative in this world and given sovereignty to the people. To sustain his argument, Montazeri pointed out that, when the people swore allegiance to Imam Ali, he told them that this oath established a contract between them and made him their representative. He invoked them to remember that he was nothing but their key-bearer and that his government was their government. No one who was not chosen by the people had the right to rule over them.[44] Furthermore, Montazeri argued, man was created free and possesses the sole right to his property, which is why only he can give the government authority to dispose over him and his property, and therefore man must be free to elect his government.[45] Even though in the absence of the Imams the jurists have been designated by God as the legitimate rulers, Montazeri argued, God has chosen no single jurist to exercise this right. Because it would result in conflict, should the jurists rule collectively it is upon the people to choose the ruler from among the jurists.[46]

In short, Montazeri's argument was that in the absence of the Imams the people have the sovereign right to chose from among the jurists the most capable person to govern them according to the laws of Islam. This election in his view establishes a contract between the ruler and the people, which on the one hand binds the people to respect the ruler's commands, while on the other hand it binds the ruler to respect the people's will and their rights. Should the ruler continuously neglect his duties or systematically violate the people's rights, the people have the right to depose him.[47] The ruler is not free to do whatever he pleases, but is bound to the rules of Islam as set out in the constitution. He cannot decide all affairs, but must seek the counsel and advice of informed individuals so that he does not decide against the will of the people.[48] Clearly preoccupied with abuse of power and violation of the law, Montazeri dealt in detail with the duties of the ruler and his agents, dedicating an entire volume to the functions of justice, the intelligence service and the treatment of prisoners.

With his idea of the popular election of the *faqih*, Montazeri returned to a view he had expressed four decades earlier. In his memoirs he related a discussion with Motahhari some time between 1942 and 1945 about the issue of leadership in the time of occultation. In this discussion, they came to the conclusion that in the absence of the Imam the people should elect their ruler from among the most able clerics. However, when they consulted their mentor Khomeini, he rejected their idea:

> At this time the Imam [Khomeini] said: No, this is not correct [...]. According to the Shiite confession the Imam must be infallible and appointed. In the time of his absence it is the fault of the people that he is hidden [...]. We must create the conditions for the return of the Imam. Upon this we said, this means that in his absence there will be disorder. And he said: This is the fault of the people.[49]

Because Borujerdi also rejected their theory, Motahhari and Montazeri dropped this idea in favour of Borujerdi's concept of the collective guardianship of the jurists over the people.[50] As Montazeri explained in *Enteqad az khod*, he held this opinion until 1979 when he revised it to argue that the collective guardianship must be exercised by a single jurist appointed by God. It was only in autumn 1985 that he once more changed his opinion to argue that the ruling jurist is not designated by God, but must be elected by the people. By this time, so Montazeri explained, he had realised that his earlier opinion was questionable not only from a religious perspective but also from a political viewpoint, as it opened the doors to despotism.[51]

Montazeri's lectures clearly showed that he wanted greater respect of the interests of the people and better control of the government, but it remained unclear how this should be achieved. In his revised version of Islamic government, Montazeri still neither allowed for direct democratic elections nor for enough checks and balances to ensure the control of the government. Furthermore, although it clearly violated the will of the people he defended the indirect election of the *faqih* and the prior review of the candidates by an unelected group of experts. In his view this was the only way to assure that the wise and worthy, and not the ignorant and corrupt, are elected. Nevertheless, although Montazeri did not transform *velāyat-e faqih* into a democratic concept his ideas stood in sharp contrast to the doctrine of the absolute guardianship of the jurist (*velāyat-e motlaq-e faqih*) which was adopted as the official doctrine in 1988. In this interpretation the leader, as God's representative on earth, has absolute power. In no way is he bound to respect the will of the people, but the people owe him total obedience. The ruling jurist is considered to stand not only above the constitution but also above the laws of Islam, which he can suspend if the interest of the Islamic state so requires.[52] In this view, the leader, not the people, is the source of political legitimacy, and any decision or institution not authorised by the leader is illegitimate. Even the decisions of parliament and the decrees of the president are invalid as long as they have not received the approval of the leader.[53] Montazeri himself had initially held this position, but during the following years political reality had made him revise his opinion. His elected, limited and conditional interpretation of *velāyat-e faqih*, developed since 1985, certainly did not solve all problems but it did open up perspectives for a democratic reform of the system.

## Conclusion

The revolution radically changed the relationship between religion and politics in Iran. The new political system which, at the overthrow of the monarchy, was enshrined in the constitution of 1979 made religion the basis of politics and thus gave the clergy a central role in the political field. If nominally their position in politics was based on their religious authority, and was thus a reflection of their standing in the religious field, they soon took over and built up positions that were independent of their religious position. The revolution thus led to the clericalisation of politics as much as to the politicisation of the clergy. Until the revolution, the political discourse had been dominated by liberal and leftist ideas to the point that even Khomeini took up parts of the arguments of his secular rivals. With the triumph of the political clergy in 1979, and the elimination of all rival forces by 1981, political arguments came to be framed in religious rhetoric. However, if nominally compatibility with religion was the primary criteria for the legitimacy of political practice, it soon became apparent that the rules and regulations of Islam were neither sufficient to administer a modern state nor always in line with the objectives of the revolution. The contradictions between the shari'a and the interests of the State led to continuous conflict between different factions and institutions that, at times, threatened to block the political process. These contradictions could often only be superficially covered up by resorting to legal tricks, which enabled controversial measures to pass but neither helped resolve the underlying conflict nor bolstered the system's claim to religious legitimacy.

In this situation the position of the ruling jurist gained additional importance. Often, he was the only mediator who could find a solution to the factional fighting and continuous conflict between institutions. The system's dependence on the position of the ruling jurist posed a serious problem. Since its inception, it was clear that the jurist's powers were closely connected to the authority and charisma of Khomeini: the jurist's powers were very much Khomeini's powers. In the event of his death the system risked sliding into a serious crisis. Therefore, the leadership decided to choose a successor while Khomeini was still alive. Since no other senior cleric endorsed *velāyat-e faqih* and no other political figure had his religious authority, Montazeri was eventually chosen as a successor even though he too was not yet recognised as a *marja'-e taqlid*, as required by the constitution.

Montazeri's position after the revolution was in many ways representative of the position of the clergy in general. His political power was only partly derived from his authority as a religious scholar, and largely depended on the network of political institutions and personal representatives he had built up since the revolution. Furthermore, many of his powers were dependent on his proximity to Khomeini. In a way typical of the informal structures of the system, Khomeini delegated numerous rights and duties to Montazeri which permitted him to exercise power in the political field without holding any official office. Although he readily engaged in politics, he never entirely succumbed to its attraction. While he was ready to compromise on the shari'a if this was in the interest of the State, he was not willing to sacrifice his principles for the sake of personal power or to close his eyes to the systematic violation of people's rights. Genuinely shocked by the excesses in the courts and prisons, Montazeri began early on to criticise in confidential letters and private meetings the state of the judiciary as well as the incompetence, inefficiency and corruption of the executive. When he realised that this was not sufficient, he turned to making his criticism public. He therewith returned to what had long been the function of the clergy as a corrective to the State and a representative of the people. In his view, criticism was not treason to the cause of the revolution but rather was necessary in order to realise its original objectives and true values. He was probably aware that with his public criticism he infringed on the rules of the political discourse, but he expected that his personal authority, his political position and his relationship with Khomeini were sufficiently secure to allow him to say that which others did not dare. However, things began to become difficult when his relationship with the leader was profoundly shaken by the affair surrounding his associate, Mehdi Hashemi.

# CHAPTER 4

# AN INCONVENIENT SUCCESSOR

## The Controversy Surrounding Mehdi Hashemi

To my regret you have acted, spoken and written under the influence of others and [on their instigation] have held public speeches and sent messages to the judiciary. In the interests of the nation, I expect you, for many years my friend [...] to clean your house of its relations to Seyyed Mehdi and to refrain from any reaction to the trial against him, which surely will end with his condemnation.

(Khomeini, in his letter to Montazeri of 4 October 1986)[1]

A certain mystery continues to surround the affair of Seyyed Mehdi Hashemi, which marked a turning point for Montazeri and the beginning of his decline. This affair, which became public with the unveiling of the secret arms-for-hostages deal with the United States in November 1986 and ended with the execution of Hashemi and several other of Montazeri's close associates in September 1987, must be read as a result of the conflict between the partisans for the export of the revolution and the proponents of a more pragmatic approach to foreign policy. However, it also represented an attempt by Ahmad Khomeini, Rafsanjani and the Minister of Intelligence, Hojatoleslam Mohammad Reyshahri, to weaken Montazeri's position and to bring the future leader under their control. The fact that in this situation Khomeini was not willing to side with Montazeri and prevent Hashemi's trial considerably embittered Montazeri and seriously strained the relationship between the longtime friends. The affair brought to light the increasing estrangement between the two men since the revolution, and highlighted the leader's growing discontent with his deputy's critical stance on interior policy as well as his free-wheeling course in foreign policy which had long been the source of conflict with other institutions of the regime.

Since the revolution Montazeri had been one of the staunchest supporters of the export of the revolution. Along with his son Mohammad, he advocated providing not only ideological but also financial and military support to foreign revolutionary groups, notably in Lebanon and Afghanistan. As he said during a Friday prayer in June 1980, 'if our Muslim brethren in Afghanistan, in Palestine, in Lebanon and in any other place are involved with the superpowers and invaders, we are involved because we are the Afghans' brethren. War against our brethren in Palestine, Lebanon, Eritrea and the Philippines are wars against us.'[2] With Khomeini's approval, Montazeri and his son founded an office in the Pasdaran in 1979 to coordinate activities in support of militant Islamist groups abroad. This Office for Islamic Liberation Movements (OILM) organised courses for cadres of these groups and held public rallies in support of the export of the revolution. Moreover, it funnelled funds to guerilla groups abroad, with Montazeri regularly calling upon the public to donate one day's wage for their support. In principle, Khomeini shared Montazeri's belief in the transnational vocation of the revolution and initially even refused to accept relations with governments deemed un-Islamic. However, he was soon forced to adopt a more pragmatic policy that favoured proper relations with all countries, and subsequently adopted an intermediate position between the radical faction and the proponents of a more cautious approach based on the interests of the State – the latter rooted particularly in the foreign ministry.[3]

The government's reluctance to support his activities embittered Mohammad Montazeri, but did not prevent him from pursuing his own projects. During his years of exile, Mohammad had come into contact with numerous militant groups and received military training in the camps of the Palestinian Liberation Organisation (PLO) in southern Lebanon. He maintained close contacts with the PLO leader Yassir Arafat as well as the Libyan leader Muammar al-Ghaddafi, who had generously financed the clerical opposition to the Shah. In September 1979, Mohammad with several dozen supporters travelled to Libya to take part in the independence celebrations. Upon his return he was arrested at Tehran airport, but subsequently freed by his armed supporters. The affair provoked such a scandal that even his father was forced to distance himself from him, and to ask the authorities to help him make his son accept medical treatment, explaining that Mohammad's incessant activities for the revolution had led to his physical exhaustion and mental troubles.[4] In December, Mohammad's plan to send an army of volunteers to southern Lebanon to support the Palestinians in their fight against Israel once more brought him into conflict with the authorities. When they refused to permit their departure, Mohammad occupied the airport lounge before being allowed to leave with a group of unarmed supporters.[5] As the Iranian volunteers represented an inconvenience for both the Syrian and the Lebanese governments they were sent to a training camp near Damascus, where they remained until the start of the war with Iraq.[6] Mohammad, however, continued his activities until his death in the bombing of the IRP headquarters in June 1981, whereupon the OILM came under the control of Seyyed Mehdi Hashemi.

Hashemi was born in 1944 into a respected clerical family in Qohdarijan, a small town near Najafabad. His father was one of Montazeri's first teachers in Isfahan, while his elder brother Hadi married one of Montazeri's daughters and later served a prison sentence with Montazeri. Together with Mohammad Montazeri, the two brothers were involved in the clerical movement since 1963 and acquired a reputation for their militancy and radicalism. Mehdi in particular was known for his often ruthless tactics as well as his unorthodox religious beliefs and his radical leftist ideas. In the 1970s, he set up a vigilante group in his native Qohdarijan, which was reportedly engaged in a series of murders of prostitutes, homosexuals and orthodox clerics. In April 1976, he was arrested and sentenced to death for the murder of Ayatollah Mohammad-Reza Shamsabadi (an incident which will be discussed later). After the revolution, both brothers were considered heroes by the political clergy; Montazeri made Hadi the director of his office in Qom while Mehdi joined the Pasdaran, where he was appointed to the central command and the ideological committee.[7] In his letter to Khomeini of 9 October 1986, mentioned in the previous chapter, Montazeri wrote about his relationship with Hashemi:

I have known Seyyed Mehdi since he was a child when he, with Mohammad [Montazeri], came to my classes. His father was my teacher, and his brother is my son-in-law. I know all his particularities. He is a devoted servant to Islam, the revolution and also to your person. He is talented, intelligent, and a gifted orator and writer. By his intelligence, leadership and planning capacities he is superior to the commander of the Guards [Reza'i] and the minister of intelligence [Reyshahri] and his commitment and piety are in no way inferior. However, he does not suffer from blindness and is not ready to blindly submit to others.[8]

Hashemi's radicalism and his refusal to submit to the authority of others led to a series of conflicts both inside the country and abroad. After the revolution, Hashemi set up a number of militias around Isfahan which sought to realise their own radical vision of the revolution, notably engaging in a controversial effort to distribute large estates to the landless. In the winter of 1979, they also clashed with the armed supporters of a rival faction of the clergy, resulting in a number of deaths. The conservative clergy, in particular, resented Hashemi's radical leftist views as well as his modernist religious beliefs. Like Montazeri, Hashemi actively sought to promote the idea of Islamic unity and reconciliation between Sunnis and Shias both on the political and the theological level. This idea had been officially adopted as the policy of the regime, but it was opposed by many conservative and orthodox clerics as it called into question some of the fundamental theological beliefs of the Shia. Hashemi was later accused of having spread 'night letters' against Khamene'i and other suspected members of the conservative Hojjatiye society, an organisation that vehemently opposed the idea of Islamic unity and which, despite its official ban by Khomeini in 1984, remained intact and active.[9] As Hashemi in other cases also did not hesitate to publicly denounce, threaten and intimidate his opponents he earned himself the lasting enmity of some of the leading conservative clerics.

His activities abroad also gave rise to controversy: Hashemi was particularly active in the support for the militant groups of the Shi'ite community in Lebanon. Following the Israeli invasion of southern Lebanon in June 1982, the Iranian Government authorised a large contingent of Pasdaran to set up their base in the eastern Beka'a Valley to organise the military and ideological training of the local Shi'ite militias, which eventually merged into the Hezbollah.[10] While a wide range of Iranian institutions was involved in this operation, Hashemi's organisation in close cooperation with the Iranian ambassador to Damascus, Hojatoleslam Ali Akbar Mohtashemi, played a central role.[11] Thus, it was under the supervision of the OILM that the leading clerics of the Hezbollah set up the charter of the new movement in autumn 1982 and laid out plans for an Islamic republic along the lines of the Iranian system. Subsequently, the OILM assumed responsibility for operative coordination with the Hezbollah.[12] In this function it was involved in both the hostage takings and the suicide bombings which earned the Hezbollah worldwide notoriety. In April 1983, a suicide bomber attacked the US Embassy in Beirut, and in October that year the group perpetrated a devastating suicide attack on the headquarters of the French and the American forces, which eventually forced them to withdraw from the country.[13] In December 1983, the clandestine Iraqi party, al-Dawa al-Eslamiya, which had its base in Iran, perpetrated a series of bomb attacks in Kuwait. Subsequently, 21 suspects were arrested and put on trial, including 17 members of al-Dawa's Lebanese sister party. Among these were two close relatives of senior Hezbollah leaders, who were therefore particularly interested in obtaining their release. Starting in February 1984, the Hezbollah abducted a number of Western citizens in order to exert pressure for the release of the 17 Dawa members. Later abductions were also meant to free other prisoners, to obtain political concessions or to take revenge for hostile actions.[14] Although the precise role of the OILM in the individual abductions and attacks is difficult to assess, its close cooperation with the Hezbollah in operative issues suggests that it played a significant role.

In Iran, the hostage issue was a controversial matter. While the radical faction regarded the hostages as a useful leverage in dealings with the West, the more pragmatic faction around Rafsanjani saw them as a liability for Iran. By consequence, it viewed Hashemi's involvement with disapproval and sought to limit his influence. In November 1982, parliament denied Hashemi's organisation its recognition, whereupon, with the approval of Montazeri, the former removed the OILM from the Pasdaran and transformed it into an independent institution based in Qom. However, Hashemi remained under pressure, and early in 1984 was forced go give up his seat in the central command of the Pasdaran. He subsequently withdrew to Qom where he concentrated on organising courses, publishing magazines and running a political library in support of the export of the revolution. Although Montazeri claimed that Khomeini did not express his opposition to Hashemi's activities prior to 1986,[15] it appears that as early as 1982 Khomeini asked the Pasdaran's intelligence service to keep Hashemi under surveillance. When in 1984 the intelligence ministry was founded, the newly appointed minister, Reyshahri, exerted increasing pressure on Hashemi's organisation to cease its activities, and apparently also misused his powers to tap the telephones of Montazeri's office. Reyshahri lacked revolutionary credentials but had the protection of his father-in-law, Meshkini, who possibly urged him to act against Montazeri in the hope that the latter's removal would clear his own way to the top.[16] Early in 1986, Reyshahri forced the OILM office in Tehran to hand over most of its weapons and other resources. In the months that followed, Rafsanjani and Ahmad Khomeini attempted to persuade Montazeri to have Hashemi posted to an embassy or cultural mission abroad. When he refused to be sent away, Reyshahri tried to discredit him by raising the issue of Shamsabadi's murder and Hashemi's alleged cooperation with the Savak. However, Montazeri saw this as another manoeuvre designed to remove Hashemi and refused to withdraw his support. To resolve the conflict Hashemi in May and June met with Rafsanjani and Ahmad Khomeini, but the meetings failed to ease tensions.[17]

While these moves must be understood as an attempt to remove a key supporter of Montazeri in order to gain control over the future leader, they were also an effort to neutralise an organisation that was increasingly out of step with the government's foreign policy. Officially, the export of the revolution remained the stated policy of the regime, but in private the leadership had decided to adopt a more moderate course. One of the reasons for this change of mind was the war with Iraq. On 22 September 1980, the Iraqi President, Saddam Hussein, had ordered an attack on the oil-rich province of Khuzestan in the hope of an easy victory. By June 1982, Iraqi forces had been expelled from Iranian territory and the city of Khoramshahr had been retaken. However, Khomeini rejected the ceasefire and reparations proposed by Iraq, and decided to continue the war until the 'liberation of Iraq.'[18] During the following years, Iranian forces managed to make some advances, and, in 1984, they conquered the Iraqi island of Majnun. In 1986, they even managed to occupy the Iraqi peninsula of Fao, but a definite victory was not in sight. While Iraq had the financial and military support of most Arab countries as well as much of the Western world, the US Government had banned the sale of weapons to Iran in 1983 and also forced its allies to adhere to this ban. The Iranians therefore had serious problems buying weapons and finding spare parts for their military equipment, which largely dated from the time of the Shah and was of Western origin. Against this background, Khomeini, in a meeting with the leadership in mid-June 1985, called for a change in foreign policy in order to end the country's isolation. Under the new policy, which was readily adopted by Rafsanjani, the regime tempered its call for the export of the revolution and sought to assure its neighbours that it was not seeking regime change. Moreover, Rafsanjani was authorised to seek a solution to the hostage issue in Lebanon, which had become one of the main obstacles for détente with the West. In a first move, he used his influence to negotiate the release of the passengers from a plane abducted in mid-June by the Hezbollah.[19] The other hostages, however, remained captive as they were a valuable bargaining chip in the nascent arms deal with the US Government.

Even before the meeting with Khomeini, Rafsanjani had engaged in secret contact with the US Government in order to purchase much-needed weapons and spare parts.[20] Contact was first established on the initiative of the Israeli Government, with the help of the Iranian arms dealer Manuchehr Ghorbanifar in April 1985. In August and September, with the approval of US President Ronald Reagan, two shipments of US-manufactured anti-tank missiles were delivered by Israel to Iran, whereupon one hostage was released in Lebanon. While these first consignments were managed entirely by the Israelis, during the following shipment of anti-aircraft missiles in November logistical problems forced the Americans to get more deeply involved. Subsequently, the Americans assumed complete control of the operation and also took the lead in the negotiations.[21] Originally, the arms deal was meant as a confidence-building measure to lay the basis for more far-reaching negotiations, but the deal was soon modified to include the release of American hostages. The talks were further complicated by the fact that both the Americans and the Israelis lacked intelligence on Iran, so that they depended on the information provided by Ghorbanifar who pretended that the weapons would go to the moderates to strengthen their position in the power struggles expected after Khomeini's demise. Moreover, in a move not approved by Reagan, parts of the arms payments were diverted to finance the Nicaraguan Contras, who had been placed under an arms embargo by the US Congress. A measure which had originally been meant to improve political relations was thus turned into a complex exchange of arms for hostages, with a dimension hidden to both the US President and the Iranian Government. As this led to a number of complications and misunderstandings, it was eventually decided to seek direct talks with the Iranians.

When, in May 1986, a meeting for further negotiations was arranged with the help of Ghorbanifar in Tehran, it soon became apparent that he had misled both sides, causing each to believe that the other was willing to give more than was actually the case. The US delegation, which arrived on 25 May in Tehran, was led by the former National Security Advisor Robert McFarlane. On the Iranian side the talks in the Hotel Estiqlal (former Hilton) were led by the deputy prime minister, Mohsen Kangarlu, who was also responsible for special operations in the Pasdaran. As McFarlane, who had been led to believe that he would talk to Rafsanjani, Khamene'i and Mussavi, insisted on speaking to more senior officials, the chairman of the foreign affairs committee, Mohammad-Ali Hadi-Najafabadi, also joined the talks. McFarlane was determined to have all four American citizens in Lebanon released, but it soon became apparent that the Iranians – or at least Rafsanjani's faction – had no direct control of the hostages. Moreover, they had been led to believe that the Americans were willing to engage in a long-term arms deal in return for their release. The Iranians also rightly felt that they were being cheated by the Americans, who, seeking to make a profit with which to finance the Contras, charged them an exorbitant price for the arms. In the end, no agreement was reached and the US delegation left Tehran empty handed on 28 May.[22]

In spite of this failure, talks continued and the two sides met again in Germany after one hostage had been released and several more arms shipments were delivered to Iran. After the fiasco in Tehran the Americans sought to cut Ghorbanifar out of the talks, as they rightly suspected him of playing his own game. Fearing to lose a lucrative business and to be stuck with unpaid bills allegedly running into the millions, Ghorbanifar became increasingly nervous. On 10 July 1986, he wrote two long letters to Kangarlu in which he complained about the outstanding payments and proposed several scenarios for the further talks. The increasingly desperate Ghorbanifar later sent copies of these letters to Montazeri, whom he knew from before the revolution, probably hoping to thus exert pressure on Kangarlu. Through these letters Montazeri and Hashemi first learnt of the meeting with McFarlane as well as of the details of the proposed deal.[23] Montazeri was alarmed that he had not been informed about the negotiations. While he was not opposed in principle to negotiations with the USA, he was scandalised that Iran should fight its Muslim brothers in Iraq with Israeli weapons. He also believed that Washington's objective was not to help Iran but to prolong the war. When he complained to Ahmad Khomeini and Rafsanjani, both were much displeased that he had learnt about the matter.

Montazeri does not indicate when exactly he received the letters, but the chronology of events indicates that it was some time in July or August 1986. Although he was clearly alarmed about the talks, there is no indication that Montazeri or Hashemi immediately took any steps to expose the negotiations. However, it is possible that Hashemi was involved when, on 9 and 12 September, two more US citizens were abducted by the Hezbollah in Lebanon. The timing of these abductions suggested that they were meant to disrupt the talks. Hashemi's involvement would also explain why Reyshahri at this point decided to intervene against the former's organisation.[24] On 11 September, the intelligence service raided a building of the OILM in northern Tehran and reputedly secured weapons, ammunition and explosives as well as forged documents. The raid was publicly presented as an intervention against an illegal group preparing attacks on the regime, and five days later Ahmad Hassani (or Arabzade), who was responsible for the site, was arrested.[25] Khomeini not only approved these steps but ordered the arrest of all persons involved in the activities of the office. Warned that this not only included Mehdi Hashemi but might also concern members of Montazeri's office, he reputedly said that if Montazeri were responsible he too should be arrested.[26] In a harshly worded letter of 4 October 1986, he admonished his longtime friend, whom he addressed by the title of Hojatoleslam, for surrounding himself with people such as Hashemi, and warned him not to interfere in the trial against Hashemi and his associates:

The greatest danger [to your reputation] is your proximity to Seyyed Mehdi Hashemi. I do not want to say that he has really committed a crime, but I want to stress that he is accused of numerous crimes, among them murder. Even if he is innocent, the relationship with him is damaging to your reputation [...]. What is certain, is that hoarding weapons, allegedly to support the so-called liberation movements, using the money of the people without the approval of the government is wrong. Whether these activities really served the assistance of these organizations or not, all illegitimate interference in the affairs of government must be stopped [...]. To my regret you have acted, spoken and written under the influence of others and [on their instigation] have held public speeches and sent messages to the judiciary. In the interests of the nation, I expect you, for many years my friend, to only consult with people who are worthy of the leadership of this country [...]. I expect you to clean your house of its relations to Seyyed Mehdi and to refrain from any reaction to the trial against him, which surely will end with his condemnation.[27]

Five days later, on 9 October 1986, Montazeri replied with a nine-page letter to Khomeini in words that betrayed the bitterness he felt about the recent events. Clearly injured by the tone of Khomeini's letter, he recalled what he had done in support of the religious and political activities of Khomeini. Should it be true, Montazeri wrote, that he was a simple-minded person who acted under the influence of others, as implied by Khomeini's letter, then it would be Khomeini's duty to rethink the question of succession without consideration for his person. Never, Montazeri claimed, did he want any post or power for himself. However, if Khomeini should find that Montazeri had merely tried to correct the failings of the system after reading the letters and listening to the complaints of citizens and officials on the problems of the country, then Khomeini should listen to what he had to say. Turning to the recent arrest of Hassani and the charges brought against Hashemi, Montazeri stressed that it was he himself who had been responsible for the founding and the running of the OILM, that its military activities had been stopped and that the intelligence service had at all times had full knowledge of its activities:

The founders of the Office for Islamic Liberation in Iran, which works towards the export of the Islamic revolution in the world, and for the support of the revolutionary forces abroad, were myself and Mohammad Montazeri [...]. The office has until today provided great service to Islam and the revolution while our Foreign Ministry has only presented empty slogans [...]. At the time of Mohammad Montazeri the power of the office was far greater and it had more money and weapons [...]. However, since Mohammad's death this work has been stopped and, about eight months ago, Mr. Hassani went to Mr. Fallahian, Mr. Reyshahri's assistant, and handed over the financial and military resources of the office. Since then, he has limited himself to cultural and propaganda work abroad. His office has always acted on the consent of the judiciary and the committees and with the knowledge of the intelligence service.[28]

Montazeri wrote that if anyone were to be held responsible for the activities of the office, it should be himself, not Hassani or Hashemi, who had only acted on his assignment. In a rare show of sarcasm, which once more betrays his bitterness, Montazeri continued:

Now that all the problems of the country, including the war, the economic crisis, the inflation and the discontent of the people have been solved, and only the problem of Seyyed Mehdi Hashemi remains, the guards, the committees and the intelligence service have assumed power. They can arrest and execute any person they want, including Seyyed Mehdi Hashemi. However, the gentlemen who for some time have been pulling the strings behind the scenes, claiming to act in your name, shall know that even if they tear Seyyed Mehdi Hashemi to pieces in my presence, I will never surrender and shall preserve my intellectual independence [...].[29]

Referring to the accusation that, at the time of the Shah, Hashemi had been involved in the murder of the court cleric Shamsabadi, Montazeri wrote that even at this time the Special Court in Isfahan had the capacity and the independence to abrogate the death sentence to which Hashemi, on the pressure of the intelligence service, had been condemned. In the Islamic Republic, however, Montazeri continued, the Minister of Intelligence and Khomeini himself were declaring that Hashemi was guilty of murder even before the trial had begun. This, Montazeri declared, was not the proper procedure:

> In a country, which respects justice, the right of prosecution for murder lies with the prosecutor, the appropriate authority is the judiciary, and the intelligence service has no right to interfere. The prosecutor must make the accusation and the judiciary must take the appropriate steps [...]. You, who are the leader of the Islamic world, and who have known Seyyed Mehdi since he was close to you as a member of the Guards, declare upon hearsay that he represents a danger. You would have done well, after all you have heard from his enemies, to summon this Seyyed, who repeatedly has asked for a meeting, and personally question him. It is not right to only listen to a person's enemies.[30]

In spite of these strong words, Montazeri's letter was to no avail: on 12 October 1986, Hashemi was arrested on the charge of 'illegal activities' and in the following days and weeks numerous other associates of Hashemi and supporters of Montazeri were thrown into prison. In total 40 men were arrested in the course of this affair, of whom 14 were ultimately executed – among them, Hashemi and Hassani. The remaining members of the group were silently eliminated without a regular trial during the prison purges in summer and autumn 1988. On 15 October, probably in the hope of bringing pressure to bear on Reyshahri and Rafsanjani, some of Hashemi's friends at Tehran University printed and distributed a leaflet in which the secret talks with the US Government were revealed. However, as no names were given and the story remained fairly vague it failed to make a deep impression.[31] As the wave of arrests continued, Hashemi's friends informed the Lebanese weekly *al-Shira'* about Hashemi's arrest as well as McFarlane's visit in Tehran.[32] On 3 November, the newspaper published an article which, for the first time, brought the details of the secret negotiations to the world's attention. However, if Hashemi's friends had hoped that this would discredit Rafsanjani, they were mistaken. While in the United States the revelations caused a major political upheaval, in Iran the news had surprisingly little effect. Although Rafsanjani was obliged the following day to admit the existence of secret talks with the enemy, this did not notably weaken his position. If his breach of one of the major taboos in

Iran went unpunished, it was because he had the protection of Khomeini. The leader had, on 27 October, charged Reyshahri with the investigation against Hashemi and his group, making clear that he was not willing to intervene in favour of Montazeri's protégé. After two months of interrogations, an extensive confession by Hashemi was broadcast on television on 12 December 1988. In a statement clearly produced under the effects of torture, he confessed to have deviated from the path of the leader and to have committed severe crimes against the cause of the revolution:

> I considered myself so great and absolute, that I lost all respect for the law. This was why, when the section of the movements [OILM] was removed from the Sepah, though I had the power to prevent it, I regrettably gave my consent that the brothers bring weapons, ammunition, explosives and documents from the Sepah.[33]

Speaking of his relationship with Montazeri, Hashemi declared that he now realised and regretted that in abuse of Montazeri's confidence, and by taking advantage of the presence of his brother and numerous friends in his office, he had turned Montazeri's religious seminaries to his own interests and transformed his office into his own base:

> In this aspect, I, who was a dirty man and had committed a series of erroneous, ignoble and divisive acts and thoughts, should not have approached the office [of Montazeri]. However, alas, it has happened and I have sought to interfere and to influence both the office and the gentleman [Montazeri] and by this I have verily committed a great treason.[34]

Hashemi had been forced by Reyshahri to make two confessions: one reserved for Khomeini and Montazeri and the other for the general public. Contrary to Reyshahri's promise, a censured and shortened version of the recording destined for Khomeini was shown on television which included points Hashemi would not have wanted to be made public.[35] Three days after the broadcast of his confession, Reyshahri went public with a long list of accusations against Hashemi. These included propaganda against the revolution and the hoarding of arms and ammunition for the overthrow of the regime. Furthermore, he was accused of the murder of Shamsabadi in April 1976.

According to Montazeri, Shamsabadi was a court cleric who, on the instigation of the Savak, had joined the campaign against the controversial book *Shahid-e javid*. On several occasions he had preached against the book and its supporters in Najafabad and Qohdarijan. As Montazeri was in prison and could not respond to the accusations, Mehdi Hashemi, together with several associates, took it upon himself to silence Shamsabadi and in the course of this attack killed the cleric.[36] At the time, the murder caused a major scandal. The regime used it against the political clergy, which was obliged to distance itself from it. Hashemi claimed that he had only wanted to frighten, and not murder, the cleric, but he was sentenced to death by a court in Isfahan. The verdict was later repealed by another court (his opponents claim, after his agreeing to collaborate with the Savak), and in late 1978 Hashemi was set free.

When, in 1986, it was announced that he should again be tried for this murder, some officials questioned the legality, as well as the advisability of such a step, but in the end Reyshahri prevailed.[37] Some days after the charges had been announced, Reyshahri declared that Hashemi and his associates would be put on trial before the Special Court of the Clergy. This court had initially been set up after the revolution, but its activities had been so controversial that after a short time it was dissolved. As it had no basis in the constitution it was considered by many to be illegal. Nonetheless, on the order of Khomeini it was revived on 16 June 1987. Ali Razini became its judge and Hojatoleslam Ali Fallahian was made its chief prosecutor. On 19 August, the trial against Hashemi was opened with the reading of the accusation. He was charged with:

(1) Setting up and directing numerous groups specialised in terrorism and abduction before and after the revolution; (2) Attempting to set up and direct an independent organisation in the Sepah and to secure its maintenance and equipment [which led to] clashes with local revolutionary committees resulting in dozens of people being killed and wounded; (3) Hiding more than 250 weapons and large quantities of ammunition belonging to the Sepah; (4) Infiltrating different institutions and offices and stealing secret and classified documents [...].[38]

He was also accused of creating discontent with the leadership by spreading false news in unsigned 'night letters', as well as disrupting the country's foreign relations with the consequence of 'hundreds of people being killed in clashes between states'.[39] Seven days after the reading of the list of accusations the trial ended with the expected verdict: Hashemi was found guilty of 'fighting against God' (*mohārabe*) and other crimes, and condemned to death.[40]

After Hashemi's arrest, his relatives pressed Montazeri to intervene in his favour. In a long meeting with Ahmad Khomeini, Montazeri criticised the fact that neither Hashemi nor the people accused of relations with him had been given the right to defence. Montazeri declared that he would not compare Khomeini to the Shah but that he certainly saw some similarities between 'the crimes of your intelligence service and the situation in your prisons' and the former regime. He concluded, 'I assumed that one day you would be cut off from the majority of your supporters, but I did not suppose that this would happen so soon'.[41] However, these complaints had as little effect as Montazeri's earlier letters. While Montazeri did manage to secure the release of Hadi Hashemi, who after his brother's confession had also temporarily been arrested and exiled, he was not able to save Mehdi Hashemi. When the death sentence against him was announced, Montazeri tried to intervene one last time: on 27 September 1987, he wrote a short note to Khomeini in which he reminded the *faqih* of Hashemi's service to the revolution and asked him to spare his life, concluding his letter with the words 'Executing is always possible, but nobody can bring the dead back to life.'[42] Apparently Khomeini was moved to show clemency. Reputedly, Reyshahri himself later confirmed[43] that one day after Montazeri had sent the note Ahmad Khomeini phoned to inform him that his father wanted the death sentence to be transformed into internal exile. To gain time, Reyshahri asked him for a written confirmation of this order. However, before the confirmation could arrive, he had Hashemi secretly executed.[44] If this account is correct, it would confirm Montazeri's claim that the driving force for the removal of Mehdi Hashemi was the group surrounding Reyshahri.

After his arrest it was also rumoured that Hashemi's elimination was part of a secret deal with the USA.[45] This thesis was sustained by Reagan's national security advisor, John Poindexter, who on 14 November in an interview declared that Hashemi, who had been linked to the hostage taking in Lebanon, had been arrested following an agreement with the Iranian government to cut its support to foreign terrorist groups.[46] Although I have found no evidence that Hashemi's name was actually discussed during the talks, the Americans were obviously keen that the Iranians end their backing for terrorist groups. The removal of Hashemi may therefore have been a welcome occasion for Rafsanjani to prove his resolve to bring about a change in foreign policy, while also permitting him to obtain fuller control of the hostages and to eliminate a key supporter of Montazeri. Montazeri himself was convinced that, from the start, the affair was directed not against Hashemi but against himself. In the light of Khomeini's advanced age and failing health, so he claimed, Reyshahri, Rafsanjani and Ahmad Khomeini had wanted to bring his house and office under their control. To establish their influence over the future leader, they had sought to remove Mehdi and Hadi Hashemi as well as a number of other people. As Montazeri wrote, they had wanted not the rule *of* the jurist, but the rule *over* the jurist.[47] Although subsequently not only Khomeini but also Rafsanjani and Meshkini publicly declared their support for Montazeri,[48] it was clear, that his position had been considerably undermined.

## Protesting against the Prison Purges

The execution of several thousand people in a few days is not an appropriate reaction and errors cannot be ruled out [...]. One should remember the following hadith: 'If possible try not to apply the Islamic penal laws to Muslims and, if you have the choice to avoid these punishments, use this opportunity. It would be better for an Imam to wrongly forgive than to wrongly punish.'
(Montazeri, in his letter to Khomeini of 31 July 1988)[49]

In July 1988, faced with military defeat at the front, economic collapse at home and growing social discontent, Iran was forced to sue for peace with Iraq. On 18 July, Khomeini accepted what he referred to as a 'poisonous chalice' and signed the UN Security Council Resolution 598 on a ceasefire agreement. Almost eight years after the Iraqi attack on Khuzestan, and more than six years after the expulsion of Iraqi troops from Iranian soil, this ended a war which had caused both sides human suffering and material damage without count. It left the Iranian people disillusioned about the revolution and distrustful of any further revolutionary undertaking. Four days after the signing of the resolution, and a few days before the ceasefire was to go into effect, the military forces of the Mojahedin-e Khalq, with the assistance of the Iraqi airforce, launched one last offensive against Iran. In the operation 'Eternal Light', their forces captured several small Iranian towns and started to march on Kermanshah, 100 kilometres from the border. However, if they had hoped to benefit from popular discontent and spark a revolt against the regime, they were mistaken. Not only was the ill-prepared offensive quickly brought to a halt and the invading forces almost entirely wiped out, but neither did the expected revolt take place.

Most Iranians were not willing to forgive the fact that the Mojahedin had taken sides with the country's enemy and were not ready to join them. Nevertheless, for the hardliners, who had long wanted to purge the overcrowded prisons, the Mojahedin's offensive offered the necessary pretext to finish them off once and for all.[50] Shortly after the invasion Khomeini issued a secret fatwa, which ordered the execution of all Mojahedin held in the country's prisons. The unsigned and undated decree, which was first published in Montazeri's memoirs in 2000, stipulated that whoever among them refused to refute their beliefs was to be considered an enemy of God:

As the treacherous monafeqin [Mojahedin][51] do not believe in Islam and what they say is deceptive and hypocritical, as their leaders have confessed that they have become renegades, as they are waging war on God, as they are engaging in classical warfare in the western, the northern and the southern fronts, as they are collaborating with the Baath Party of Iraq and spying for Saddam against our Muslim nation, and as they are tied to World Arrogance [USA], and in light of their cowardly blows to the Islamic Republic since its inception, it is decreed that those who are in prison throughout the country and remain steadfast in their support for the monafeqin, are waging war on God and are condemned to execution. The task of implementing the decree in Tehran is entrusted to Hojatoleslam Nayyeri, the religious judge, Mr Eshraqi, the Tehran prosecutor, and a representative of the Intelligence Ministry. Even though a unanimous decision is better, the view of a majority must prevail. In the provincial prisons, the views of a majority of a trio consisting of the religious judge, the revolutionary prosecutor, and the Intelligence Ministry representative must be obeyed. It is naive to show mercy to those who wage war on God [...]. Those who are making the decisions must not hesitate, nor show any doubt or be concerned with details. They must try to be 'most ferocious against infidels.' To have doubts in matters of revolutionary Islam is to ignore the pure blood of martyrs.[52]

Apparently, the decree was issued on Thursday 28 July, one day before the withdrawal of the remaining Mojahedin forces from Iranian soil. On the following Saturday, a copy of the order was transmitted to Montazeri by a prison official from Qom, who was alarmed by the way the decree had been put into practice. He told Montazeri that the intelligence service pressed the prosecutors and judges to rapidly proceed with the executions. In interviews, which often lasted not more than a few minutes, the prisoners, who had no knowledge of what was at stake, were asked by the commission if they remained steadfast in their political beliefs. If they replied yes, they were immediately executed. Shocked by what he had heard, Montazeri asked the chief justice, Musavi-Ardebili, to intervene with Khomeini. It was not right to execute prisoners for an action they had had no part in, and often not even any knowledge of. To condemn a person who had already been condemned on other charges, and who had not committed any new offence, was against the law, he maintained.[53] Apparently, Musavi-Ardebili thereupon called Khomeini's office, but rather than directly relate Montazeri's criticism he preferred to frame it in the form of questions. These questions were later written by Ahmad Khomeini on the back of Khomeini's decree:

Does the decree apply to those in prison who have already been tried and sentenced to death, but have not changed their stance and, where the verdict has not yet been carried out, or are those who have not yet been tried also condemned to death? Are those Monafeqin prisoners who have received limited jail terms and already served part of their terms but continue to hold fast to their stance in support of the Monafeqin, also condemned to death? In reviewing the status of the Monafeqin prisoners is it necessary to

refer the cases in counties with an independent judicial organ
to the provincial centre or can the county's judicial authorities
act autonomously?[54]

Khomeini's answer to these questions was brief and left little doubt
about his intentions. Clearly he was not concerned with the legality of
his order:

> In all the above cases, if the person at any stage or at any time
> maintains his [or her] support for the Monafeqin, the sentence is
> execution. Annihilate the enemies of Islam immediately. As regards
> the cases, use whichever criterion speeds up the implementation of
> the verdict.[55]

To this day it is disputed whether the order was really written by
Khomeini. Montazeri suggested that the text was issued on the initiative
and under the influence of members of Khomeini's office, who had
assumed control over the ageing leader. He pointed out that, at the time
of its publication it was said that the letter was in Ahmad Khomeini's
handwriting.[56] However, the fact that Khomeini did not write the text
by his own hand does not rule out the possibility that he dictated the
words. And, while it is quite possible that Khomeini was influenced by
others to issue the order, there is no proof that it was issued without his
consent. In any case, the decree was quickly put into effect: On 29 July,
the prisons were sealed off, visits by relatives and friends interrupted,
and access to television and newspapers stopped. Survivors of the purges
later recalled that this day marked the beginning of intense activity in
the prisons: some inmates were moved to other facilities, others were
transferred to solitary confinement and the first batch of prisoners was
taken to interrogation. At night, prisoners heard the sounds of the firing
squads and saw the dead bodies loaded onto trucks. In many prisons,
those condemned to execution were hanged from cranes, six at a time.[57]
When Montazeri saw that the executions were continuing unabated in
spite of his intervention, he decided to write a letter to Khomeini. He
recalls that before writing the text he consulted with his associates, Hadi
Hashemi and Qazi Khoramabadi. Both men advised against intervening
over the executions because it would only anger Khomeini who, after the
Mojahedin offensive, was not willing to show any clemency. However,

Montazeri felt that, as the deputy leader, he would be held responsible for the killings and that it was his duty to prevent harm to religion and the revolution. After reading his prayers and consulting the Qur'an, he therefore sat down to draft the text:

> Concerning your Excellency's order for the execution of the imprisoned monafeqin: The execution of those arrested during the recent events [the invasion] is accepted by the nation and society and apparently has no contrary effect. However, the execution of those who have been imprisoned for a long time will under the present circumstances be seen as revenge and disappoint and hurt many families generally loyal to the revolution. Although many of these prisoners no longer persist in their former positions, certain radical members of the executive behave as though they do [...]. The sudden execution of prisoners who have been condemned by the courts to minor sentences according to the law, and who have not committed any new offence, will lead to indifference towards the judicial principals and the courts' rulings [...]. So far, the executions and the brutal proceedings have not had any positive result but only increased the propaganda against the system, as well as the interest in the monafeqin and the enemies of the revolution [...]. Should you maintain your orders, at least insist that decisions be based on the collective ruling [...] and that no more women are executed [...]. The execution of several thousand people in a few days is not an appropriate reaction and errors cannot be ruled out [...]. 'It would be better for an Imam to wrongly forgive than to wrongly punish.'[58]

On 31 July 1988, Montazeri sent one copy to Khomeini's office and another copy to the chief justice, Musavi-Ardebili. To make sure that the letter actually reached Khomeini, he called the members of his office and told them to immediately forward it. However, he never received a reply. When, a few days later, Mohammad-Hossein Ahmadi,[59] a religious judge from Khuzestan province, reported to him on the hasty and often unlawful way in which the prisoners were sent to the gallows, Montazeri decided to write a second letter to Khomeini in which he recounted what the judge had said:

Three days ago a shari'a-judge from the province, who is a reliable man, came to me in Qom. He was much alarmed by the way your recent decree was put into action. He told me: The officer of the intelligence service questioned a prisoner whether he persists in his beliefs. He asked him: Are you ready to condemn the organisation of the monafeqin? The answer was: Yes. Are you ready to go to the front and fight against Iraq? – Yes. Are you ready to step on a mine? – Are people ready to step on mines? One should not expect too much of me, I have only recently become a Muslim. – Then it is clear that you persist in your former position. And the officer behaved as though the prisoner had not repented.[60]

Montazeri sent the letter on 4 August. Two days later, he received a brief reply from Ahmad Khomeini in which he was advised not to worry about the executions: God would punish the Mojahedin.[61] In his memoirs, Montazeri insisted that it was not out of love for the Mojahedin that he intervened, but out of concern for the reputation of religion and the revolution. He was not generally opposed to executing political opponents, notably if they had taken up arms against the regime, but he was outraged at the unlawful killing of people who had often not done more than distribute tracts or shout slogans. Over the course of the following days, Montazeri learnt more details about the proceedings from one of his representatives in the prisons and a prosecutor in Fars province.[62] On 15 August, Montazeri called the officials of Evin to his office: the prison's shari'a judge Hossein-Ali Nayyeri, Tehran's prosecutor Morteza Eshraqi, Tehran's deputy prosecutor Ebrahim Ra'isi and the Deputy Minister of Intelligence Mostafa Pur-Mohammadi. When he asked them to immediately stop the executions, Nayyeri replied that they had already executed 850 prisoners and would stop the executions once they had killed the other 200 prisoners already tried. This response very much angered Montazeri. He told them that, should Mojahedin continue to agitate in the prisons and to propagate their beliefs, they should be tried for these offences by a regular court. Should one find that, according to the law, they deserved the death sentence, they should be executed. However, to execute a person condemned only to a minor prison sentence would not only be unlawful, but also un-Islamic. It would harm Islam, the system and the revolution and would help the Mojahedin.[63] Montazeri's notes of this meeting were later published in Ahmad Khomeini's *Ranjname*, as well as his own memoirs:

> I have suffered more harm and beatings from the Mojahedin than all of you, both inside and outside of the prison. They have martyred my son and if anyone should seek revenge, it should be me. However, I bear in mind the interests of Islam, the revolution, the country, the prestige of velāyat-e faqih and Islamic government, and the judgement of the future, and of history. Such a massacre of prisoners without proper trials will surely in the long term benefit [the Mojahedin], will encourage them to pursue their fight and the world will condemn us. It is wrong to combat ideas and thoughts by executions [...]. The Mojahedin-e Khalq are not a person, but rather a way of thinking. It is a kind of logic, and one must confront the wrong logic with the correct logic and the correct arguments. Killings will not make it disappear but rather encourage it.[64]

In early September, Khomeini reportedly issued a second secret decree in which he ordered the execution of all non-religious prisoners, e.g. the communists. Since the text of this decree never surfaced, its exact content remains unknown. Montazeri recalled that, when this decree fell by chance into the hands of President Khamene'i, he became very angry and ordered an immediate halt to the executions. When Montazeri asked him why he was so upset by this second order but had done nothing to stop the execution of the first decree, Khamene'i was surprised because, or so at least he pretended, he had not known of this decree.[65] Prisoners reported that by mid-August the first wave of executions was over, probably because most Mojahedin had been killed by this time. It was only after the second fatwa that the trials and executions resumed. While the Mojahedin were executed for their political beliefs, the communists were killed for their refusal to pray and recognise God. It remains an open question as to whether the massacres were primarily politically or religiously motivated. Khomeini's fatwa called the Mojahedin enemies of God, but also accused them of siding with the enemy and fighting against the regime. Although the communists were clearly judged according to their religious belief, their execution as heretics can also be understood as an attempt to give a political decision a religious legitimation.

While Tehran was the centre of the purges, executions also took place in most other cities. Only the Isfahan prison escaped the purges because it was still under Montazeri's control. Apparently the massacre was also used to execute a number of other opponents, among them 11 supporters of Montazeri.[66] Ultimately, all of Montazeri's actions were to no avail. According to his memoirs, between 2,800 and 3,800 political prisoners were executed in the country's prisons in the summer and autumn of 1988.[67] In 1990, a report of the Mojahedin-e Khalq put the number of prisoners executed in August 1988 at 1,300. Later, they published a list with the names of 3,208 of their supporters who fell victim to the purges. Amnesty International estimates that around 2,000 people were killed, but declared that it has no evidence as to the exact extent of the massacre.[68] Thus, the number of people murdered during the purges remains unclear.

By late September or early October 1988, the worst of the massacres was over and the prisons were partly reopened. Although family members were again allowed to visit prisoners, the relatives of the victims were kept in the dark regarding their kin's fate, and even their burial places were kept secret. In spite of these attempts to stop information from leaking out, international human rights bodies quickly learnt of the massacres. In October, the UN special representative for human rights in Iran presented an initial report on the executions, but then did not further follow up on the information regarding the massacre. The regime continued to deny all accusations, and to this day has not officially confirmed the executions.[69]

## Montazeri's Call for Liberalisation

> On many occasions we showed obstinacy, shouted slogans and frightened the world, who thought our only task here in Iran was to kill. We should not stop at making promises about freedom of speech and freedom for political parties [...]. Unfortunately, we see good people who are afraid of persecution. They cannot breathe in peace. This is wrong.
>
> (Montazeri, in his speech on 11 February 1989)[70]

With the end of the war in 1988, the political debate turned to the reconstruction of the country which, after eight years of conflict, was suffering a major economic crisis. Not only had large parts of the border regions been destroyed or damaged, as well as many of the major ports, industries and refineries, but the whole economy had been destabilised by the war. Shortages were common, inflation was rising, and unemployment was widespread. During the last phase of the war, Iraqi air strikes had caused significant damage to the cities, so that the housing crisis caused by the refugees from the border regions had been further exacerbated. While, during the hostilities, these social and economic problems had been overshadowed by the military crisis, and all resources had been directed at winning the war, now that the conflict was over attention focused on the resolution of the economic crisis. The people, who for many years had silently suffered the constraints and restrictions imposed by the war, were increasingly unwilling to accept the situation. While, through the war years, the political leadership had been able to blame the enemy for all problems, now the leadership itself, as well as its incompetence, inefficiency and corruption, were increasingly held responsible.

The disillusionment of the soldiers returning from the front further added to this social crisis. Many of these combatants, who had risked their lives and suffered adversities and injuries, had to discover on their return that both state and society preferred to forget about the war as soon as possible. Those who had volunteered to defend the revolution out of idealism were especially disappointed to find on their return that society had turned its back on many of the original ideas, values and objectives of the revolution, and that many of the officials were less concerned with the revolution than with their own advantage. Echoing the preoccupations of the people, Montazeri in a letter to Prime Minister Mussavi complained about the incompetence, inefficiency and corruption of many officials. In his letter of 1 October 1988, which was leaked to the public the following month, he also criticised the faulty structures of the system:

After the end of the war there is the expectation that the economic and political situation and the treatment of the people will fundamentally change. Shortages, injustice, inflation, lack of income, irrational price differences, many of which are caused by the government itself, as well as the incompetence, ruthlessness and narrow-mindedness of certain trade officials in the country's import-export sector and the interference in commerce of unaccountable organisations such as the Revolutionary Guards and the Martyrs' Foundation have led to the total paralysis of the economy.[71]

Montazeri added that while even the socialist countries had recognised their mistakes, opened the political sphere and given more power to the people, in Iran politics 'has fallen into the hands of inexperienced children whose policies cause numerous shortages and injustices'. The intelligence and security services must mend their ways, as 'the numerous arrests, beatings and killings' have had no benefit but fuelled the discontent of the people. He recommended that the government replace 'narrow-minded, heavy-handed and inconsiderate' officials, eliminate duplicate offices, end rationing and encourage investment in industry and agriculture. He also asked that the government propose a general amnesty to entice the millions of educated Iranians living abroad to return home. Only a small portion of those living in exile was really opposed to the system, he asserted, whereas the others were willing to return if they were given the assurance that they would not be troubled. Their continuous presence abroad threw a negative light on the system, Montazeri warned, as it testified to the existence of fear and violence in the country. While he was certainly not the only one to address these problems or to propose such reforms, the words of his letter were harsher than those employed by other leading politicians. At the approach of the tenth anniversary of the revolution he went even further, and in an interview on 23 December 1988 accused the political class of having turned its back on the original ideas and values of the revolution:

> Unfortunately, we have shouted slogans rather than implement and protect the values [of the revolution], and instead of giving priority to the people and the people's protection, we have increasingly alienated and marginalised the enlightened and knowledgeable forces. Clearly, the situation has reached a point that, for our own protection, we have to violate our own original objectives and forget all values.[72]

Taking up these very words in another interview published on 8 February 1989 in the daily *Keyhan*, he continued in what was no longer the mere criticism of some isolated points but rather a sweeping assault on the leadership and a direct attack on Khomeini:

> I agree with the new generation of the revolution that there is a great distance between what we promised and what we have achieved [...] mismanagement, a failure to give jobs to the right people, exaggeration, self-centredness, monopolisation, factionalism, the denial of people's rights, injustice and disregard for the revolution's true values have delivered the most severe blows against the revolution to date. Before any reconciliation [takes place], there must first be a reconstruction of the country's thinking about administration and its quality, and there must be a political and ideological reconstruction in the management of the country. This is something that the people expect of the leader.[73]

Three days later in a speech for the tenth anniversary of the revolution, Montazeri continued this attack. Criticising the large sums of money spent on vain and futile festivities while the people suffered from shortages and power cuts, he admonished the officials to do more to help the poor and the invalids of the war. Rather than repress all dissent, the leadership should open the media to the citizens so that they could express their opinion and their criticism. Turning to Iran's foreign policy, Montazeri openly questioned the necessity of continuing the war:

> Did we do a good job during the war? Our enemies, who imposed the war on us, emerged victorious. Let us count the forces we lost, the young people we lost, how many towns were destroyed [...] and then let us repent recognising that we made these mistakes. On many occasions we showed obstinacy, shouted slogans, and frightened the world who thought our only task here in Iran was to kill. We should not stop at making promises about freedom of speech and freedom for political parties. Our behaviour and actions should be such that all devoted revolutionaries who have ideals can state them in the interests of the revolution and for the development of the country without fear of persecution. Unfortunately, we see good people who are afraid of persecution. They cannot breathe in peace. This is wrong.[74]

In the end, echoing an idea he had earlier expressed in an interview, Montazeri went so far as to say that if government violated the values of religion and the revolution, it was better not to have any government at all: Rather not rule than rule in violation of one's own principles. His speech was a transgression of the rules and limits of the discourse, which could not stand without response or sanction. If his position as the deputy leader and a source of emulation had so far allowed him to say what others dared not express, he had now crossed the 'red line'. With his speech he had infringed upon several rules of the political discourse:

1. Not to express criticism in public. As long as Montazeri had only expressed his criticism in private letters to the leadership, this had been accepted as a tiresome but permissible form of protest. However, when he turned to criticising the government in public speeches and interviews, it was no longer tolerable as it could no longer be ignored and brought the dissension among the leadership to the public's attention.

2. Not to question the central policies of the government. As long as Montazeri had only criticised the failures and deviations of individual officials and institutions, as was the case when he condemned the squander of certain officials and the broadcasting of un-Islamic programmes in the media, this was to be tolerated. However, when he turned to criticising the failures of the government to fulfil its own promises, this put into question the entire regime.

3. Not to attack the ruling jurist. Khomeini was not officially considered infallible, but to publicly accuse him of mistakes was unacceptable. When Montazeri not only admonished him to see to the ideological and administrative restructuring of the country – therewith indirectly holding him responsible for the current dismal situation – but also questioned Khomeini's decision to continue the war, he went too far.

In contrast to Khomeini, who had several times changed the red lines, Montazeri did not have the authority to redefine the rules of the discourse nor to redraw the limits of the discursive field. His political position by this time was already severely weakened. He had lost the confidence of Khomeini and had, through his constant criticism, angered

**Plate 1**   Having obtained the degree of *ejtehād*, Montazeri, here in a photo from 1957, wore the characteristic white turban and dark cloak of the clergy. (Source: © courtesy of the Office of Ayatollah Montazeri)

**Plate 2**   During the protests against the reforms of the Shah in 1963, Montazeri with other young clerics set out to mobilise the students of the seminaries in Qom. (Source: © courtesy of the Office of Ayatollah Montazeri)

**Plate 3** At the opening session in August 1979, Montazeri was elected chairman of the Expert Assembly, but mostly left the chair to his deputy Beheshti. (Source: © courtesy of the Office of Ayatollah Montazeri)

**Plate 4** Montazeri and Beheshti were considered the main advocates of *velayat-e faqih* in the Expert Assembly and strongly pushed for its inclusion in the constitution. (Source: © courtesy of the Office of Ayatollah Montazeri)

**Plate 5** In autumn 1979, Montazeri served for several weeks as Tehran's Friday prayer leader, but after his return to Qom he left the post to Khamene'i. (Source: © courtesy of the Office of Ayatollah Montazeri)

**Plate 6** Montazeri and Khamene'i had closely collaborated during the struggle against the Shah, but after the revolution maintained only a distant relationship. (Source: © courtesy of the Office of Ayatollah Montazeri)

**Plate 7**  Although Montazeri, here during a speech in 1980, did not hold any formal office after the revolution, he regularly intervened in the public debate. (Source: © courtesy of the Office of Ayatollah Montazeri)

**Plate 8**  Montazeri, here during Tehran Friday prayers in February 1980, was known as good natured, humorous and amenable. (Source: © courtesy of the Office of Ayatollah Montazeri)

**Plate 9**  Shortly after the revolution, Khomeini placed Montazeri in charge of choosing and training the Friday prayer leaders for whom he set up a special school in Qom. (Source: © courtesy of the Office of Ayatollah Montazeri)

**Plate 10**  As one of Khomeini's closest students and supporters Montazeri was chosen in 1985 as his designated successor, but during the following years, he maintained his intellectual independence. (Source: Kaveh Kazemi/ Getty Images)

**Plate 11** In November 1997, in his famous speech at his *hosseiniye* in Qom, Montazeri attacked Khamene'i for obstructing reforms and disputed his claim to the *marja'iyat*. (Source: © courtesy of the Office of Ayatollah Montazeri)

**Plate 12** Following his release from house arrest in January 2003, Montazeri despite his advanced age and frail health continued to work on his religious and political writings. (Source: © courtesy of the Office of Ayatollah Montazeri)

Rafsanjani and Khamene'i. However, even now, Khomeini hesitated to depose his designated successor.

In an apparent attempt to divert attention and to gain time, the leader turned to another question: Salman Rushdie's *The Satanic Verses*. The book contained a passage that referred to an episode from the Prophet's life according to which he had at one point been unable to distinguish between Godly revelation and the whispering of Satan. In Khomeini's view this passage was an insult to Islam, the Prophet and the Qur'an, even though the related episode was mentioned in several Islamic histories. In a short fatwa broadcast on the morning of 14 February 1989 on Tehran Radio, Khomeini called upon all Muslims to kill the author and the publishers of the novel. That Khomeini chose this moment to issue his fatwa was clearly politically motivated. *The Satanic Verses* had been accessible in Iran soon after it had been published in September 1988. Extracts and reviews had been broadcast on Persian-language radio stations abroad, and reviews had appeared in the Iranian press. Later, a scholar had presented an extensive refutation of the novel to Khomeini, but the latter had dismissed the issue saying that there had always been people who spoke nonsense, and that this book was not to be taken seriously.[75] By December 1988, the book had been banned in five countries but it could still be freely imported into Iran. It was only after violent protests erupted in Islamabad and Kashmir on 12 and 13 February that Khomeini broke the silence he had so far maintained on the matter. When he issued his fatwa, his objective was twofold: he was able to present himself as the leader of the Muslim masses, and he could show to his internal critics that, despite his failing health and advanced age, he still held the reigns of the country. The fact that no other Muslim country was willing to condone his death sentence against Rushdie, and that his fatwa once more exacerbated Iran's isolation, were accepted as unavoidable, if not actually welcome, side effects. When, on 18 February, Rushdie issued a statement regretting the distress his book had caused to many Muslims, Khomeini refused to accept this apology. He not only declared that Rushdie should be killed even if he became a devout Muslim, but also offered a reward to any non-Muslim willing to kill the author.[76]

It was amidst the outrage caused by his fatwa that, on 22 February, Khomeini turned on his critics in a long letter to the clergy. In what was a veiled response to Montazeri's criticism, he refuted the accusation that the revolution had failed to reach its objectives, defended his policies during the war and warned against compromise with the regime's opponents. Even though Iran had not reached its final aims in the war, he wrote, it had in no way been defeated. Rather, the war had been a 'blessing' to the country: it had revealed Iran's oppression by the imperialist powers and taught it to stand on its own feet.[77] Addressing the question of an amnesty for political refugees, which would allow Iranians abroad to return home, Khomeini declared that anyone willing to serve the country was welcome to return. However, it would not be tolerated should they question the revolution or criticise the regime's past or present policies. Khomeini apologised to the veterans of the war for the 'erroneous analyses made these days', but declared that he would not repent or apologise for the conduct of the war, which he reminded his readers had been 'fought to fulfil our religious duty', while its 'result is a marginal issue'. Without explicitly naming Montazeri, he declared that questioning the achievements of the revolution would lead to the loss of the people's confidence. He warned all revolutionaries against listening to the 'liberals' of the Nehzat-e Azadi. Otherwise they would regain their former position in the system, which, he maintained, they had never deserved. The letter was a clear warning to Montazeri and a signal to his opponents that he no longer held the leader's support. Immediately, the efforts for Montazeri's removal were intensified and by the end of the month rumours were circulating that his deposition was imminent.

## The Fall of Montazeri

> Since it has become clear that after my death you are going to hand over this country, our revolution, and the people of Iran to the liberals, and thereby to the monafeqin, you have lost the legitimacy to succeed me as the leader of the state [...]. Since you are naive and easily influenced, do not interfere in political matters, and perhaps God will forgive you your sins.
>
> (Khomeini, in his letter of dismissal to Montazeri of
> 26 March 1989)[78]

Montazeri's speech had been a transgression of the rules and limits of the political discourse and it was clear that such a violation would not stand without response. If his political position as the deputy leader had so far permitted him to say what others dared not express, this time he had gone too far. With his speech he had provided his opponents with the opportunity to openly attack his position, and in the following days and weeks numerous articles and editorials appeared in the press meant to undermine his authority and thus to pave the way for his removal. At this point not only Khomeini but also the other members of the leadership knew that the leader's death was imminent. Suffering from an advanced state of cancer, Khomeini's health was rapidly and visibly deteriorating. When, on 19 March, Khomeini asked Montazeri to return a sealed letter that was only to be opened after his death, Montazeri knew that the decision for his deposition was irreversible. On 22 March 1989, Khomeini publicly declared that 'I have not signed a contract of brotherhood with anyone. The framework of my friendship depends on the correct behaviour of each individual'. Thereupon, Montazeri decided to write a letter to Khomeini to offer his resignation:

> I have so far been convinced that my criticism and my remarks
> do not weaken the system, but that they give hope to the majority
> of the people, and that the officials lend more attention to these
> questions, and that they thus strengthen the system and the
> revolution. However, should you decide that this is not in the
> interest [of the state] and that it weakens the revolution and the
> system, I will give priority to your opinion. Never have I had
> anything else in mind but the good of Islam and the revolution.[79]

This letter was sent on 24 March. However, the following morning the text of Montazeri's letters to Khomeini protesting against the 1988 prison purges were broadcast on the BBC. Thus, for the first time, the existence of an official order for the execution of the prisoners was confirmed. The letters had been transmitted to Banisadr's office in Paris, which had forwarded them to the BBC. How they had reached Paris is not clear,[80] but it is likely that opponents of Montazeri had passed them to Banisadr in the expectation that their publication would hasten the former's deposition – a supposition that was to prove correct. On 26 March, Khomeini sent a scathing letter to Montazeri in which he accused him of collaboration with the Mojahedin and the liberals, forbade him to further intervene in politics and deposed him not only as his successor but also as his religious representative:

My heart is broken and filled with blood now that I write a few words to you. Perhaps one day the people will realise the truth by reading this letter. In your recent letter, you said that, in accordance with the shari'a, you would give priority to my views over your own. God is my witness when I point out the following points: as it has become clear that after my death you are going to hand over this country, the revolution, and the people of Iran to the liberals, and thereby to the monafeqin, you have lost the legitimacy to succeed me as the leader. In your letters, speeches and statements you have shown that you believe that the liberals and the monafeqin should rule this country. Since it was clear that your remarks were dictated by the monafeqin, I did not see the point in sending a reply. The monafeqin took advantage of your speeches and writings in their defence to promote their comrades, who had been condemned to death on the charge of waging war against Islam and the revolution, to positions of power. Can you see what valuable service you have offered arrogance [United States]? Concerning the murderer Mehdi Hashemi, you considered him to be one of the most religious persons in the world. Although it was proven to you that he was a murderer, you continued to ask me to spare his life [...]. You no longer have the power of representation on my behalf [...]. It breaks my heart and my chest is full of pain when I see that you, the product of my life, are so ungrateful. Relying on God, I give you these words of advice, and you will decide whether you heed them or not: (1) Try to change the members of your house so as to not further nourish the monafeqin, the liberals and Mehdi Hashemi's group from the donations of the Imam. (2) Since you are naïve and easily influenced, do not further interfere in politics and maybe God will forgive you your sins. (3) Do not ever write to me again, and do not allow the monafeqin to pass state secrets to the foreign radio. (4) Since you became the voice of the monafeqin and your speeches have, through the media, conveyed their wishes to the people, you have severely damaged Islam and the revolution. This is treason against the unknown soldiers of the Hidden Imam [the intelligence service], and against the sacrifices made by the martyrs of Islam and the revolution. If you wish to be saved from hell, you should confess your sins and mistakes and maybe God will help you. I swear to God that from the start I was against choosing you as my successor, but I did not realise you were so easily influenced. I never believed that you were a resourceful manager, but I thought you were an educated man from whom the seminaries could benefit. If you continue on this path, I will be obliged to act against you, and you know I never neglect my duties. I swear to God that I was also against appointing Mehdi Bazargan as prime minister, but I considered him to be an honest man. I swear to God that I also did not vote for Banisadr as president. In each case I followed the advice of my friends [...]. I ask God to forgive me and to take me away from this world so that I no longer have to taste the bitterness of my friend's treachery. We all submit to God. We have no power without God. Everything comes from Him.[81]

On the morning of 27 March, the letter was delivered to Montazeri by a member of Khomeini's office. Two hours later, Khomeini's representative to the Pasdaran, Hojatoleslam Abdollah Nuri, arrived from Tehran and warned that the 'gentlemen' wanted to have the letter read on the radio. As this would not only have been humiliating to Montazeri but also harmful to the system, Nuri urged him to write an apologetic reply accepting his deposition. On the way from Tehran he had drafted a letter in which Montazeri admitted to having let the Mojahedin infiltrate his office. Hojatoleslam Qorban'ali Dori-Najafabadi, who had replaced Hadi Hashemi at the head of Montazeri's office, also urged him to prevent a further escalation of the situation.[82] Montazeri refused to admit to something he considered false, but after Nuri's departure he wrote a letter, which, if not apologetic, was accommodating, and, despite the harsh tone of Khomeini's letter, humble and polite:

Just as I have, since the beginning of the uprising until the present day, been a selfless and obedient soldier at your side on the path of religion and the revolution, so I am today obliged to obey your orders because the preservation of the Islamic system demands that one obey the leader [...]. Concerning my designation as deputy leader, I have been opposed [to this decision] since the beginning, and, in the face of the numerous difficulties and the heavy burden of responsibility, I had written to the Expert Council, that my designation was not in the interest [of the state]. Today, I again clearly announce that I am not ready [to assume this post], and request you to instruct the Expert Council to keep the future interest of Islam, the revolution, and the country in mind. And I ask you to grant me permission that I may, as in the past, devote myself under your guidance as a small and humble student in the seminaries to my studies, my teachings, and the service to Islam and the revolution. And should mistakes occur, as is often found in human nature, things will, if God permits, be set right under your guidance. Concerning the decision of the leader and the experts, I beseech the honoured brothers and sisters that they refrain from any action or words in my defence, because the leader and the experts act solely for the benefit and in the interest of Islam and the revolution.[83]

Some hours after Nuri delivered the letter to Khomeini, the former called Montazeri to tell him that Khomeini had torn up his earlier letter and requested Montazeri to do the same. Should the text ever be made public, it would be his fault.[84] Furthermore, Nuri told Montazeri that in spite of his deposition as political leader he remained Khomeini's representative in religious matters.[85] The following day, state radio broadcast the text of Montazeri's letter of 27 March, together with Khomeini's reply. Written less than 48 hours after the first letter, the tone was completely changed – a fact that later led many to doubt that the first letter was of Khomeini's hand.

As you have written, the leadership of the Islamic Republic is an arduous task and a heavy responsibility that demands more patience and perseverance than you possess. This is why we both have been opposed to your designation since the beginning. In this point we were of the same opinion but, since the experts had decided otherwise, I did not want to intervene against their rightful decision. Now that you have announced that you are not ready to assume the post of deputy leader, I approve your decision and honestly thank you for it. Everybody knows that you have been the product of my life and I remain profoundly beholden to you. So that the past mistakes are not repeated I request that you clean your house of dishonest people and that you refrain from further contact with the opponents of the system who under the pretence of being inclined towards Islam and the Islamic Republic have infiltrated [your house]. I have already given you this advice after the affair of Mehdi Hashemi. I am convinced that you are a scholar from whose advice both the system and the people can benefit. Do not let yourself be perturbed by the lies of the foreign radio stations. The people know you well and they see through the ploys of our enemies [. . .]. In Islam the interests of the state are paramount and all else and everything else must be subordinate to them. If God permits, you will give warmth to the seminary and the system with your teachings.[86]

The man, who for more than eight years had been considered a father of the revolution, a leading scholar and had been addressed as a 'pillar of Islam' and the 'hope of the people' was thus deposed. From one day to the next his pictures were removed from offices, the publication of his lectures stopped and any reference to him, both in the media and during prayers, was forbidden. His books were taken from the shops and his seminaries placed under tight control. The general public was taken by surprise by his deposition and not all were willing to silently accept his removal. After all, Montazeri was not only a central figure of the revolutionary movement, but also a respected scholar whom many recognised as their source of emulation. Many members of the political and religious elite had attended his lectures, and many officials in the various institutions of the regime numbered among his supporters. Although many laughed at his simple manners and his rural dialect, many more among both the common people and the intellectual elite respected him for his modesty, his courage and his outspoken criticism of the failures of the regime. These people had set their hopes on him to put an end to the worst excesses and improve the conditions of the opposition once he assumed power. They were therefore disappointed when they learnt of his dismissal, and in Najafabad, Qom and other cities hundreds poured out onto the streets in spontaneous protests. It was only after a letter from Montazeri calling for restraint had been read to the protesters that the situation again calmed. Protests also erupted in parliament when his removal was discussed. To prevent a further escalation, Khomeini sent a letter to the deputies on 15 April in which he explained and justified Montazeri's dismissal.[87] His opponents realised that to silence him, it was not enough to withdraw his title. Amid a flurry of defamatory articles and editorials in the press, on 29 April 1989, Ahmad Khomeini published a book containing a lengthy list of accusations against Montazeri, along with a number of hitherto unpublished documents meant to break his authority.

The booklet, termed *Ranjname* (*Letter of Suffering*) was at first only distributed among Ahmad's friends and allies, but in mid-May, *Resalat* and *Al-Abrar* published long extracts before it was widely disseminated by the propaganda office.[88] The book was meant to prove Montazeri's deviation from the path of the revolution and to justify his removal from the post of deputy leader. It was intended to show to the surprised public that the dismissal of one of the fathers of the revolution and one of the pillars of Islam was a regrettable, but necessary, step in the best interest of the country. Ahmad claimed that his father had for the last two years been increasingly sceptical about Montazeri's personal aptitude and political ability to succeed him as the leader of the State. Due to Montazeri's naivety and simplicity he had been misused and manipulated by the liberals, the leftists and the Mojahedin, Ahmad claimed.[89] Several of his letters had been written on the initiative, or under the influence, of the members of his office. Even though Montazeri had not been personally plotting against the regime, he was unfit to rule the country. Montazeri, Ahmad declared, should repent for the fact that the latter's father 'for months and years [...] has patiently endured the whip of your unfounded accusations'.[90]

Ahmad quoted extensively from Mehdi Hashemi's confessions to prove how Hashemi and his brother had sought to influence Montazeri. As Ahmad wrote, the public had to be thankful for these confessions, because 'if these letters, interviews and writings of Mehdi Hashemi did not point to you [Montazeri] and the members of your house, we could not prove today that you became the mouthpiece of the monafeqin and the liberals'.[91] However, as these confessions had clearly been produced under torture they were hardly a credible source of evidence. Ahmad also included a selection of Montazeri's and Khomeini's letters from 1986 to 1989 in order to discredit Montazeri. However, these letters not only showed the growing dissent between the leader and his deputy, but also documented how Montazeri had sought to put an end to the worst excesses in the courts and prisons. To the more liberal classes of society this was not treason to the cause of the revolution, but rather an attempt to preserve its original objectives. That *Ranjname* allowed such a positive reading was not the only reason many members of the leadership were unhappy about its publication. In their view, it was not in the interest of the regime to further discuss such sensitive matters as the secret negotiations with the USA or the prison purges. However, Ahmad did not heed such objections because with the book he not only meant to damage Montazeri's authority but also to enhance his own position in the race for his father's succession. At its publication in May it was not printed, as might have been expected, with a photo of Montazeri on its cover, but rather with an image of Ahmad with a quotation from his father: 'You are honest and intelligent and I consider you an expert in social and political matters.'[92]

At the time of its publication the question of succession was clearly on everybody's mind. When, on 26 March, Khomeini had written his first letter to Montazeri he had also called his son Ahmad, Rafsanjani, Khamene'i, Meshkini and Ebrahim Amini, an influential member of the Expert Council, to discuss the question of succession. To the question of who should replace Montazeri, Khomeini reportedly replied 'you have Khamene'i who is eligible'.[93] Legally, he did not have the right to appoint his successor, but it was clear that his opinion in this matter would be decisive. Apparently he briefly considered Ahmad, but either he had doubts about his abilities, or he feared that this would look like the hereditary succession of a monarchy.[94]

When Khomeini died of a heart attack in his house in Jamaran on 3 June, the revision of the constitution had not been completed nor had a successor been chosen. Therefore, upon the news of his death, frantic activity set in.[95] To gain more time the information of his passing was initially kept secret, his residency sealed off and all communication interrupted. Only on the morning of 4 June, after the Expert Council had assembled, was the news of Khomeini's death officially announced. The session of the council began with the solemn reading of Khomeini's last will to the deputies by Khamene'i. Of the subsequent debate, no minutes exist. Reportedly the debate turned first on the question of whether to prefer a single leader or a leadership council, most delegates opting for the first, before turning to the question of who should be this leader. As it was clear that they would not find a candidate conforming to the criteria specified in the constitution, Meshkini, the chairman of the council, at this point read out the letter Khomeini had written to him shortly before his death. In this letter he asserted, that it would not be necessary to be a *marja'-e taqlid* to be eligible as *faqih* and that he had never claimed this to be the case.[96] This cleared the way for Khamene'i. Reportedly it was Sadeq Khalkhali who first brought up his name, but it was Rafsanjani who decided the matter when he spoke up for his longtime friend and rival in the subsequent debate. He first related an account of a meeting in 1986 or 1987, when Montazeri had already fallen out of favour, during which Khomeini had pointed to Khamene'i as his preferred successor. He then spoke of the meeting during the previous March, when Khomeini had once more recommended Khamene'i. Although there was no independent confirmation of his account, it was difficult to ignore Khomeini's presumed will so shortly after his death.

Thus, on 4 June, Khamene'i was elected as the new leader, with 60 votes out of 70 and the support of Rafsanjani, Meshkini, Khalkhali and other leading figures.[97] Officially Khamene'i was the sole candidate, but in 1997 Rafsanjani revealed that another candidate had stood against him. Reports indicated that this was Musavi-Ardebili, then the head of the judiciary. This would mean that the debate was more controversial than is commonly reported.[98] It must be noted that, at this time, the constitution had not yet been changed. The election of a cleric lacking the qualification of *marja'iyat* was hence illegal. It was only after Khamene'i's election that, in the course of the revision of the constitution, the criterion that the leader be a *marja'-e taqlid* was dropped. The first steps towards a revision had been taken several months before the crisis of succession made such a change unavoidable. In December 1988, 100 delegates had sent a formal request to Khomeini asking his permission for the revision of the constitution. The division of competences between the president and the prime minister had for years posed a serious problem to the functioning of the executive. Furthermore, the conflict between parliament and the Guardian Council had only partly been resolved with the creation of the Expediency Council. It had been created by decree of the *faqih*, and still lacked a basis in the constitution. Because the constitution did not provide for its own revision, Khomeini asked Montazeri, as the former chairman of the Expert Assembly, to convene a commission to tackle this task. However, Montazeri considered the moment inappropriate so soon after the war. It was only on 24 April 1989 that Khomeini ordered an assembly to be convened.[99]

The assembly, under the chairmanship of Meshkini, was composed of 66 members. Ten deputies had been appointed by Khomeini; the others were members of government, parliament, the judiciary and the Expert, Guardian and Expediency Councils.[100] The assembly was not only given the task of including an article on the Expediency Council, and of resolving the conflicts between the different legislative and executive institutions, but also of revising the articles pertaining to the qualifications of the *faqih*. This was essentially meant to eliminate the clause that the candidates for the post of *faqih* must hold the rank of *marja'*. The assembly completed its work only after the election of the new leader on 4 June. The revised version, presented to a national referendum on 9 July, considerably changed the allocation of powers between the various legislative and executive institutions. Thus, it weakened the Guardian Council by setting up the Expediency Council as a permanent institution. It abolished the post of prime minister and considerably strengthened the position of president, who received the task of supervising the cabinet. At the same time, the job of coordinating the legislative, executive and judiciary powers was given to the *faqih*, whose rule was termed 'absolute' (*motlaq*).

While the *faqih*'s political power was strengthened by this reform, his political and religious authority was diminished. Not only did the revised version no longer require the *faqih* to be a *marja'*, but it also dropped any reference to his popular legitimation. While the original version had required that the *faqih* be 'recognised and accepted as leader by the majority of the people' (Article 5) and that he be a man of 'learning and piety as required for the function of *marja*" (Article 109), in the revised version he was only required to be elected by the Expert Council and to have qualifications 'as required for performing the function of mufti'.[101] Unlike the president, the *faqih* in this system was only indirectly legitimised by the vote of the people, and unlike the *maráje'-ye taqlid* he did not possess supreme religious authority. Consequently, it was not only possible that his religious decrees could be overruled by one of the *maráje'* but also that the president might gain a stronger popular legitimacy than the *faqih*.

The separation of the function of *faqih* and *marja'* did not mean the separation of religion from politics, but rather established the supremacy of politics over religion. Henceforth, the State did not receive its legitimacy from the *faqih*, but the *faqih* depended on the State for his own legitimacy. Originally, the *faqih*, as the most learned scholar, had been meant to supervise the three branches of government in order to ensure that their policies conformed to Islam. It was his personal religious authority that constituted the final and supreme guarantee of the Islamic character of the regime. Without this authority the Islamic legitimacy of the regime was considerably shaken, and it would be more so if the *faqih* laid claim to the right to override the laws of the shari'a – an entitlement that Khomeini had arrogated for this post. As the guardianship of the jurist had been termed 'absolute', the *faqih* now legally possessed this right, but if he were really to use it he risked straining his authority.

After Khamene'i's election, Montazeri initially seemed willing to avoid an open conflict. In a short message to Khamene'i he congratulated him on his election, and in a demonstrative show of unity for several weeks took part in the Friday prayers in Qom. In return, Khamene'i allowed him to resume teaching in the hope that he would concentrate on his religious activities. However, the relationship between the two men remained tense, and while Khamene'i's supporters continued to attack Montazeri in the press his allies also continued to express their discontent at his removal. Thus, in early June, 200 deputies sent a letter to Montazeri to offer their condolences on the death of his father, who had passed away in Najafabad some days before Khomeini. With this letter, they not only expressed their grief at the demise of his father but also their discontent with his dismissal.[102] In December 1989, his supporters went further and started distributing 'night letters' in Qom and other cities, in which they questioned Khamene'i's religious qualifications and his suitability for the office of *faqih*.

As the defamation campaign against him continued, Montazeri too dropped his initial restraint. When he learnt of the government's intention to take up foreign loans to finance the post-war reconstruction, he asked parliament not to approve the plan. In a letter of 28 December 1989, he claimed that Khomeini had, in their last meeting, expressed his opposition to foreign loans, and warned that 'the colonialist governments [...] have never yet had the good and the benefit of our people, the growth and prosperity of our economy in mind'.[103] When his appeals to the majles were to no avail, Montazeri in a speech called on the people to intervene against the government's plan. In this speech, delivered on 1 January 1990 to a group of visitors from Najafabad and other cities, he pointed out that the revolution had begun in 1963 with Khomeini's protest against the decision of the Shah to take up a loan of $200 million. Now the government planned to take up a loan of $120 billion, Montazeri alleged, although the constitution clearly stated that safeguarding the economic independence of the country was one of the principal goals of the revolution.[104] When 136 of his students expressed their opposition to the plan in an open letter, Montazeri once more became the target of a violent press campaign. His house and office were attacked and ransacked by the militias, and he was briefly detained. In a humiliating move, he was forced to appear without his turban, the symbol of the clergy, with just a white cap on his head.[105] Even so, Montazeri refused to be silenced. Although during the following years the ban of his publications and the boycott by the media considerably limited his means of expression, he continued to intervene in the public discourse and he remained a rallying point for the Islamic left.

## Conclusion

After the revolution, Montazeri had helped institute a system that reserved many of the political posts for the clergy and concentrated much of the power in the hands of the *faqih*. He had supported the elimination of armed resistance and the repression of the liberal opposition as a necessary step for the preservation of the regime. In contrast to other clerics, he had remained silent when the regime censored the press, banned all parties and protests and instituted a reign of terror far worse than that seen under the Shah. However, early on Montazeri was alarmed by the excesses of the security forces and genuinely scandalised by the violation of the people's rights. From 1981 onwards, in private letters and meetings he criticised the excesses and called for restraint. His main points of criticism were:

1. The constant and systematic violation of the law, which was in contradiction to the revolution's promise to realise a reign of justice. He was particularly sensitive to this issue since he himself had suffered imprisonment, injustice and torture under the reign of the Shah. He favoured a more lenient approach to those who did not actively oppose the regime, fearing that otherwise the people would be alienated from it.

2. The concentration of power in the hands of a small clique of leaders, and their refusal to listen to the criticism and complaints of the people. He believed that rather than close one's eyes to the problems, it was necessary to listen to all sides and to seek the participation of all parties in order to find a solution. He advocated the liberalisation of the press and the legalisation of parties so that everybody could express their opinion and contribute to the political process.

3. The general corruption and decadence of the new political class, which stood in stark contrast to the ideal of selflessness and self-sacrifice preached by the clergy. He was alarmed by the impudence with which some officials used their power to their material advantage and their personal advancement. He rejected the intrigues and factional infighting of the political field – especially when he himself became the victim of one of these intrigues.

The removal of Mehdi Hashemi considerably embittered Montazeri. He was deeply disappointed that his friend and mentor Khomeini failed to support him in what he perceived as an attempt by his opponents to bring him under their control. To see his closest associates publicly humiliated and sentenced to death in what was apparently a politically motivated trial only served to make him more sympathetic to the plight of the political prisoners, and possibly contributed to his intervention in 1988. As the leadership refused to react to his appeals, ignoring the criticism he voiced in private meetings and letters, he went public with his protest. As deputy leader he could voice what others could not express, but he was repeatedly warned that his post did not grant him impunity. When, in February 1989, he held the leader personally responsible for the failures and deviations of the regime, he must have been conscious that he therewith overstepped a red line. However, for Montazeri the preservation of power did not justify all means. When he declared that it was preferable not to rule rather than to rule in violation of one's own values, he meant what he said and was ready to suffer the ultimate consequence – to renounce his post and power. That he dared speak his mind was considered foolish by some, and both friends and foes wondered why he had not waited until his rise to power to then initiate reforms. However, the fact that he refused to sacrifice his principles for the sake of power earned him respect and enhanced his credibility as a defender of public freedoms and human rights.

Of course, Montazeri was by no means the only figure to criticise the failures and deviations of the regime. Many other clerics, officials and intellectuals shared his concern over the inefficiency, ineffectiveness and corruption of the new government bodies, as well as the often arbitrary administration of justice. By the late 1980s, the inability of the regime to realise its own promises was difficult to ignore. While many of the social and economic problems could be blamed on the war, it was clear that the lack of accountability, the lack of participation and the exclusion of any opposition from the political field considerably contributed to the problems. Disillusioned by the political developments and frustrated by the lack of progress, many members of the revolutionary movement began to question the policies of the regime. In restricted circles and small-circulation periodicals these clerics, politicians and intellectuals began to analyse the problems and to reflect on the causes of the failure to achieve the original objectives. In the beginning they did not constitute a coherent network with a clear political project. However, when, in the wake of economic reconstruction, the control of the political field was somewhat relaxed, the discourse on reform intensified.

# CHAPTER 5

# POLITICAL CRISIS AND THE DEBATE ON REFORM

### Social Discontent and Intellectual Resurgence

The goal of Islam is to attend to both the material and the spiritual well-being of humans, and Islam has specific plans for this [which involve] an emphasis on work, production and resource extraction [. . .]. There are people who still believe that Islam and other holy religions do not concern themselves with the material lives of people, that they have plans for heaven and not for earth.

(Rafsanjani on the need for a new approach to Islam, 26 November 1989)[1]

The death of Khomeini, who by his religious authority, his tactical ability and his charismatic personality had been the undisputed leader of the State for a decade, marked a turning point in the history of the Islamic Republic. The new leader, Khamene'i, was certainly an able politician, but he possessed neither the religious authority nor the personal charisma of his predecessor. Whereas Khomeini had enjoyed a quasi-sacred status by remaining aloof from daily politics and factional disputes, Khamene'i's legitimacy was never undisputed. On the one hand this led him to seek recognition of his status as *marja'-e taqlid*, and on the other hand it forced him to garner the support of the conservative faction. This personal crisis of legitimacy coincided with a more general one, as the country faced a profound economic and social upheaval after the end of the eight year war with Iraq. While before it had been possible to justify the economic and political restrictions imposed on the population by the conflict, there was now no longer any excuse for the desolate state of the economy or for the restriction of freedoms. With the external threat and existential danger removed, the population started to ask why the regime had failed to realise its promise of social justice or to improve the general economic situation.

One decade after the revolution, inequality had not diminished but continued to grow. By the early 1990s, the richest 950 families held 40 per cent of the country's wealth, while the poorest 40 per cent of the population possessed but 3 per cent.[2] If Khomeini and other leaders maintained a modest and at times even ascetic lifestyle, many other members of the new elite had used their position and power to amass considerable wealth for themselves and their families. Notable among them were the religious foundations, which had taken over the former elite's assets to support the dispossessed but used their vast funds for the regime's clientèle. After eight years of war, large parts of the economic infrastructure were damaged or destroyed, and those which were not also suffered from shortages and inflation. The oil industry had particularly suffered from the conflict, so that oil revenues, which constituted the State's main source of income, were much reduced. The economy desperately needed investment, but foreign banks and companies were reluctant to invest in Iran and Iranian exiles were hesitant to return. Rationing of basic commodities continued after the war, shortages were common and inflation was high. Unemployment was widespread, the young having particular difficulty finding a job.

In the 1980s, the country had witnessed a period of unprecedented population growth, with a yearly rate of 3.5 per cent. In 1979, according to the United Nations, Iran's population had been 37 million, but by the end of the war it had risen to 53 million. By the early 1990s, the government had given up its former family policy and introduced measures for birth control, so that in the period from 1990 to 1995 the growth rate sank to 1.7 per cent. However, in 1995, no less than 53.6 per cent of the population were under 20 years of age, and the government still faced the problem of providing education and employment for an increasing number of young people. By the early 1990s, the regime of the Shah and the revolution were no more than a distant memory for most school and university students. They had grown up with the Islamic Republic and with the shortages and restrictions imposed by the regime. Faced with the difficulty of finding a job or starting a family, many among the urban middle class asked what the regime had to offer but slogans. They not only grumbled at the lack of economic prospects but also at the absence of personal freedom. After all the years of political turmoil they wanted to live a normal life, and had had enough of the State's intrusion into their daily lives.

A decade after the revolution, the time of ideals and illusions was over. The export of the revolution had proved as impossible to realise as the dream of social justice had proved illusory. The new leadership was aware that it would be measured by its capacity to improve the situation of the populace. The pragmatic Rafsanjani therefore made the reconstruction of the economy his priority, and introduced a number of reforms that sought to modernise the economy and cut back the social and political restrictions imposed on the population. The first five year plan, presented in 1989, was meant to radically liberalise the economy, which was still largely controlled by the State. Rafsanjani reduced subsidies for basic commodities, abolished the parallel exchange system and launched an ambitious programme for the reconstruction of the country's infrastructure and industries. In the early 1990s, the economy grew at an annual rate of 8 to 10 per cent. However, to satisfy the growing demand for consumer goods imports were considerably increased, which led to a growing trade deficit and rising foreign debt.[3] The radical liberalisation and privatisation of the economy was accompanied by more cautious social and political reforms. In cabinet, Rafsanjani replaced some of the most radical figures of the Islamic left with technocrats who favoured a practical rather than ideological approach, and whose concerns were primarily economic not political. He also cut back the influence of revolutionary organisations, abolished some of the harsher cultural policies and generally reduced the State's intrusion into the daily lives of its citizens.[4]

During the early 1990s, Rafsanjani also allowed a cautious opening up of the political discourse. After 1981, it had been limited to a small number of newspapers, which operated under strict state control, but during the tenure of the Minister of Culture and Islamic Guidance, Hojatoleslam Mohammad Khatami, things began to change. As he applied a more liberal press policy, the number of titles increased from 102 in 1988 to 369 in 1992. Many of these new newspapers offered space for new ideas and new groups, and thereby laid the ground for the emergence of the discourse on reform.[5] The most important forum for this discourse was the monthly journal *Keyhan-e Farhangi*. Founded in 1984 as the cultural magazine of the daily *Keyhan* by a group of religious intellectuals around Reza Tehrani and Mostafa Rokhsefat, it not only published texts on poetry, theatre and literature but also quickly became the forum for a controversial debate on politics, religion and philosophy. It offered its pages to liberal clerics as well as to progressive intellectuals, the most important of whom was the philosopher Hussain Dabbagh, more commonly known by the name of Abdolkarim Soroush.

Because of the publication of Soroush's controversial theory on the limitation of religious knowledge the journal was closed in 1990, and only allowed to reappear one year later after the original staff had been replaced. However, the journal's founders, Rokhsefat and Tehrani, did not let themselves be discouraged, and with the former *Keyhan* editor Mash'allah Shamsalva'ezin launched the bimonthly journal *Kiyan* in November 1991. Although this new periodical had an edition of just 2,000 it soon reached a readership of up to 50,000, and for almost a decade remained the most influential publication in intellectual circles as well as the principal forum of the discourse on reform. Designed along much the same lines as *Keyhan-e Farhangi*, it published essays on religion, politics and philosophy along with articles on poetry, theatre and the arts – all texts illustrated with abstract and surrealist black-and-white drawings. It addressed the relationship of religion to reason, science, pluralism, secularism and democracy, and regularly published the translation of articles by contemporary Western sociologists, theologians and philosophers whose works were otherwise not available in Iran.

Although the journal had just five permanent staff members, it soon attracted a wide circle of young progressive intellectuals, journalists, politicians, scientists and clerics. Most of them had been committed revolutionaries and many had held important political and military functions, but over the years they had come to realise the necessity of reforms. Besides Soroush, who wrote for almost every edition, regular contributors were Hojatoleslam Mohammad Mojtahed Shabestari, Hojatoleslam Hassan Yussefi Eshkevari, Hamid Reza Jalaiepour, Ali-Reza Alavitabar, Akbar Ganji (who also used the pseudonym Hamid Peydar) and Sa'id Hajjarian (who wrote under the name Jahangir Salahpur). Many of the ideas which were first developed and discussed in

*Kiyan* were later spread by the popular daily *Salam* to a wider public. Founded in 1989 by Hojatoleslam Mohammad Khoa'iniha, the latter quickly became the leading voice of the Islamic left and, from 1992, a prominent advocate of reform. The journals *Iran-e Farda* (founded in 1992 by Ezatollah Sahabi as the voice of the religious nationalists) and *Asr-e Ma* (founded in 1994 by Behzad Nabavi as the voice of the Islamic left), as well as the popular daily *Hamshari* (established in 1992 by the mayor of Tehran, Gholamhossein Karbastchi) also contributed to the propagation of the ideas of reform.

During this time, a number of periodicals were founded which addressed a separate, but no less important, aspect of reform – the question of women's rights. Notably, the monthly journal *Zanan* played a central role in the effort to realise social and legal equality and to reform the discriminative legislation targeted at women. Established in 1991 and directed by Shahla Sherkat, it discussed women's rights from an Islamic perspective but also drew on secular feminist concepts from the West. Regular contributors were the secular jurist Mehrangiz Kar and the religious scholar Hojatoleslam Mohsen Saidzadeh, who advocated a liberal and feminist interpretation of Islam.[6] The magazine was designed in the same style and published by the same company as *Kiyan*. However, if the close connection between the two publications was testimony to the importance accorded women's rights by the *Kiyan* circle, the fact that they did not address this question in their own journal was symptomatic of the way the issue was generally treated by the reformers. They certainly recognised the importance of women's rights, but preferred to leave their promotion to others. What is more, when questioned on them they often revealed positions not dissimilar to the patriarchal and traditional stance of their opponents.[7]

Women's rights was not the only issue to which some reformers' commitment was rather superficial. Many of the politicians, scholars and clerics who joined the reform movement in the late 1980s were genuinely concerned about the abuse of human rights and recognised the necessity of reform to realise freedom and social justice. Many, however, only began to protest against the repression of the opposition when they themselves were excluded from power. For many members of the Islamic left, the real turning point was not 1989 but the parliamentary elections in April and May 1992. In these campaigns, the long-running struggle for power between the Islamic left and the joint forces of the conservatives and the pragmatists came to a head. During the screening by the Guardian Council many candidates of the Islamic left were rejected for lack of 'practical commitment to Islam and the Islamic government'.[8] The Islamic left was alarmed to suddenly find itself excluded from the revolutionary movement, and even those who had previously not been known for their respect of divergent opinions or their support of the rule of law now called for tolerance and respect for legal procedures. However, their protests were to no avail. When the election results were announced they exceeded the worst fears of the Islamic left: while the pragmatists and conservatives secured more than 70 per cent of seats, many leaders of the left failed even to obtain a mandate.[9]

However, while the manipulative tactics of their opponents had certainly played a role it could not be denied that the main reason for their defeat was rejection by the voters. In many aspects the Islamic left at this point was no longer a progressive force but a conservative group that sought to block many reforms and to maintain the outdated policies of the 1980s. Its defeat in the elections was only the beginning of its political marginalisation, as the new pragmatist and conservative majority set about removing leading figures of the Islamic left, who had long been a thorn in its side. The first prominent victim was Khatami, the Minister of Culture and Islamic Guidance, whose liberal press policy and tolerant position on music and film had long been offensive to the conservatives. In July 1992, after a controversy over the film maker Mohsen Makmalbaf, they secured Khatami's dismissal. Under his successor, Ali Larijani, many of his policies were reversed and the pressure on the press once more increased. Next on the list was the Director of Radio and Television. This post was held by Mohammad Hashemi, the younger brother of Rafsanjani, who had long been criticised by conservatives for his liberal position. After a parliamentary inquiry into the scheduling of the state broadcaster found that it was not sufficiently Islamic, Khamene'i replaced him with Larijani in November 1993. The post of Minister of Culture and Islamic Guidance was in turn assumed by Mostafa Mir-Salim, who continued his predecessor's policy of fighting Western influence in the arts, the press and public education, and promoting the further Islamisation of Iranian culture.[10]

Another target of the conservatives was the Centre for Strategic Research in Tehran. This institute had been founded as a consultancy of the president, but under the direction of Khoa'iniha it had become the

centre of a group of leftist and liberal intellectuals. Among them were
the former intelligence officer Sa'id Hajjarian, the sociologist Alireza
Alavitabar, the liberal cleric Hojatoleslam Mohsen Kadivar and the
*Salam* editor Abbas Abdi. After the 1992 elections they were joined by a
number of politicians removed from their posts, such as the former Vice-
President, Ata'ollah Mohajerani, as well as Khatami.[11] Kadivar and
Alavitabar were deeply influenced by Montazeri. As Alavitabar later
explained, Montazeri's removal from power had made him question the
course of the regime and realise the necessity of reform. He admired
Montazeri as a model of tolerance, and taking inspiration from him had
with several others written a letter of protest against the prison purges of
1988. According to Alavitabar, most members of the centre were
initially critical of Montazeri, but he and Kadivar changed their opinion
in his favour.[12] However, in 1992 the conservatives removed Khoa'iniha
and imprisoned Abdi and Alavitabar.

For many liberal intellectuals and politicians of the Islamic left, the
years after 1992 were a time of reflection, discussion and sometimes self-
criticism. Removed from power and banished to the margins of the
political field, they began to reconsider their former positions, to discuss
new concepts and to think about a reform of the system. However, the
reformers were not a uniform group, but rather a mix of radical and
moderate, Islamist and secular, authoritarian and republican elements
with different, and at times divergent, origins and objectives. While
some had long been dissatisfied with the repressive policies of the
regime, others only recognised the value of pluralism, freedom and
tolerance once they themselves became the object of repression. Some
were genuinely convinced that reforms were necessary to preserve the
revolution's original values of freedom and social justice, while others
only began to advocate reform when they realised that otherwise they
would not be able to return to power. Some were aware that their call for
the respect of civil rights stood in sharp contrast to their earlier, often
authoritarian, positions, but few openly admitted as much.

## Rethinking the Official Reading of Religion

Utter submission to change and renewal leaves no permanence
and thus no religion worthy of the name; while insistence on

permanence, and obstinate resistance to change, will render religious
life in the contemporary world impossible. Therefore, reconciling
the two is the great challenge of benevolent theologists of today.
(Soroush on religion and religious knowledge)[13]

Islam's relationship with modernity had occupied thinkers in Iran as in
much of the Islamic world, since the nineteenth century. The question of
how religion could retain its relevance in a changed and changing world,
and how it should react to the challenges of modern science and Western
thought, had for many years been the object of intense debate among
Islamic clerics, scholars and intellectuals. When reformist thinkers in
the late 1980s and early 1990s began to reconsider the official reading of
the scriptures and to discuss a new understanding of religion, they did
not enter virgin territory but rather took up a debate begun many years
earlier.[14] However, the context of this debate and the rules of the
discourse had changed since the Iranian revolution. In the new system,
the religious and political fields were closely connected. While this
meant that religion determined politics and that the clergy controlled
the State, it also meant that political considerations influenced the
interpretation of religion and that the State interfered in the affairs of the
clergy. Islam was used and misused by all political parties to legitimise
their own factional interests while the regime tried to impose its official
reading of religion, denouncing all dissent as opposition not only to the
system but also to Islam. In this context, pluralism was conceived by
many clerics no longer as a threat to the clergy's unity but rather as the
precondition of its autonomy from the State and as the basis of a free
and open debate. Not only the traditional clergy but also many of the
revolutionary clerics increasingly regarded the subjection of religion to
politics as a threat to their individual freedom, as well as to the
credibility of religion and the collective authority of the clergy. When
the religious reformers called for a separation of politics and religion, it
was less to save politics from religion than to preserve religion from its
further corruption by politics.

In the late 1980s, the two most interesting and most influential
religious reformers in Iran were Abdolkarim Soroush and Hojatoleslam
Mohammad Mojtahed Shabestari. Born in 1945 into a pious family in
southern Tehran, Soroush was as a youth deeply interested in religion
and, after his graduation from school, briefly studied theology and

philosophy in Qom. He then changed to pharmacology and chemistry, and after his graduation from Tehran University worked for some years in pharmaceutical research. In 1973, he went to London to complete his studies with a doctorate in analytical chemistry, but then changed to philosophy of science. This continued to be his main preoccupation during the following decades, but his approach remained marked by his training in science.[15] During his studies in Tehran he regularly attended the lectures at the progressive Hosseiniye Ershad and came to know Beheshti, Motahhari and Shari'ati, all of whom deeply influenced his thinking. When he moved to London, he started to give lectures to counter the influence of leftist ideas among Iranian students. During this time he wrote a number of books on the interrelation of religion, science and philosophy, which were published between 1977 and 1979. His treatise on traditional metaphysics, *The Dynamic Nature of the Universe*, earned the attention and praise of Motahhari, Khomeini and other clerics.[16] A series of televised debates with the Marxists about their theories made him a well-known figure in Iran.[17]

After the revolution Soroush was appointed to the chair of the Islamic department of Tehran's teachers college. When the universities were closed down in April 1980, he was named one of the seven members of the Setad-e Enqelāb-e Farhangi (Advisory Council for the Cultural Revolution). As the council was responsible for the Islamisation of the curriculum of the universities and for the eviction of ideologically unreliable individuals, he was later severely criticised for taking on this appointment. Although his work for the council contradicted his later convictions, Soroush never publicly disassociated himself from it. Like many reformers, rather than self-critically admit having made a mistake he sought to justify his earlier activities by citing the needs of the times, and claimed that he had not been involved in anything reprehensible. After his resignation from the council in 1983, Soroush began to teach philosophy at the university in Tehran and the seminaries in Qom. From 1988, he gave weekly lectures at Imam Sadiq University in the capital, which were particularly popular among the students.

Soroush regularly published in *Keyhan-e Farhangi* and *Kiyan*, which soon became closely associated with him. His controversial theory on the nature of religious knowledge was first published in *Keyhan-e Farhangi*, beginning in May 1989, as a series of articles entitled '*Qabz va bast-e teorik-e shariat*' (*The Theoretical Contraction and Expansion of Religion*).

This epistemological theory was based on the distinction between religion and religious knowledge. It held that religion as revealed by God was absolute, complete and unchangeable, but that human knowledge of religion must be understood as limited, fallible and changeable:

> Yes, it is true that sacred scriptures are [. . .] flawless, however, it is just as true that human beings' understanding of religion is flawed. Religion is sacred and heavenly, but the understanding of religion is human and earthly. That which remains constant is religion; that which undergoes change is religious knowledge and insight. Religion has not faltered in articulating its objectives and its explanations of good and evil; the defect is in human beings' understanding of religion's intents. Religion is in no need of reconstruction and completion; religious knowledge and insight that is human and incomplete, however, is in constant need of reconstruction. Religion is free from cultures and unblemished by the artefacts of human minds, but religious knowledge is, without a shadow of a doubt, subject to such influences.[18]

Religious knowledge is influenced by the cultural and temporal context as well as by other sciences, Soroush argued. It is not only the product of a specific time and place, but also marked by the personal predilections of the interpreter. Thus, a philosopher has a different approach to a jurist or a mystic. As it is impossible to obtain full knowledge of God's intent, nobody can claim to possess the one and only truth. As Soroush wrote, the Prophet was the last prophet, but no interpreter can claim to be the last interpreter: 'The last religion is already here, but the last understanding of religion has not arrived yet.'[19] Based on this theory, Soroush distinguished between the essential and the accidental elements of religion. Among the first he counted the central Shi'i dogma: the Imamat, the prophecy of Mohammad, the justice and unity of God, and the belief in resurrection. All other rules, norms and principles should be considered the result of the historical, cultural and social situation in which Islam developed. Soroush did recognise the importance of rules and rituals for religion, but did not consider them an essential part of it. This gave him the freedom to do away with outdated traditions. However, even liberal theologians complained that his distinction between the essential and the accidental remained arbitrary.[20]

Based on his idea of the relativity of knowledge, Soroush in a speech at Tehran's Shahid Beheshti University in March 1991 argued for a free debate, as only the free exposition and exchange of rational arguments allows the discovery of truth. Only those, he argued, who believe that they possess the absolute truth do not need and do not want freedom. Not only is freedom the condition for the exercise of reason and thus for finding the truth, but more generally an imposed truth is without merit. Only the free adoption of religion and the free submission to its rules is of value. In the absence of freedom, erroneous ideas and ideologies such as Marxism go unchallenged, Soroush argued, in a veiled attack on *velāyat-e faqih*:

> Do not assume that only your enemies err and wallow in falsehoods while your minds are the overflowing fountain-heads of pure, unadulterated truth. Allow your own errors to be exposed as well. Do not assume that truth and falsehood are so clearly delineated in the absence of a free sphere. What caused all that corruption was the intellectual guardianship of Marx and Engels, and the same will ensue wherever such guardianship [*velāyat*] exists.[21]

In the 1980s and 1990s, no other intellectual had as profound an influence on the discourse as Soroush. However, it has been pointed out that many of his ideas were not new, and his argumentation often lacked theoretical rigidity, coherence and structure.[22] His unbroken belief in modernity, science and progress was criticised as naive, as the belief in humankind's ability to control nature and to form society had given rise to some of modernity's worst aberrations. He also often appeared to give precedence to beauty over clarity of expression, and commonly quoted classical Persian poetry although it often did little to sustain his arguments.

The theories and theses of Shabestari were in many aspects similar to Soroush's, but his approach and line of argumentation were different. Born in 1936, he received a traditional religious training in the seminaries of Qom before being appointed the director of the Islamic Centre in Hamburg. The years in Germany brought him into contact with modern Western philosophy and Christian theology. Upon returning to Iran in 1978, he was elected to the first parliament after the revolution. Having left parliament after one term he was appointed professor of theology and Islamic studies at Tehran University.[23] Besides Islamic philosophy he specialised in comparative studies of religion and actively participated in the inter-religious dialogue. He was strongly influenced by Motahhari and Iqbal as well as modern Christian theologists such as Paul Tillich, and Western philosophers, such as Hans-Georg Gadamer. Shabestari was especially interested in hermeneutics, epistemology and the historical-critical approach, according to which religious texts must be understood as the product of a specific historical situation. Compared to Soroush his writings were less elaborate in style but clearer, and his arguments were more systematic, coherent and convincing.[24]

Much like Soroush, he criticised earlier religious reformers for having misused religion for social and political ends, and accused the traditional clergy of having totally failed to address the question of modernity. In a number of articles published in *Kiyan* over the course of several years, Shabestari tried to come up with his own response to this question. Rejecting both the approach of the traditionalists, whom he accused of wanting to preserve all religion from change, as well as the modernists, whom he blamed for seeking to change all religion, he advocated a critical and rational approach to religion. The question of how to adapt religion to a changing world led Shabestari in 'Mabani va mekanism-e sabat va tahul-e ma'refat-e imani' ('Basis and Mechanism of Continuity and Change in Religious Interpretation'), published in *Kiyan* in January 1992, to seek a distinction between the permanent and the non-permanent. Much like Soroush, he argued, that an absolute truth exists, but that this truth is hidden from humanity. Human beings can only approach, but never reach, the complete truth of godly revelation. Therefore, there is not just one true interpretation, and several divergent interpretations can exist side by side, each containing part of the truth. Addressing the question of how to approach the truth, Shabestari in 'Tchera bayad andishe-ye dini ra naqd kard?' ('Why Must Religious Thought be Criticised?'), published in *Kiyan* in April 1994, argued for a rational and critical approach to religious thought. Religious thought, he explained, is closely connected to the believer (or the society of believers) and cannot be separated from it. It must therefore not be confused with religion:

> The study of the history of Islamic theological and philosophical sciences in Muslim societies shows that they always recognised the difference between the revelation of the Prophet and their own

theological and philosophical thought and that, for them, the
change in theology and philosophy did not mean the change of the
Prophetic revelation.[25]

Religious thought can be criticised, even though it is based not only on
logic but also on belief, Shabestari argued, distinguishing thus between
an outer and an inner criticism. While the first intends to disprove and
thereby destroy religion, the second seeks to improve the understanding
of religion. The permanent criticism of religious thought is necessary,
Shabestari insisted, to prevent its stagnation and ossification. Only by
permanently reassessing religious positions in the light of present
developments can man's relationship with God be kept alive. Criticism
makes man conscious of religion's essence and intent, and leads to new
theological, mystical and poetic approaches:

> If today we see that our heritage has gained great breath and many
> sides, the reason is that in the course of history there has been
> profound and perpetual criticism of religious thought in an
> atmosphere of freedom or semi-freedom [...]. We must remain
> conscious that the inner criticism of religious thought is to the
> advantage of belief and piety. [Therefore], we must preserve an
> atmosphere open to such criticism.[26]

To come to a modern understanding of religion, Shabestari argued, Islam
should adopt the method of historical criticism. In 'Motun-e dini va
jahanbini-ye naqd-e tarikhi' ('The Religious Texts and the World-view
of Historical Criticism'), published in *Kiyan* in August 1995, he
discussed the implications of this method for modern Christian theology.
The method of historical criticism, Shabestari wrote, views a text as the
product of a specific historical situation and attempts to reposition it in
its original context. In modern Christian theology 'this new interpretation
has brought into existence important and interesting theological theories,
and one can say that the Christian religion has in the past two centuries
been fundamentally changed'.[27] To him this new approach was not a threat
but a promise, as it opened up new perspectives for the interpretation of the
scriptures. He was convinced that it would only destroy false beliefs and
traditions, not religion or religiosity itself. However, even liberal clerics
protested that the complete congruence of religion and reason could

only be achieved at the expense of de-sacralising religion and reducing it to a secular philosophy. The traditional clergy for their part rejected Shabestari's ideas, as he challenged not only the clergy's status as the sole legitimate interpreters of the scriptures but also the very basis of the traditional interpretation of religion. To treat the Qur'an as an historical document and to submit its contents to a rational and critical analysis was, in their eyes, totally unacceptable. Nevertheless, the reaction of the clergy and the regime to Shabestari was less vehement than to Soroush. On the one hand this was due to the fact that the former was a cleric, and thus a member of their own caste, and on the other that he was less polemical and less explicitly political than Soroush.

Many of the ideas first discussed by Soroush and Shabestari were later developed by Hojatoleslam Hassan Yussefi Eshkevari. Born in 1949 in the town of Eshkevar in the province of Gilan to illiterate peasants, Eshkevari studied at a local *maktab* and went to continue his studies in Qom in 1965. Initiated into politics during the events of 1963, he chose Khomeini as his *marja'-e taqlid*. He read the works of Bazargan, Sahabi, Motahhari, Taleqani and Allameh Tabatabai, but was most impressed and influenced by the writings of Shari'ati, whose lectures at the Hosseiniye Ershad he regularly attended.[28] From 1968, Eshkevari regularly wrote for religious and political journals. In 1972, he married Mohtaram Golbaba'i, the pious daughter of a middle-class family in Tehran, with whom he engaged in religious and political propaganda work. Because of these activities he was imprisoned in 1974 and 1975. After the revolution, he briefly worked for a radio station before being elected to parliament in 1980. At the end of his mandate he disengaged from politics, but continued to write for a variety of papers and journals. He also gave courses at university, before being expelled for giving a speech at the funeral of the religious-nationalist politician Kazem Sami, who was murdered in November 1988 – probably on the order of the regime. From 1992, Eshkevari worked for the daily *Iran-e Farda* and repeatedly wrote for *Kiyan*. His style was simpler and clearer, and his articles often more coherent, than Soroush's.

In December 1997, he published 'Kasrat gera'i dar nazar va vahdat gera'i dar amal' ('The Diversity of Intentions in Thought and the Unity of Intentions in Action'). In this article Eshkevari dealt with the question of freedom and pluralism in Islam. Inspired by Islamic mysticism, he argued that belief is not limited to the recognition and outward respect of the rules and principles of religion, but that it is the inner experience of the absolute truth and the reality of God. He wrote,

> Therefore, one must be conscious that belief [imān] and religion
> [din] are not one, but that belief is the essence, the truth and inner
> religiosity. A faithful person is someone who has arrived at belief
> [...]. With other words, every believer [mo'meni] is also a faithful
> [dindār], but it is possible that not every faithful [dindāri] is also a
> believer [mo'men].[29]

As reason and reality prove, the inner experience of Godly truth differs according to personal predispositions. Even if not everyone can and will experience the full and entire truth, everyone can obtain a glimpse of it. As in the story of the three blind men who touch an elephant and each arrive at a partial and different but nonetheless true image of the elephant, so humans may arrive at images of the truth that, though different, are nonetheless part of the same truth, Eshkevari wrote.

One may conclude from this that there is not just one but several religious beliefs, which in spite of their differences all refer to the same truth. The Qur'an too has recognised that the experience of the sacred truth is both personal and direct. Based on the diversity of approaches to the same truth, one can say that diversity is in unity and unity is in diversity. If it is correct that there are different approaches to the same truth, and that the experience of this truth is both personal and direct (in which, as a consequence, nobody else can take part, and for which nobody else can assume responsibility), Eshkevari asked, then how can one impose a definition of belief which everybody must follow lest they be considered deviants? The prophets have exposed the message of God to the people, Eshkevari argued, but the people are free to accept or reject this invitation to the truth. Every human is responsible for his or her beliefs and behaviour, and nobody can take this responsibility from him or her. Nobody should therefore blindly follow and imitate the example of another, even if it be the Prophet. A belief that is not freely and consciously adopted is without value or merit. Even if one follows the example of the Prophet, one still bears responsibility for one's beliefs and behaviour:

> Even if I honestly recognise and respect the orders which have been
> revealed by the Prophet from God or himself, the responsibility

will not be taken from me. This is why piety without knowledge has been prohibited in Islam and why at the time of resurrection neither God nor the Prophet will answer for our deeds. On this ground, religiosity [ta'abod] and rationality [ta'aqol] are two sides of one coin.[30]

Montazeri did not share many of the ideas developed by reformers like Soroush, Shabestari or Eshkevari, but he recognised their contribution to the discourse. In 2008, in response to several writings of Soroush on revelation (vahi), which had caused some controversy among the clergy, Montazeri published a small book under the title Safir-e haq va safir-e vahi (The Messenger of God and the Sapphire of Revelation), in which he criticised Soroush's views and laid out his own understanding of this subject. Although he did not agree with Soroush, he took the latter's views seriously.[31] Montazeri generally advocated the discussion of new ideas and argued for a rational exegesis of the scriptures, although his own approach to religion remained marked by tradition and he continued to regard the clerics as the most qualified interpreters of the subject. His contribution to the discourse lay less in the debate about the understanding of religion than in the discussion about its relation to politics. Notably, his advocacy of a more democratic reading of the theory of Islamic government opened up the debate to new ideas.

## Reconsidering the Theory of Islamic Government

What transpires among us humans, whether in the name of God or otherwise, is of necessity, human and fallible. It should thus be open to rational supervision and scrutiny. The social and political admits of no irrational and supernatural displays commanding passive witness and submission. Everything that enters nature, including religion and revelation, bends to its ways. Everything that enters human society becomes social and human.

'(Soroush on the place of religion in politics)[32]

In his lectures on velāyat-e faqih Montazeri had proposed an alternative reading of the doctrine, which sought to limit the powers of the faqih and to strengthen the people's participation in politics in order to safeguard their will and to prevent the abuse of their rights. Although these lectures received only limited public attention at the time, several intellectuals realised their potential for reforming the system. Montazeri's ideas were certainly not free of contradictions, and he failed to address some crucial questions. However, his reading of *velāyat-e faqih* did present the possibility of changing political practice without actually breaking with the basic doctrine of the system. In July 1993, Ganji addressed some of the ideas raised by Montazeri. In an article in *Kiyan* entitled 'Mashru'iyat, velayat va vekalat' ('Legitimacy, Guardianship and Representation') he discussed different concepts of legitimacy, distinguishing between the concepts of guardianship (*velāyat*) and representation (*vekālat*). In the view of the partisans of *velāyat*, among whom Ganji counted Fazlollah Nuri, Khomeini and Mesbah-Yazdi, the *faqih* is the guardian of the people and his legitimacy derives directly from God. In this view it is not through the people but through the *faqih* that the other organs of government receive legitimacy. By contrast, in the view of the partisans of the second concept, among whom Ganji counted Na'ini, Montazeri, Motahhari and Salehi-Najafabadi, the *faqih* is the representative of the people and his legitimacy depends on their consent. In this view the people have not only duties but also rights, which the *faqih* is bound to respect.[33] Ganji cited several passages from Montazeri in which the latter rejected the idea of a divine designation of the jurists and argued for the election of the *faqih* by the people. Although Ganji did not actually challenge the official doctrine, he suggested that there are different concepts of legitimacy, and that the concept of *velāyat* is by no means the most convincing.

Soroush too, without directly questioning the concept of *velāyat-e faqih*, challenged the idea of a state based on divine legitimacy. Drawing on his theory of the distinction between religion and religious knowledge, Soroush, in a series of lectures at Tehran's Imam Sadiq University in December 1994, argued that no government can lay claim to divine legitimacy and infallibility, since human rule is necessarily based not on religion but on religious knowledge, which is human, limited and fallible. Human rule should always, even if it claims to act in the name of religion, be open to rational supervision and scrutiny, Soroush wrote,

What transpires among us humans, whether in the name of God or otherwise, is of necessity, human and fallible. It should thus be open to rational supervision and scrutiny. The social and political admits of no irrational and supernatural displays commanding passive witness and submission. Everything that enters nature, including religion and revelation, bends to its ways. Everything that enters human society becomes social and human.[34]

In March 1993, Soroush published an article in *Kiyan* entitled 'Hokumat-e demokratik-e dini?' ('Religious-Democratic Government?'), which launched a new and more far-reaching debate on the relationship of religion to politics. This article was set against a debate triggered by a controversial lecture by Bazargan in January 1992, in which he had demanded a complete separation of politics and religion because, in his view, the purpose of the prophets was 'to alert people to the existence of God and to prepare them for the hereafter, not to tell them how to conduct their policies and run their affairs in this world'.[35] In response to this lecture Soroush sought to develop a system that respected the rights both of the people (*khalq*) and of the creator (*khaleq*). He argued that a religious society should have a religious regime, as a secular regime would be a violation of the people's will and nature. As secularism and liberalism, in the sense of a relativism of beliefs, are not necessary conditions for democracy, Soroush argued, this regime could very well be democratic. To be ethically and rationally acceptable this religious-democratic regime must be based on collective reason, founded on rational values such as truth, justice and public interest, and recognise human rights. Although these principles are of extra-religious origin, Soroush argued, any religion must recognise them so as to be ethically persuasive in the modern world. Hence, rather than founding a government on Islamic principles, Soroush incorporated the principles of democracy in Islam:

> In order to remain religious, they [democratic religious regimes], of course, need to establish religion as the guide and arbiter of their problems and conflicts. But, in order to remain democratic, they need to dynamically absorb an adjudicative understanding of religion, in accordance with the dictates of collective 'reason.'[36]

In response to these ideas Ganji, under the pseudonym Hamid Peydar, in May 1994 published an article in which he rejected the idea of the compatibility of democracy and Islam. In 'Paradoks-e eslam va demokrasi' ('The Paradox of Islam and Democracy') Ganji played the role of 'devil's advocate', adopting a conservative interpretation of the scriptures. He accused Soroush of adopting a normative rather than a positivist approach and rejected his claim that a truly Islamic society can be nothing but democratic as historically and theoretically false, arguing that democracy can only be achieved if society is secularised. While democracy recognises the indeterminacy of truth and leaves its citizens free to choose according to their personal belief, Islam does not recognise the believer's right to choose his religion, but demands submission to God, Ganji maintained. It commands the execution of apostates, enjoins the fight against infidels and does not recognise the idea of sexual and religious equality, but accords different rights according to sex and religion. Quoting Mesbah-Yazdi's assertion that democracy allows man to decide whatever he wants while Islam requires man to follow God's commands, Ganji argued that the two are irreconcilable opposites.[37] This article led to a vehement response both by Soroush and Eshkevari. While Soroush adopted an outer-religious approach, Eshkevari in 'Paradoks-e eslam va demokrasi?' ('The Paradox of Islam and Democracy?') sought to prove the compatibility of democracy and Islam from an inner-religious perspective. He refuted Ganji's claim that because Islam does not recognise freedom of choice, man could not be made responsible for his own acts:

> If there were no self-determination [ekhtiār] and no choice [entekhāb], the ethic musts and must-nots and good and evil, which is the basis of the prophetic message, would be without meaning [. . .]. According to the fundamental teachings of monotheist religions, God has made man in this world and the hereafter 'answerable for his deeds' and considers him 'responsible'. It is obvious that responsibility is the consequence of self-determination [. . .]. It is clear that 'reason' only finds its meaning and significance in connection with 'freedom'.[38]

The fact that man is free to decide, Eshkevari argued, does not mean that there is no difference between good and evil: religion shows man the right path, but man is free to follow this way – and bear the consequences for his decisions. Coming to Ganji's claim that the modernists who consider Islam compatible with democracy have misinterpreted the scriptures, as their interpretation contradicts Islamic tradition, Eshkevari wrote,

> Every kind of interpretation of the Qur'anic verses is bound to a different historical period and most are under the influence of the period's conditions and culture. How does one know that the past interpreters have necessarily understood correctly? Have the present interpreters not the right to arrive at a new understanding of the Qur'anic verses? Not only is a new understanding no sin and no crime but it is even desirable. If he [Ganji] has reasons [to believe in] the falsity of the new understanding he can present the proof [. . .].[39]

While Eshkevari referred to the Qur'anic passages on freedom of choice (*ekhtiār*), the use of reason (*ta'aqol*), the oath of allegiance (*be'yāt*), the idea of counsel (*shurā*), the openness of interpretation (*ejtehād*) and the general indeterminacy of the political system in order to prove the compatibility of Islam and democracy, Soroush chose an outer-religious perspective. In 'Modara va modiriyat-e mo'menan – Sokhani dar nesbat din va demokrasi' ('Tolerance and Governance – A Discourse on Religion and Democracy') he bluntly dismissed any attempt to found democracy on religious law. Rather than try to deduce democratic values from religion, they should be introduced to Islam:

> The present argument, unlike the writings of some Islamic thinkers, makes no attempt to place the entire weight of the conceptual edifice of democracy upon the frail shoulders of such (intra-religious) precepts as consultation [*shurā*], consensus of the faithful [*ijmā'*], and oath of loyalty to a ruler [*bey'āt*]. Rather, the discourse on religious government should commence with the discussion of human rights, justice, and restriction of power (all extra-religious issues). Only then should one try to harmonise one's religious understanding with them.[40]

Soroush criticised Ganji for reducing religion to religious law while ignoring its ethical and mystical dimensions. Democracy cannot simply be judged by its compatibility with religious law, he asserted, but rather the whole of religion must be taken into account. Soroush also alleged that Ganji falsely assumed that democracy required people to give up their beliefs. In democratic societies, Soroush pointed out, there also exist certain beliefs – such as individual autonomy, legal equality and the right to self-determination – which are considered durable, universal and inviolable. In a similar way, the people in a religious democracy can freely agree to recognise and respect the inviolability of certain religious principles, which thereby acquire a rational quality. Soroush also rejected Ganji's argument that Islam does not recognise freedom of choice. Rather freedom of faith is fundamental to Islam as to all religions, as only a freely accepted religion is of merit. As faith can only be voluntary and personal, one should accept the diversity that this implies rather than suppress faith by imposing a single interpretation of religion. Only a free society can be a truly religious society, Soroush asserted, and only if the society is truly religious will it also have a religious government. All this brought Soroush to the conclusion that a truly religious society not only *can* but *must* be democratic.

The idea of freedom was also central to the thought of Hojatoleslam Mohammad Khatami. Born in 1943 in the central city of Ardakan, the son of a highly respected cleric, Khatami received a religious education in Qom. He attended courses by Khomeini, Motahhari and Montazeri before continuing his studies in philosophy at Tehran and Isfahan. Although interested in politics, he was not actively engaged in the clerical movement. In 1978, he succeeded Shabestari at the head of the Islamic Centre in Hamburg but returned to Iran in 1979. The following year, he became the leader's representative in the *Keyhan* group before being appointed Minister of Culture and Islamic Guidance in 1982. Increasingly critical of the restrictive and repressive cultural and educational policies of the regime, he pressed for more tolerance and greater diversity in film, music and the press. In spite of the criticism and hostility of the conservatives, he retained his post under Rafsanjani. He partly managed to liberalise the rules in the cultural field, but was forced to resign in July 1992. Appointed Director of the National Library, Khatami only played a marginal role in politics during the following years, but, like other members of the Islamic left, actively participated in the discourse on reform.[41]

Although he was highly critical of the West's imperialist politics and its materialistic lifestyle, he did not approve of its wholesale rejection but wanted to critically adapt its cultural, political and philosophical heritage. Notably, the idea of individual freedoms and inalienable rights appealed to him. He was convinced that citizens, as autonomous individuals responsible for their own actions, have the right to determine their own fate. As he argued in his book *Bim-e mouj* (*Fear of the Wave*), published in 1994, the principle attraction of the West is its promise of freedom, which he considered a universal aspiration of mankind:

> The West says: In the system we propose, man can achieve his wishes and no limits but those he defines himself will restrict his actions, so that, in this way of life one of the greatest objectives of humankind, man's aspiration for freedom, is realised. In the course of history, man has desired nothing as much as freedom and for perhaps no objective has sacrificed as much as for freedom. Today man stands face to face with a system which invites him to eat freely, to dress freely, to speak freely, to think freely and to live freely.[42]

In Khatami's view, the challenge for religious intellectuals is to develop an interpretation of Islam in accordance with the needs of the time and the aspirations of society. This new reading must be based upon the universal and eternal aspiration of mankind – that is, freedom. While Khatami was unequivocal in his support for freedom, he emphasised that it should be limited by the law, which is based on religion. In contrast to the West, where humans alone define the limits of their actions, he argued, in an Islamic society humans recognise the limits set by Islam.

The idea that Islam should be reinterpreted in order to integrate the democratic values of freedom, pluralism and participation was later taken up by Khatami's collaborator Sa'id Hajjarian. Born in 1953 in Tehran, the latter studied mechanical engineering and later received a degree in political science. He sympathised with the Mojahedin-e Khalq, and worked to strengthen the influence of Islam in the universities. After the revolution he became co-founder of the new intelligence service, where he was Vice-Director until the late 1980s. Although he reputedly played a moderating role, he was at least indirectly responsible for the repression of the opposition.[43] As one of the leaders of the Mojahedin-e Enqelab, Hajjarian was removed from his political posts in the early 1990s. He soon joined the Centre for Strategic Research in which, along with Khatami and other members of the Islamic left, he sought to reformulate the latter's programme and rebuild its movement with a view to regaining power. In 1994, together with Nabavi, he founded the influential biweekly *Asr-e ma*, whose director he remained until its closure in 2004.

Although actively engaged in the discourse on reform, Hajjarian was less a scholar than a strategist. For him, the reform of politics and religion was more a means to regain power than an end in itself. His objective was to preserve the structure of the system, but to change its contents by prioritising the republican over the religious elements. To give legitimacy to this project, he proposed a republican reinterpretation of Khomeini's theory and praxis of governance. According to this interpretation, the constitution of 1979 had established a contract between the leader and the people, who had delegated the sovereignty that it had received from God to the leader. The leader thus became God's representative on earth, but remained bound to respect the rights and the will of the people.[44] According to Hajjarian, Khomeini during his rule prioritised the interests of the people over the principles of Islam. He acted as arbiter and remained aloof from daily politics and factional conflicts. With this interpretation, Hajjarian managed to superficially resolve the contradictions between the republican and religious elements of the constitution, but he was not able to explain the patrimonial and authoritarian character of the regime in the 1980s. His description of Khomeini's theory and praxis of governance was less dictated by historic facts than motivated by the desire to legitimise his own faction's programme of participation, pluralism and the rule of law.

Unlike Soroush, Hajjarian did not reject the subjection of religion to politics and its transformation into an ideology, but criticised its rigid and traditional interpretation by the conservatives. In 'Din-e demokratik-e hokumati' ('The Religion of Democratic Government'), published in *Kiyan* in May 1994 under the pseudonym Jahangir Salahpur, he advocated a dynamic and contemporary interpretation of religion as the only possible basis for a religious democracy. Such an interpretation recognises the relativity and plurality of opinions and constantly adapts religious law to the needs of the times, the will of the people and the interests of the State. This, Hajjarian admitted, will necessarily make religion more worldly:

> This signifies that this religion and jurisprudence will [. . .] have to go along with the state and the ruler who are centred on the

rationally defined common and worldly interests. One example of this is the experience of the theory of *velāyat-e faqih* which would not have been able to survive without accepting the principle of interest {*maslahat*}.[45]

Thus Hajjarian, much like his conservative opponents, came to the conclusion that the rules and principles of Islam should not determine politics, but rather that the needs and interests of the State should determine the interpretation of Islam. While the conservatives used this argument to legitimise the absolute powers of the *faqih*, Hajjarian used it to legitimise a religious democracy. Both claimed to act in the interest of the Islamic state, but in the end both left the question unanswered as to how a state can be Islamic if it subordinates Islam to the interests of politics. In a similar way, Soroush's argument that Islam is compatible with democracy because democratic principles are rational and universal, and not because they are inherent to Islam, raised the question of what remains of religion if it can adopt any principle that human society deems rational or useful. Of course, the debate did not end here nor was it limited to Montazeri, Khatami and the *Kiyan* circle. Rather, the ideas broached by Montazeri, Soroush and others were discussed then and later in other periodicals, newspapers and public lectures as well as in seminaries, universities and certain mosques by both supporters and opponents. Also, the debate on the theory of *velāyat-e faqih* and the compatibility of democracy and Islam were only part of a wider discourse on the relationship of politics to religion. This discourse during the early 1990s found its most concrete expression in the controversy over Khamene'i's claim to the *marja'iyat*.

## The Controversy Surrounding the *Marja'iyat*

The Shi'i *marja'iyat* has always been an independent spiritual power, this independence should not be broken by you and the houze elmiye should not become the employee of the government as this would be harmful for the future of Islam and Shi'ism. Whatever your supporters may try, you will find no evidence for the scholarly position of the late Imam [Khomeini].

(Montazeri, in his letter to Khamene'i of 3 November 1994)[46]

In spite of the conservatives' triumph at the elections in 1992, their control over the political and religious discourse remained incomplete. Ever since the election of Khamene'i as *vali-ye faqih*, the legitimacy of the system and the authority of the leader were shaken. *Velāyat-e faqih* was based on the idea that the State is ruled by the most qualified jurist in order to guarantee its Islamic character, but, for political reasons, the Expert Council in 1989 had chosen not one of the recognised sources of emulation but a mid-ranking cleric, who was not even considered an ayatollah. Hence, many questioned his qualification for the exercise of this post. According to the original version of *velāyat-e faqih*, the *faqih* is first the supreme religious authority and only then the supreme political authority: he only becomes the ruler of the State because he is recognised as the most learned jurist by his peers. This presupposes the independence of the religious from the political field, as well as the dominance of religion over politics. In this view it is religion that provides the norms and determines the structures and policies of the political system, with the *faqih* at its top to see that the religious laws are respected and correctly enacted. He is the guardian of religion and the guarantor of the religious character of the State. However, in the absence of a politically suitable *marja'-e taqlid*, the assembly for the revision of the constitution in 1989 changed the articles pertaining to the *faqih*, giving priority to political over religious qualifications. According to the revised version of the constitution, the *faqih* no longer has to be a *marja'-e taqlid* recognised by his peers and the people (in whatever way this was to be verified) but is elected by the Expert Council whose members are elected according to political rather than religious criteria, and who do not represent the traditional clerical elite of the *marāje'-ye taqlid*. The revision of the constitution thus emphasised the *faqih's* political over his religious legitimacy.[47]

This revision of the constitution was in accordance with the general tendency since the revolution. If, in theory, religion determined politics, in practice Khomeini gave precedence to the interest of the State over the rulings of religion. When the Guardian Council threatened to block the legislative process with its strict reading of religion he set up the Expediency Council, whose objective was not the preservation of Islam but the interest of the State. In the end Khomeini even went so far as to claim that the interest of the State had priority over religious law, and that the *faqih* could overrule the most central commandments of

Islam.[48] This raised the question of how a state can be Islamic if it does not respect the most fundamental rulings of Islam. Obviously the election of Khamene'i did little to resolve this problem, but further undermined the religious legitimacy of the regime. Even though the constitution no longer required the *faqih* to be a *marja'*, many felt that Khamene'i lacked the necessary qualification.

One solution to the legitimacy crisis was to replace Khamene'i by a higher-ranking cleric such as Montazeri. Parts of the political and clerical elite backed this solution and actively promoted the latter's return to power. Thus, on 17 November 1991, 100 deputies visited Montazeri in Qom to pay their respects and to seek his guidance as *marja'-e taqlid* in the question of the Madrid Peace Conference.[49] When this visit became public knowledge it caused a political scandal, as it was rightly perceived as an affront to Khamene'i. Although officially the deputies had merely sought Montazeri's guidance as a religious authority, implicitly they had expressed their support for his return to the political field. As Montazeri wrote, the deputies were accused of having brought back to life he who had already been dead.[50] In the ensuing debate, the leader of the faction, Morteza Alviri, justified their visit with Khomeini's words from his letter of deposition: 'If God permits, you [Montazeri] will, with your teachings, give warmth to the seminary and the system.' However, the conservatives retorted that the sentence had to be understood in its context, and attempted to bring Alviri to the Special Court of the Clergy. It was only on the intervention of Khamene'i, who feared a further escalation of the debate, that this was prevented. Later however, two other leaders of the faction were tried and sentenced by the court.[51]

The regime was worried by the continuing support for Montazeri, and sought an occasion to intimidate him. When Montazeri in a speech on 10 February 1993 criticised the regime for denying the existence of political prisoners even though only recently several of his supporters had been detained under the pretext that they had planned a coup d'état,[52] the regime used this opportunity to order an attack on his house. The following day, his residence was ransacked by a mob under the protection of the security forces. Along with his office and lecture hall the one-storey house, built in yellow brick after the revolution, formed a small compound about 300 metres south of the city's main sanctuary. It lay at the angle of a small alley where it joined the riverbank road (named Shahid Mohammad Montazeri) with his sons living next door, while several senior clerics had their houses and offices nearby. The attacks on the compound continued over three days and several of his students were detained, forcing Montazeri to close his seminary. On the evening of the fourth day his office was surrounded by several hundred security officers who broke into his house, ransacked his office and pillaged his archive. Although they did not produce an official warrant, they carried away numerous books, tapes and files – among them, important letters and documents.[53]

A second solution to the legitimacy crisis was to promote a *marja'-e taqlid* as the State's spiritual guide. Thus, from July 1989, Khamene'i and his supporters promoted Mohammad Reza Golpayegani and Grand Ayatollah Mohammad-Ali Araki as the highest sources of emulation. A group of clerics declared that Khomeini's followers should henceforth consider Araki as their *marja'-e taqlid*. Araki in return declared that these followers could continue to pay their religious taxes to the persons authorised by Khomeini. Furthermore, they could continue to use his *resāle-ye amali-ye*, although traditionally a *marja's* fatwas lose their validity after his death.[54] Although both Araki and Golpayegani kept out of politics, they did not openly question the doctrine of *velāyat-e faqih* and were both willing to issue fatwas in support of the regime.[55] By publicly endorsing their *marja'iyat*, the regime benefited from their religious authority and strengthened its own legitimacy. However, in the long term this solution was untenable as it meant accepting the separation of political and religious authority. To the leader and his supporters the only viable solution was to raise the status of Khamene'i and to promote him as *marja'-e taqlid*. Given the traditional reluctance of the clergy to accept the interference of the State in its affairs Khamene'i sought to tighten control.

In February 1992, during a visit to the Madresse Feiziyeh in Qom, Khamene'i called for a sweeping reform of the seminaries. He criticised the lack of coordination between the seminaries, and the neglect of missionary activities and foreign-language publications. He recommended expanding the teaching of modern sciences and foreign languages, to employ more computers and to privilege *excathedra* teaching over the more traditional didactic methods.[56] Above all, taking up Motahhari's plans from the 1960s, he pressed for the creation of a central financial fund and a central administrative council to improve coordination between the seminaries. According to this plan, religious donations should no longer be paid to the *marāje'-ye taqlid* but should go directly into the central fund.[57] Many of these demands had long been discussed among the more progressive clerics, who were aware of the necessity of adapting the methods, contents and structures of the *houze elmiye*[58] to the needs of the contemporary world. On their initiative, modern subjects like sociology, psychology and economics as well as comparative study of religions had been introduced, new methods adopted and new publications established. However, if by the 1990s the seminaries were no longer the self-centred circles focused on obscure debates without practical relevance once criticised by secular scholars and progressive clerics, a profound reform had been prevented by the conservative clergy.

Each seminary remained linked to a *marja'*, who controlled its administration; determined its curriculum; and, with the donations from his followers, assured its financing. Its teachers and students depended on the *marja'* for their wages and stipends, and faithfully followed his guidance. Consequently the seminaries were personal fiefdoms of the *marāje'*, largely independent from the State as well as from other clerics.[59] The creation of a central financial fund, as proposed by Khamene'i, was meant to deprive the *marāje'* of their main source of income and to make them dependent on the benevolence of the State. These efforts to tighten the control of the State were regarded with hostility not only by the traditional clergy but also by many progressive clerics, who believed in the need for modernisation of the seminaries but opposed the State's further intrusion into the religious field. The increasing politicisation of the clergy had shown that position (and title) in the religious field risked losing its credibility and value if it was no longer the result of religious learning but the reflection of position (and power) in the political field. Progressive and traditional clerics alike feared that the *marāje'* would lose their autonomy and authority should they become subservient to politics. Hence, Khamene'i's efforts to be recognised as a *marja'-e taqlid* were met with opposition and his first attempts to assume the succession of a deceased *marja'* failed.

When, on 8 August 1992 in Najaf, the death was announced of Grand Ayatollah Abolqasem Mossavi Kho'i, who was considered by many as the most learned *marja'-e taqlid* of his time, Khamene'i attempted to be recognised as his successor. In a number of sermons and publications in

Syria and Pakistan, the supporters of Khamene'i declared their recognition of his *marja'iyat*.[60] However, Kho'i had been an outspoken opponent of the politicisation of Islam, and had openly rejected *velāyat-e faqih*, which he considered to be based on an erroneous interpretation of the scriptures. His students and supporters were therefore not willing to accept Khamene'i as their new *marja'-e taqlid*. Faced with their opposition, Khamene'i silently dropped the claim.[61] When Golpayegani died in Qom on 9 December 1993, the situation was different, and Khamene'i's supporters seized the opportunity to promote him as his successor. As the sermon at the funeral of a *marja'-e taqlid* is traditionally held by his designated successor, Khamene'i asked to be allowed to hold this address. However, Golpayegani's family and friends quickly buried the *marja'* in order to not have to accord Khamene'i this honour. Following this second defeat, Khamene'i and his supporters declared their support for Araki, who by this time was over 100 years old, in the hope of assuming his succession at his death. In the following months as Araki's health deteriorated, Khamene'i's supporters intensified their efforts. They argued that the informal, and often non-transparent, designation of the *marja'-e taqlid* by his peers and the pious masses was no longer timely. The Shi'i community needed not only a central leader, but also one capable and willing to address the social and political problems of the world. On 18 November 1994, the head of the judiciary, Ayatollah Mohammad Yazdi, declared in a sermon that religious and political leadership should be united. What he meant was not that a *marja'* should become the *rahbar* (leader), but that the *rahbar* should be recognised as a *marja'*. In another sermon, Ayatollah Ahmad Jannati, a senior member of the Guardian Council, proposed that a council of clerics should be formed to elect the *marāje'-ye taqlid*. Although he did not specify who should be members or what the criteria should be for their decision, this council was clearly meant to strengthen the State's control.[62]

When Araki died in Qom on 28 November 1994, the fight for his succession broke out in earnest. While Khamene'i's camp intensified its campaign, Montazeri's supporters did not remain inactive either. On 30 November, in an interview with BBC Farsi, Montazeri's son, Ahmad, confirmed that 14 prominent members of the state clergy had signed a declaration in support of his father. The existence of this text was confirmed some days later, when the signatories were asked by a group of students in the weekly newspaper *Keyhan-e hava'i* to withdraw the declaration. Interestingly, several conservative clerics such as Ayatollah Mohammad Reza Mahdavi-Kani were also reported to have signed the declaration. Although it was never officially published, and the signatories were reported to have denied their participation, its existence was once more confirmed when, in the London weekly *al-Wasat* of 2 January 1995, the now 20 signatories affirmed their support for Montazeri.[63] Khamene'i responded to the challenge posed by the declaration with a harsh attack on Montazeri during Friday prayers on 2 December 1994. With this sermon he also reacted to a letter of 3 November, in which Montazeri had warned against the politicisation of the *marja'iyat* and the violation of the autonomy of the religious field.

The message had originally been written in mid-July, but Montazeri had only decided to send it when the debate on the *marja'iyat* intensified. It was sent along with several letters, declarations and the recordings of speeches by supporters of Khamene'i in support of his claim to the *marja'iyat*, in which Montazeri and other clerics were attacked. The message was transmitted by Ayatollah Mohammad Mo'men, a member of the Guardian and the Expert Council, who shared Montazeri's views. Another cleric refused to accompany Mo'men because he rightly feared that the passage on the *marja'iyat* would provoke the leader's fury.[64] This passage read:

> The Shi'i *marja'iyat* has always been an independent spiritual power, this independence should not be broken by you and the *houze elmiye* should not become the employee of the government as this would be harmful for the future of Islam and Shi'ism. Whatever your supporters may try, you will find no evidence for the scholarly position of the late Imam [Khomeini]. Do not permit the authority and spirituality of the *houze* to become mixed up with the political work of [government] bodies [...]. It would be in the interest of Islam, the seminary and yourself that your office officially announces: Because he has much work and the responsibility of administering the country lies on his shoulders, he does not respond to religious questions [...] and you should refer to the *houze* for scholarly and religious advice and for donations.[65]

On 1 December, the conservative clergy published the names of three clerics who were considered equally qualified for Araki's succession.

At their head was Khamene'i, followed by the Grand Ayatollahs Mirza Javad Tabrizi and Mohammad Fazel-Lankorani. The following day the Jāme'e Modaressin Houze Elmiye Qom (Teachers' Society of the Seminary of Qom) published a second list with seven names – at their head: once again, Khamene'i. The most respected grand ayatollahs, such as Ali al-Sistani in Najaf, did not appear on the list while traditional clerics such as Mir Mohammad Ruhani in Qom and Hassan Tabatabai-Qomi in Mashhad, who had fallen out with the regime because of their rejection of *velāyat-e faqih*, were also omitted.[66] According to Montazeri, it was only on the insistence of the supporters of Khamene'i, who organised a demonstration in front of the society's office, that the Teachers' Society issued the list. On 4 December, a group of 150 deputies under the leadership of the President of Parliament, Ali Akbar Nateq-Nuri, sent a letter to Khamene'i in which they addressed him as Grand Ayatollah and called him the most qualified person to lead the Islamic community. On 7 December, a group of 100 clerics from inside and outside the country published a declaration in *Keyhan-e hava'i* in which they recognised Khamene'i as the sole *marja'*. The list of signatories was headed by Yazdi, Jannati and Nateq-Nuri, but most others were minor members of the state clergy.[67]

In spite of this public support, the clergy was critical of Khamene'i's claim to the *marja'iyat*. Not only did the great mass of the traditional clergy not support it, but even some of the conservative members of the political clergy were not willing to recognise him as *marja'*. Notably the influential editor of *Resalat* and secretary of the Jāme'e Modaressin, Azari-Qomi, was highly critical of his bid for the *marja'iyat*, and in private letters to members of the leadership advised against it. There was even the risk that political heavyweights like Musavi-Ardebili, Mahdavi-Kani, Mostafa Mohaqqeq-Damad, and Mo'men might publicly express their support for Montazeri. As this would not only have been a rejection of his religious authority but also an attack on his political authority, Khamene'i felt that it was preferable to end the debate before it caused further damage. In a speech on 14 December, he denied that there was a dispute over the *marja'iyat* and claimed that he had never actively sought recognition as *marja'-e taqlid*. Although he would accept this responsibility should it be in the interest of Islam, as he had also accepted the post of *rahbar*, he had never claimed the title himself. It had been his supporters, he maintained, who, without his consent, had placed his name on the list. As there were enough qualified clerics to give guidance, he had also not sought to publish a *resāle-ye amali-ye*. Therefore, he renounced the *marja'iyat*, at least in Iran:

I have to tell you that I am already burdened with a very heavy responsibility. Being the leader of the Islamic republic along with the great responsibilities in the world is a weight as heavy as the burden of several *marāje'* [. . .]. The present situation is not that urgent. Thanks to Allah, there exist so many *mojtaheds* [. . .]. This is why I refuse to accept the responsibility of being a *marja'* [. . .]. Of course, outside Iran, things are different. I accept the burden [. . .]. Today, I accept the request of Shi'ites outside Iran, as there is no alternative.[68]

The official recognition of a separation between the *marja'iyat* inside and outside the country was unprecedented in the history of Shi'ism, whose tradition and theology knows no borders.[69] Khamene'i's claim that no cleric outside Iran qualified as *marja'* was also not well received by non-Iranian clerics. Many of them preferred Sistani, and were reluctant to recognise the regime's claim to religious supremacy. If Khamene'i nonetheless insisted on his recognition as *marja'-e taqlid* outside Iran it was because he feared that his authority would be challenged outside rather than inside the country, where few dared openly question the leader.[70] Although Montazeri too had not publicly challenged Khamene'i's claim to the *marja'iyat* and had instructed his supporters to remain silent, he was perceived as one of the leader's principal rivals. Therefore, after Friday prayers on 23 December, dozens of Khamene'i's supporters assembled in front Montazeri's house and *hosseiniye* (lecture hall), and the following day a violent mob broke into the building. The attack was not as ferocious as in 1993, but numerous students and clerics voiced their protest. Montazeri's son Sa'id also wrote a long letter of complaint to the leader but, as on earlier occasions, it went unanswered.[71] In the end, the debate on the *marja'iyat* succeeded in establishing Khamene'i in the official discourse as Grand Ayatollah, but it also highlighted how controversial his claim to this title was. For the State, the ultimate outcome of the debate was a defeat. It had tried to establish its supremacy, to impose its choice on the clerics and to change the rules of the religious field – and it had failed.

## Conclusion

The discourse on reform in Iran in the early 1990s was a continuation of the discourse on religion, politics and modernity begun in the mid-nineteenth century. However, given the changed political, cultural, and social context, this discourse followed different rules and had new objectives. This change was caused by a triple crisis of legitimacy in Iran: a crisis of the regime, which had proved to be as corrupt, repressive and inefficient as its predecessor; a crisis of leadership, which, after the transition to Khamene'i, no longer fulfilled its own criteria; and a crisis of religion, which, because of its constant political abuse, increasingly lost its credibility and authority among the people. The restrictions on individual freedoms imposed by the State in the name of religion were increasingly at odds with the aspirations of large parts of society. According to Pierre Bourdieu, the social function of religion lies in its ability to justify the existing social order. If it does not fulfil this function for a social group, this group will either turn its back on religion or seek to adapt it to its needs.[72] In Iran the growing discontent with the official reading of religion led reform-minded clerics, politicians and intellectuals to seek an alternative reading more in line with the aspirations of society for fear that it might permanently turn away from religion. The participants in the reform discourse were by no means a homogeneous group, but came from different backgrounds and had different perspectives. While some had long been alarmed by the violation of rights, others only came to value freedom, pluralism and the rule of law once they themselves became the object of repression. Some only wanted to return to power, while others genuinely wished to change politics. Some wanted to preserve and perfect the current system, while others sought a transition to democracy. And while some held on to the traditional approach to religion, others went beyond this approach or completely dropped all reference to tradition.

Although critical journalists, dissident clerics and liberal politicians were prosecuted, imprisoned and banned from elections, while numerous reformist newspapers were closed down, the reformers not only managed to pursue their debates but also to change the rules and limits of the discourse itself. Thus, new concepts and subjects were introduced: Montazeri brought up the question of rights and duties, political legitimacy and popular sovereignty. Soroush raised the issue of the plurality of opinions, the position of the clergy and religious democracy, while Shabestari introduced to the discourse the question of religion's relation to reason, criticism and freedom. Their ideas were rejected by their opponents, but they could not be ignored since their authors were respected and recognised authorities. Rather than try to disprove the legitimacy of their ideas, their opponents sought to physically silence the reformers and to undermine their position in the field. In the end, the response to their ideas was so great that conservative thinkers such as Ali Motahhari, Azari-Qomi, Mesbah-Yazdi, Javad and Sadeq Larijani were compelled to discuss them and to recognise them as legitimate parts of the discourse. Khamene'i, too, was forced repeatedly to respond to their views, but even he was only temporarily able to stop the debate. Despite appearing theoretical, the ideas of the reformers had practical political implications. While, out of prudence, many authors left it to their readers to spell out the consequences, the debates on pluralism, freedom, reason and democracy in the *Kiyan* circle were never purely theoretical but were meant to help develop a plan for reform. When in the mid-1990s the reformist politicians around Hajjarian and Khatami set out to formulate a new political programme, they could draw on the concepts developed and discussed over the previous few years. And in 1997, when the elections were due, the reformists were ready to challenge the conservatives' hold on power.

# CHAPTER 6

# POWER AND IMPOTENCE OF
# THE REFORM MOVEMENT

### Cultural Change and the Hope for Reform

Protecting the freedom of individuals and the rights of the nation
[...] is a necessity deriving from the dignity of man in divine
religion [...] [It requires] provision of the necessary conditions for
the realisation of the constitutional liberties, strengthening and
expanding the institutions of civil society [...] and preventing any
violation of personal integrity, rights and legal liberties.

(Khatami, his inaugural speech on 4 August 1997)[1]

In 1995, a group of reform-minded politicians and intellectuals of the
Islamic left, who had been forced to the margins of the political field,
formed around Hajjarian, Khatami and the reformist journalist Mostafa
Tajzadeh to discuss the creation of a new journal. Although this
publication never appeared, the group's discussions helped set the agenda
for the reform movement, and its members became the strategic and
organisational centre of the 1997 election campaign. Drawing on the
discourse initiated by Soroush, Shabestari and Montazeri, and inspired by
their ideas on the reinterpretation of religion and its relationship to
politics, this group developed its own distinct political programme. Its
members realised that in the face of social change the regime had to adapt
its discourse and its policies. By 1996, nearly 75 per cent of the population
of Iran was below the age of 35. The proportion of Iranians with a formal

education had risen to nearly 80 per cent, and women accounted for 43 per cent of those passing the entrance exams to university. Field surveys showed that with the increasing urbanisation of the country, the importance attributed to religious mores, values and traditions had sharply decreased. This notably affected the relationship between men and women, as well as the importance accorded to the family.[2] By 1997, the official discourse was increasingly out of touch with the aspirations of the country's youth, and legislation was growing more and more at odds with the social situation of women. To the young, who by now had no personal experience of the revolution, the official culture of sacrifice, suffering and abnegation appeared outdated and obsolete. They resented the State's interference in their lives and rejected its control over their bodies and identity. Certainly not everyone wished to live a Western secular lifestyle, but all wanted to decide the way in which they lived and sought to reaffirm their individual autonomy from the State.[3] Within the family, the traditional patriarchal model gave way to relationships based on equality and dialogue. The absolute authority of the husband and father was no longer accepted by wives and children. Similarly, in the public sphere, women and the young questioned the authority of the State. As women affirmed their role in the public sphere, they were less and less willing to tolerate their legal discrimination under the pretext of religion. Over the years the women's movement succeeded in establishing in the public discourse its demands for a reform of the discriminative laws on divorce, inheritance and child custody.[4]

At the approach of the presidential election, the Islamic left presented the former prime minister, Mir Hossein Mussavi, as its candidate in July 1996. However, this choice was met with such opposition by the conservatives that Mussavi rescinded the offer. It was later reported that Khamene'i had refused to accept a layman as president. When the Islamic left asked Khatami to run, he initially also hesitated as he had not planned to return to politics. In the end he accepted on the condition that his candidature was approved by Khamene'i. It was only after he had obtained the leader's promise to remain neutral that his candidature was officially announced in early 1997. Khamene'i probably believed that the little-known and soft-spoken Khatami would be no match for his own candidate. Although he had not officially endorsed his bid, it was clear that he supported Nateq-Nuri, who had announced his candidacy for the conservatives in July 1996. As President of Parliament, he had been one of the principal opponents of Rafsanjani's course of state-controlled modernisation and privatisation.[5] Khamene'i was convinced that the race would be made between Nateq-Nuri and Hojatoleslam Mohammad Reyshahri, who had also declared his candidacy. Apparently Khatami himself did not initially believe that he could win, and only saw the campaign as an opportunity to present his programme of pluralism, participation and civil society to the wider public.[6]

That Khatami nevertheless ultimately won the elections was based on his personality, his campaign and his success in enlisting the support of the pragmatists. With his black turban, grey beard and wide cloak, Khatami appeared as a typical member of the revolutionary clergy, but his friendly, smiling and cultivated manner distinguished him from the solemn and stern appearance of other clerics. His activities before and after the revolution proved him to be a true supporter of the Islamic Republic, but his advocacy of greater diversity in culture, education and the media secured him the support and sympathy of intellectuals, students and the ethnic and religious minorities. Unlike many members of the Islamic left he had not been involved in the repression of the opposition, and, unlike other members of the state clergy, he was seen as modest, honest, hard working and not corrupt. That he did not appear well-versed in the power plays of politics was perceived as a plus point by his electorate. Among the religious elements of the population his authority as a respected cleric and a descendant of the Prophet (*seyyed*) won him confidence, while his liberal views earned him the support of the more modern sections of society. In many ways, Khatami appeared as a symbiosis of tradition and modernity, religion and reform.

His efficiently managed campaign made use of, and further contributed to, this image. Khatami's campaign team worked to emphasise both his image as a religious scholar and a man firmly rooted in everyday life. In their campaign, which began in early March 1997 with a bus tour through the provinces, they could draw on the support of leftist parties and student groups as well as writers, artists and actors, who used their celebrity to promote his candidacy. His friend, Hojatoleslam Mohammad Taqi Fazel-Meybodi, meanwhile gathered statements of support from the religious and political elite to strengthen his image as a true son of the system.[7] Furthermore, Khatami managed to enlist the support of Kargozaran. The party of the pragmatists had initially hoped to change the constitution in order to allow Rafsanjani a third term in office. However, unable to enlist sufficient support for this plan or to find a suitable candidate of their own, it decided to endorse Khatami.[8] Thanks to its support the reformers gained access to the municipal infrastructure of Tehran. Although legally all offices were required to remain neutral, Gholamhossein Karbastchi, the leader of Kargozaran and mayor of Tehran, put the city's billboards and its popular daily, *Hamshari*, at the reformers' disposal.

The clergy's position in the elections was divided: the Jāme'e Modaressin of Qom had declared its support for Nateq-Nuri early on, but several members later complained that they had not been consulted.[9] Montazeri did not openly express his support for any of the candidates. A friend of Khatami's father, he had also been Khatami's teacher in Qom, but they were not particularly close. Nevertheless, on 27 April, Montazeri issued a statement calling on the officials to allow for free elections and to permit 'no group or faction, pretending to be the guardian of the people [and to act] in their interest' to impose their choice on the people so that they 'lose control of their own destiny'.[10] Khamene'i affirmed that he would not allow anyone 'to give himself the right to cheat in the elections', but on 23 June, the day of election, Khatami's supporters registered 570 cases of voting irregularities. Faced with the victory of the reformers, the commander of the Pasdaran, Mohsen Reza'i, reportedly proposed to Khamene'i to crush any protest should the leader decide to nullify the results. However, Khamene'i refused to intervene and when the results were announced he duly accepted the victory of Khatami.[11] Neither the conservatives nor the reformers had foreseen the extent of this victory: on a turnout of 88 per cent, Khatami won 69 per cent of the 29.7 million votes cast. Polls later showed that people from all sections of society had voted for him. Khatami had done equally well in urban and rural areas, in rich and poor districts – and even among the Pasdaran, many had given him their vote. However, his main base of support were the women, the young, and the country's ethnic and religious minorities.[12] In his inaugural speech on 4 August, Khatami promised to respect individual rights and liberties and to accept the diversity of society:

Protecting the freedom of individuals and the rights of the nation, which constitute a fundamental obligation of the President upon taking the oath, is a necessity deriving from the dignity of man in divine religion [...]. [It requires] provision of the necessary conditions for the realisation of the constitutional liberties, strengthening and expanding the institutions of civil society [...] and preventing any violation of personal integrity, rights and legal liberties.[13]

Khatami did not want to remove religion from politics, society and culture, but rather proposed a more flexible, tolerant and modern interpretation of religion in order to open the space for different positions, opinions and ways of life. He wanted to break the conservatives' hold on culture, religion and politics in order to reintegrate the groups and classes of society which had progressively been excluded after the revolution. For the conservatives, the reforms proposed by Khatami posed a threat not only because they endangered their control over politics and the social and financial capital attached to it, but also because they threatened their discursive hegemony. The reforms were a challenge to their culture, their identity and their world view, all three of which were based on the fundamental distinction between the 'own' (*khodi-hā*) and the 'others' (*kheir-khodi-hā*). In the view of the conservatives, the 'others' were the liberals, the leftists, the monarchists and all others who did not share their traditional Shi'i culture with its specific rituals, rhetoric and codes. In their view this culture, despite its triumph in the revolution, remained threatened by foreign ideas, codes, and lifestyles. As its religious character gave it an absolute quality in the eyes of the conservatives, it was legitimate to resort to violence in order to defend it.[14] To the conservatives, the reformers were all the more dangerous as they belonged to their own class. The bearded Khatami with his black turban and clerical gown was no Westernised liberal in suit and tie, but one of the 'own' who had made the revolution and built the regime at their side. Like Montazeri or Soroush he was dangerous because his ideas could not easily be dismissed as foreign, secular and thus illegitimate. Furthermore, the results of the election unequivocally proved that the reforms proposed by Khatami had the approval and the support of the people.

However, it soon became clear that although the electorate had given him a mandate for reform, they had not handed him the power for its execution. The elections had given the reformers control of the executive, but the legislature and the judiciary – as well as the Guardian, Expert and Expediency Councils – remained firmly in the hands of the conservatives. Furthermore, over the previous few years the latter had seized control of many of the revolutionary offices and organisations, such as the Friday prayer leaders, the religious foundations and the Pasdaran. Finally, the conservatives retained control of the office of the ruling jurist, who with his thousands of representatives in all institutions of the country effectively constituted a rival power structure alongside the government. On 27 June 1997, four days after the elections, Montazeri warned Khatami of the dangers and difficulties ahead. In an open letter he congratulated him on his victory, which he called a 'popular revolt against the current situation' and a 'resounding message to all honoured officials of the country'. The election, he wrote, had been a vote against discrimination, mismanagement and the 'monopolisation of power by factions, and the dismissal of meritorious forces under empty pretexts'. Montazeri reminded Khatami of his heavy responsibility, and, in a direct reference to the leader, warned him not permit others to obstruct reforms:

> In order to strengthen the system and the country, it is your duty to enforce the respect and the authority of the constitution and the laws of the country in all fields and among all classes. All groups and individuals are equal in the eyes of the law, and the rights and powers of the nation, the president of the republic, the other officials and even the revolutionary leader have been defined in the constitution [...]. Servile people seeking power, whose condition under the present circumstances is regrettably much advanced, shall not through pressure and intrigues establish their influence over you, so that in the end only the person of the president has been changed, and you lose your present authority, and your voters, the absolute majority of the country, become disappointed with the leadership.[15]

Montazeri outlined the economic difficulties of the country, which was still suffering from the consequences of the war. He called on Khatami to address growing inequalities, widespread corruption and ethnic discrimination; to seek the return of Iranian exiles; to invest in the reconstruction of the country's infrastructure; to improve public healthcare; and to stop emigration to the cities, which, he warned, could leave the villages deserted and make the country dependent on foreign imports. He then returned to the question of civil rights and political reform:

> The entire nation expects the upholding of the rights of the people, and the freedoms enshrined in the constitution. The first slogan of the revolution was 'Independence, Freedom, Islamic Republic.' Freedom is of course limited by the principles of Islam and the rights of others, but according to the shari'a and the constitution, the control of beliefs is forbidden. The bugging [of telephones] and all kinds of surveillance is forbidden, the honour, the life and the property of individuals must be preserved. No one can be arrested but by order of the law and with a written indictment. Publications and the press must be free unless they are against religion or public morality. In the contemporary world, newspapers are the voice of the people and all classes can address those responsible through them. They shall not only act as the organ of the government and be obliged to print the news of those in power. Political parties must be free within the framework of Islam. People of all classes must be able to become members and express their opinion, so that through the exchange of ideas the people find political progress and the government finds support [...]. It is wrong that at the time of elections hastily established groups engage in banal propaganda. The participation of the people in the elections shall be free and with prior knowledge and preparation; the way to this is the creation of parties [...]. [I hope] that by appointing good people and abolishing unnecessary extravagances and removing superfluous organisations you can save the country and the revolution from its enemies. In any case, try to remain on the side of the people.[16]

The letter provoked different reactions on the political scene. While the conservatives were outraged that Montazeri had dared to publicly challenge the absolute powers of the ruling jurist, Khatami's response to the letter was muted as he did not wish to openly confront Khamene'i. He certainly shared most of the opinions expressed in the letter, but he feared that being too closely associated with Montazeri would only increase the opposition of the conservatives for whom Montazeri remained a source of contention. Khatami hoped that if he could not obtain the leader's active support, he might at least gain his tacit toleration of his government. He was well aware that the conservatives retained sufficient posts and power to obstruct his reforms, and felt that he would have to advance cautiously if he did not want to provoke their outright opposition.

The first test for the reformers was the nomination of the new cabinet. Khatami was willing to retain several of the technocrats from the previous cabinet but sought to place his own supporters in key posts. His choice of Mostafa Moin, Abdollah Nuri and Ataollah Mohajerani for the Ministries of Education, Interior and Culture respectively was met with resistance from the conservatives, but the most difficult task proved to be replacing Ali Fallahian. The hardline Minister of Intelligence was considered one of the master puppeteers of the repression of the opposition, and in April 1997 was famously found guilty by a Berlin court of having ordered in September 1992 the murder of three Kurdish opposition leaders in that city's Mykonos restaurant. Although Khatami eventually managed to obtain his removal, Khamene'i rejected 14 of his candidates before finally, in June 1998, approving Hojatoleslam Qorban'ali Dori-Najafabadi, who was considered to be more liberal than his predecessor but was not seen as a reformer.[17] Khatami also managed to obtain the dismissal of Reza'i, but had to accept that he was replaced at the head of the Pasdaran by his deputy, Yahya Rahim-Safavi.

While in the economic field the reformers sought to continue the course of privatisation and liberalisation pursued by the previous government, in the political field they had an ambitious agenda. Their objective was to enforce the rule of law and respect for civil rights, and to advance gender equality and political participation. Although in the end they failed to change the structural balance of power and remained powerless to prevent the conservatives from reversing their reforms, they did initially manage to open the political field and the public discourse to new groups and ideas. Three acts were of particular importance in enhancing political participation. The first was the creation of local councils. The constitution had provided for these councils and an executive bill had been passed in 1982, but no action had been taken to put it into practice. It was therefore only on the initiative of the reformers that elections were finally held in February 1999. Although the remit of these councils was limited, they offered the groups and classes of society that over the years had been excluded by the conservatives a new opportunity to take part in the political process. They also gave politicians a space to gather experience, which they could employ in national politics.[18]

The second act was the founding of political parties. The party law had been put into effect in 1988, but by 1997 only six parties and 29 interest groups had registered. When, in 1997, the reformers gained control of the Interior Ministry, which was in charge of registering parties, they encouraged political groups to seek recognition. By 2004, the number of parties had risen to 114, and the number of interest groups to 171. The most important new party was Mosharekat (Participation), founded in December 1998 and led by Khatami's younger brother, Mohammad Reza. It advocated peaceful and gradual reform, and sought to encourage the inclusion and participation of all groups and segments of society. The number of non-governmental and community-based organisations also rose to an unprecedented level – among them, numerous groups of women and ethnic and religious minorities.[19]

The third act for opening up the discursive field was the diversification of the media sector. In September 1997, Ahmad Burqani, the Deputy Minister of Culture and Islamic Guidance, placed the journalist Isa Saharkhiz in charge of the affairs of the press. In one of his first acts he replaced the informal system of pre-publication censorship with a system of legal sanctions after publication. Should publishers violate the press law, they were to be held responsible exclusively by the special press jury. Saharkhiz was convinced that everyone should have his or her say, and in his first six months in the post issued 141 new press licences. One of the earliest publications to receive recognition was the daily *Jāme'eh*, later described as the first truly independent newspaper in Iran for half a century. Launched in February 1998 by Hamid Reza Jalaiepour, Mohsen Sazegara and the former chief editor of *Kiyan*, Mashallah Shamsalva'ezin, it sought to actively contribute to the transformation of society and to encourage reforms. With colourful photographs, daring headlines and reports on sports, culture and lifestyle, it aimed to break with the culture of suffering, sacrifice and mourning that had dominated the public discourse.[20]

Apart from popular participation, the advancement of women's rights took a prominent place in the reformers' discourse. Women had voted in large numbers for Khatami in the hope that he would change discriminative laws, improve access to the job market, ease gender segregation and generally allow women more freedom in public. However, to their disappointment Khatami failed to appoint a single female minister. The nomination of Ma'sumeh Ebtekar as Vice-President for Environmental Affairs remained a mainly symbolic act, as Khatami failed to place the reform of the discriminative laws on divorce, inheritance and child custody at the top of his agenda. Even worse, Khatami was unable to prevent parliament from further tightening gender segregation in schools and public transport in autumn 1997.[21] For the conservatives, the place of women in society was the touchstone of the Islamic character of the system. Any change to this particularly sensitive issue needed to be based on a revised reading of religion, but, with few exceptions, the religious reformers did not devote much attention to women's rights and many continued to advocate a traditional role model. Montazeri was no exception in this respect. In an interview in November 2003, he argued that women, as human beings, have rights that should be respected. However, while they should have the same political rights as men, in the social domain the natural differences between the sexes should be recognised. Although he advocated an interpretation of Islam that takes better account of men's duties and women's rights, he argued that, all things considered, men's privileged position in Islam is justified by their greater abilities and their greater productivity.[22] As the reformers were reluctant to challenge the conservatives' views, they failed to attain discursive hegemony. In the face of opposition and obstruction by the judiciary and the legislature, the initial enthusiasm of the reformers soon gave way to a feeling of concern. Many feared that if the President did not take more decisive action, the conservatives would once again reverse the timid advances achieved since the election. They felt that if the conservatives were not willing to bend to the people's will, it was necessary to adopt a more radical course. Encouraged by the transformed political context, they set out to expose more radical ideas and to call for more far-reaching action. One of the first to 'enter the ring' was, once again, Montazeri.

## Montazeri's Challenge to the Leader

The meaning of leadership is that the leader supervise the country so that nobody infringes on the shari'a [. . .] but he should not set

up a royal guard and office greater than those of the emperors of
the world to which nobody has access and which interferes with
the ministers, interferes with the governors, interferes in all places
[...] this is wrong. This way the country does not progress.

(Montazeri, in his speech on 14 November 1997)[23]

On 14 November 1997, Montazeri, clad in his habitual black cloak and
white turban, stepped onto the podium of his *hosseiniye* to deliver his
most scathing attack on the system and the leader himself. Although by
then a frail and grizzled man in his seventies, Montazeri once more
proved to be one of the most outspoken critics of the regime. In his
characteristic high-pitched voice, he admonished Khamene'i that in a
republic the will and the rights of the people must be respected, and
freedom of expression and association guaranteed, and that the leader
should play a role of guidance and supervision and not directly interfere
in the affairs of government. If this were not enough, for the first time he
publicly challenged the leader's religious authority. With this speech
Montazeri reacted to the continuing obstruction of reform and to the
fierce press campaign launched against him after his open letter to
Khatami. Furthermore, it was a response to Khamene'i's renewed bid for
the *marja'iyat*. The leader apparently felt that in the face of his electoral
defeat he needed to strengthen his position, and once more tried to
obtain his recognition as *marja'-e taqlid*. During a visit by the Jāme'e
Modaressin of Qom in Tehran, he demanded that the number of
members of the society be increased, and that in future it name not seven
but just one candidate for the *marja'iyat* – himself.[24] However, this
intervention in the religious field, just as three years earlier, met with the
resistance of the clergy. Several high-ranking clerics such as Musavi-
Ardebili, Mahdavi-Kani and Mo'men declared their opposition to this
bid. When, in November 1997, the head of the judiciary, Mohammad
Yazdi, declared that the range of the leader's fatwas was sufficient to be
regarded as a *resāle-ye amali-ye*, Makarem-Shirazi objected that these
fatwas mainly consisted of Persian translations of the Arabic fatwas of
the leader's office director, Mahmud Hashemi Shahrudi.[25] This renewed
debate on the *marja'iyat* also revived the debate on the powers of the
*faqih*. In the third week of October, in an unprecedented move, 3,000
students staged a demonstration at Tehran University to demand a
reform of the *faqih*'s role. In a speech to the crowd, the student leader,

Heshmatollah Tabarzadi, demanded that the *faqih* be directly elected by the people for a limited term, that his powers be restricted and that he be accountable to the Expert Council. If necessary, the constitution should be adapted accordingly. These were the very demands of Montazeri.[26]

At almost the same time, Ahmad Azari-Qomi addressed an open letter to the President in which he bitterly complained about the leader's intervention in the religious field, disputed his religious qualifications and advised him to leave religious questions to Montazeri. For many years, Azari-Qomi as the editor of *Resalat* had counted among the leading voices of the conservatives, but he had fallen out of favour when he had expressed his disapproval of the leader's claim to the *marja'iyat* in December 1994. He was consequently banned from publishing in *Resalat*, and, in autumn 1995, forced to resign from his posts as editor and as secretary of the Jāme'e Modaressin. In January 1996, he wrote in a letter to Khamene'i that he could accept his political leadership but not his religious authority.[27] In his 24-page letter to the President, dated 27 October 1997, Azari-Qomi wrote that for years he had sought to make his criticism heard but that nobody had paid attention. He criticised the leader's continual intervention in government affairs and chided the Expert Council for failing to hold him to account. He complained that the clergy had become subservient to politics, and that religious titles were no longer assigned according to merit. Under pressure from the intelligence service, the clergy had been forced to stop publishing the rulings of senior clerics like Montazeri, Shirazi and Ruhani. Holding Khamene'i personally responsible, Azari-Qomi criticised the attack on Montazeri's house as well as the mistreatment of other clerics, mentioning in particular the torture of a son of Shirazi. Seeking to obtain his recognition as *marja'-e taqlid* the leader had ordered the intelligence service to launch a campaign, Azari-Qomi alleged. The support of himself and other conservative clerics in the Jāme'e Modaressin for the leader's bid for the *marja'iyat* in December 1994 had been wrong, he wrote, because Khamene'i did not possess the necessary religious qualifications. They had been pressured to put him on the list by Yazdi, Jannati and other hardliners, who had given out the slogan 'one marja, one rahbar'. Although nobody but Yazdi had recognised Khamene'i as the most learned of, or even as equally qualified as, the other *marāj'e*, Yazdi during Friday prayers had declared him to be the most highly qualified. The hardliners had presented their support for

Khamene'i to be in the interest of the system, but in truth their action had caused damage not only to religion but also to the system. Having the State appoint the *marāj'e* was against Shi'i tradition, and following a *marja'* who does not possess the required qualifications is without value, Azari-Qomi maintained. During the revision of the constitution he had pushed for including the term *motlaq* (absolute), but he had believed that the leader's powers should be limited to political affairs and that he could only assume the religious functions of a *marja'* if he was also qualified for this position. As this was not currently the case, Azari-Qomi declared, Khamene'i should concentrate on his political functions and leave religious issues for Montazeri or the highly respected Grand Ayatollah Mohammad-Taqi Behjat to decide.[28]

The letter caused considerable turmoil as it was passed from hand to hand in the seminaries of Qom. Later, excerpts were broadcast on foreign radio stations and printed in the exile press. However, the broader public only indirectly learnt of the letter and the conflict it had provoked when the conservative press published a statement that Azari-Qomi had been excluded from the Jāme'e Modaressin for having undermined the authority of the *faqih*. On 7 November 1997, supporters of Khamene'i staged a protest in front of Azari-Qomi's house in Qom, and three days later physically attacked him in his seminary.[29] It can be assumed that Montazeri was aware of the content of Azari-Qomi's letter, and it is quite probable that he was prompted by it to launch his own attack on the leader. For his speech, he chose the Friday prayers on the birthday of Imam Ali on 14 November. Photographs show the modest lecture hall adjacent to his house packed with students, supporters and fellow clerics. As required by tradition, Montazeri began with a long sermon on Imam Ali, interspersed with citations from the Qur'an and the hadith before, in response to a previous question, he came to speak of political parties:

> In the contemporary world the government lies in the hands of the nation. We called {our state} an Islamic Republic {which means} that the people themselves must administer the country. They must become organised, bring able forces together and draw up good programmes [...]. [However] at the time of elections you have seen some gentlemen promote a candidate and set up transitory groups which they try to forcefully advance taking advantage of the people's ignorance and their absence from the

political scene. This is wrong. The people themselves have to be mobilised and have to organise their own groups and cadres [. . .]. The people's organisations should possess newspapers and the radio and television should be under their [the people's] control [. . .]. When the people speak, the radio and television must spread their words and the newspapers must publish their views and ideas. This is the way of the world and if we do not follow suite we will stay behind. If two or three people sit together and take all decisions for the country it will not progress in the present world. 'Republic' means 'government of the people'.[30]

Montazeri then came to speak of the role of the ruling jurist, as well as the recent attacks against himself in the conservative press:

Along with this, *velāyat-e faqih* is also mentioned in our constitution. But this does not mean that the ruling jurist should decide all. That would make the republic meaningless. The conditions and duties of the ruling jurist are defined in the constitution, the most important of his duties being to supervise the affairs of society so that its policies do not deviate from the standards of Islam and truth [. . .]. They [the leader and his allies] have no right to set aside someone who is worthy from a religious perspective, and also knowledgeable in political, cultural and economic matters, who is not subservient and who is independent [. . .]. *Velāyat-e faqih* is not compatible with a royal office, luxurious travel [costing] billions and other such things. The gentlemen tell me I was against *velāyat-e faqih*. God forgive! I was the first to talk of *velāyat-e faqih*, to propagate the idea, I have written a book about it and now I am against *velāyat-e faqih*? A handful of kids, who at the time we undertook this work were not even conceived, now cry I was against *velāyat-e faqih*. Shame upon you, what is this work?[31]

Montazeri then went on to speak of the relationship of the leader and the president, and Khamene'i's continuing interference in the work of Khatami's government:

The ruling jurist must, like the leader of the faithful [Imam Ali], supervise the country, the parties, the government, but he must not interfere in all areas. In the Islamic Republic the government must be independent, that is, it must be able to do its work. Truly this is one of the problems of the president Mr Khatami [...], I have warned him in a message that you cannot work this way. The president of the government cannot take a single step, if his ministers and governors do not cooperate. I told him, that if I were in your place, I would go to the leader and tell him: your position and authority are secure, but 22 million people have given me their vote knowing that the leader of the country preferred someone else [...]. It means that they don't agree with what you [Khamene'i] say [...]. The meaning of leadership is that he [the leader] supervise the country so that nobody infringes on the shari'a. Should the president or a minister deviate from the shari'a, he should prevent this, but he should not set up a royal guard and office greater than those of the emperors of the world to which nobody has access and which interferes with the ministers, interferes with the governors, interferes in all places [...] this is wrong. This way the country does not progress. A country which has several governing bodies, a separate government, a separate Expediency Council and a separate leader's office, which all want to exert their power, this is no way to administer a country. And the absolute rule in the way that two or three people define the country's fate and the people have no role in the contemporary world leads to defeat [...]. The ruling jurist must be the most highly qualified [...] Mr Khamene'i has himself insisted before [1989] on the highest qualification of the *marja'-e taqlid*. But I say to him: You are not a *marja'-e taqlid* and you bear no resemblance to a *marja'-e taqlid*.[32]

Montazeri then quoted the passage from his letter to Khamene'i of 3 November 1994, in which he warned the latter not to lay claim to the status of *marja'iyat* as he did not possess the necessary scholarly status. This passage had also been quoted by Azari-Qomi in his letter to the President. Although Azari-Qomi therein had also questioned the leader's qualifications for the *marja'iyat*, Montazeri's speech was the first time anyone dared publicly challenge his religious authority. He not only admonished Khamene'i to refrain from further interference in the affairs of government but also challenged his right to the post of leader. This was not a violation of the red lines of the discourse but the negation of their very existence.

Montazeri's supporters were soon forced to stop the distribution of cassettes of his speech, but its content continued to filter out. The first to feel the conservatives' fury was Tabarzadi, who on 15 November was attacked and severely beaten in his office by members of the Hezbollah.[33] When subsequently brought to court, the student leader was condemned to a long prison sentence. While criticism continued to mount, the regime called a day of nationwide protests for 19 November. On this day in Qom all courses were cancelled, the bazaar was closed and a large demonstration was organised. In an address to the crowd assembled at the central mosque of the shrine, the conservative Ayatollah Abdollah Javadi-Amoli attacked Montazeri for his criticism of the leader. It was wrong to pretend that *velāyat-e faqih* merely implied *vekālat* (representation) or *nezārat* (supervision), he declared and stressed, that *velāyat-e faqih* was an essential and sacred principle of Islam. The crowd then marched to Montazeri's house and office, where they broke open the doors and windows, ransacked his library and archive and mistreated several of his students and supporters, who had come to read the prayers at his house.[34] According to Montazeri, the mob, which was mainly composed of young men from Tehran, Isfahan and other cities, then ordered him to leave the house, but he refused. When they began to argue how to further proceed, his family and friends barricaded the door, while the neighbours stopped the attackers from breaking it open. It was rumoured that the mob had orders to seize Montazeri and kill him. According to Montazeri's account, the attack was directed by the chief of the judiciary, Mohammad Yazdi, who had come especially from Tehran. It was later said that the former Minister of Intelligence, Fallahian, also helped coordinate the attack by telephone. While the mob occupied Montazeri's house and employed the loudspeakers of the *hosseiniye* to shout slogans against Montazeri, the Jāme'e Modaressin sent a prosecutor as its emissary to the attackers. He praised them for their valorous defence of the leader, but ordered them to end their occupation of the house. The same day, the mob also attacked the house of Azari-Qomi. Together with Montazeri's son, Ahmad, Azari-Qomi was arrested and detained for several days.[35] It was rumoured at the time that Montazeri too was arrested and deported to an unknown location, but Montazeri did not confirm this in his memoirs.

On 22 November 1997, the conservative newspaper, *Abrar*, published Khomeini's previously unknown letter of dismissal of 26 March 1988.[36] In a televised speech on 27 November, Khamene'i criticised Azari-Qomi and Montazeri, calling the latter a 'politically bankrupt, pathetic and naive cleric who has taken an erroneous and clumsy stance against the spine of the revolution'. However, at the same time he ordered his supporters to end the attacks. The leader hoped to calm the situation ahead of the summit of the Organisation of the Islamic Conference, which was to be held in mid-December in Tehran.[37] Several conservative hardliners asked to have Montazeri brought to court and executed for high treason, but ultimately the judiciary did not take further action for fear of provoking renewed protests. Nevertheless, the National Security Council decided that Montazeri be placed under house arrest and barred from further receiving visitors, giving courses or issuing statements. All but one of the entrances to his compound were walled up, and a permanent guard placed in front of his house.[38] Azari-Qomi fared a similar fate, and until his death in February 1999 remained under arrest in his house in Qom.[39]

Khatami's response to the speech was ambiguous: on the one hand he criticised the violent attack on Montazeri, on the other hand he distanced himself from his demands and expressed his loyalty to the leader. He quickly made clear that a revision of the constitution was not on his agenda, and that he was not going to challenge the powers of the *faqih*. He apparently still hoped that it would be possible to change policies without changing the structures of the system. He also feared that if he were to openly question the official version of *velāyat-e faqih* he would definitely be branded an enemy of the system. Montazeri, however, later argued that it was impossible to open up the system without challenging the absolute powers of the leader. To accept and respect the red lines laid out by the regime would render any criticism of the central problems, and thus any serious reform, impossible.[40] Following his speech, few people dared publicly defend Montazeri. Among those to speak out in his defence were the former delegate Azam Taleqani and the veteran politician Ebrahim Yazdi, who was thereupon arrested and detained in Evin prison. Ayatollah Taki-Behjat closed his seminary in a sign of dissent, and Makarem-Shirazi resigned from his post at the head of the Jāme'e Modaressin.[41] In Isfahan, Najafabad and Mashhad people also demonstrated against his arrest, and during the student protests in Tehran in 1998 and 1999, many expressed their solidarity with Montazeri.

## Montazeri under House Arrest

In his interviews and books, by following the theories of [...] Ayatollah Montazeri, he [Kadivar] tries to resolve the problem by [arguing] that the clergy, even the *vali-ye faqih* have a supervisory role [not a mandate to rule] [...]. Thus, in practice there will be no problem and freedom, democracy and political parties will function. But what is the nature of this supervision? This has not been clarified, or at least in the theories of Mr Kadivar is not that evident. (Eshkevari on Montazeri's and Kadivar's theories)[42]

When Montazeri was placed under arrest in Qom, no visitors apart from his closest family members were allowed to enter his house, and contact with the outside world was strictly controlled. Although his wife Khadija shared with him his arrest as she had shared the time of his exile, and his sons continued to regularly provide him with news, he was for the following five years almost completely cut off from his friends, students and supporters. His isolation and the restriction to the limited space of his small house negatively affected his health. Deprived of regular medical treatment, his long-running heart condition and diabetes not only deteriorated but he also suffered from severe depression. Nevertheless, he continued to take an active interest in the events of the country and to participate in the political discourse wherever he could. At first the only way to speak to him was through the intercom from his son's house next door, but in the later years of his arrest he was allowed to use a telephone. He was also quick to realise the benefit of the internet for expressing his views. Thus, in 2000, with the help of his sons and students, Montazeri launched his own internet site – amontazeri.org – which over the years became his most important means of expression. Like the sites of other *marāje'-ye taqlid*, it contained a question-and-answer section in which Montazeri replied to the queries of his disciples on ritual and religious affairs, as well as biographical information and a large collection of historical photos. Furthermore, it contained his principal books in digital form as well as a section with his most recent political declarations, interviews and letters. The regime repeatedly tried to block the site but never actually managed to shut it down.

Thanks to modern communication technology, Montazeri was able to break his isolation and respond to the numerous questions that continued to be sent to him by students, politicians and journalists. In the five years until his release, his collected publications *Didgah-ha* (*Viewpoints*) listed no less than 92 letters, fatwas, interviews and other documents. He published his criticism of the arrest of dissidents, his condolences at the death of old friends and his remarks on major political events. From 2000, he also regularly gave interviews to foreign media, which could then be cited in the Iranian press. Furthermore, from the isolation of his house he continued to contribute with several major texts to the debate on *velāyat-e faqih*, which he had launched with his speech. For, if the violent reaction to that speech had shown the danger of questioning the official doctrine it had not managed to bring the debate to an end. When, two weeks after Montazeri's speech, Akbar Ganji, who had emerged as one of the most outspoken advocates of a more radical course of reform, was brought to court in Tehran for a lecture he had given several months earlier, he used his trial to continue his attacks on the conservatives and their reading of *velāyat-e faqih*.

In his speech of 21 June 1997, the journalist and sociologist had attacked what he termed the fascist reading of religion.[43] In his defence he continued his attack on the 'religious fascists', and on the judiciary, which he accused of condoning their violent tactics. The fascists, so he declared, were those who patronised the youth, who attacked books and films and disrupted meetings and lectures although they had been officially approved. They were those who 'claim that the people have erred in the elections and must therefore be brought back to the true path. And, above all, it is those who by a fascist reading of religion give these acts an ideological legitimation.'[44] *Velāyat-e faqih*, Ganji argued, is no essential element of religion and its rejection should therefore not be punished. Taking up a central argument of Montazeri, Ganji argued, that the *faqih's* election by the Expert Council proves that he draws his legitimacy from the people and must be considered their representative. Referring to a statement of Motahhari, he argued that the *faqih* should not govern the country but should only supervise the country's government. Obviously these arguments did not convince the court, and in March 1998 Ganji was sentenced to three months in prison and nine months' probation.[45]

In spite of his imprisonment, Ganji, with other reformists, founded the weekly *Rah-e nou*, which rapidly became a central platform of intellectual debate. In 1998, the periodical published a series of articles by Kadivar in which the latter offered a highly critical analysis of *velāyat-e faqih* from a theological, philosophical and jurisprudential point of view. This careful and detailed study, which was later published in *Hokumat-e vela'i* (Government of the Guardian),[46] established Kadivar as one of the leading voices of the reform discourse. Born in 1959 and from a modern religious family near Shiraz, Kadivar began to study engineering in 1977 but under the influence of the revolution changed to religious studies in Shiraz. Having moved to Qom in 1981, he attended the courses given by Montazeri, who became his most influential teacher. Parallel to his religious studies at the seminary in Qom, he studied philosophy and religious science at Tarbiyat Modarres University in Tehran. Having obtained the level of *mojtahed* in 1997 and having completed his doctorate, he worked as a university lecturer in Islamic philosophy and political science.[47] In the early 1990s, he worked in the reformist Centre of Strategic Studies on questions of Islamic theory, and later continued to write on religion and politics.

In 1994, he published the controversial study *Nazariye-ha-ye doulat dar feqh-e shi'e* (*Theories of State in Shi'i Law*), in which he distinguished nine different views in Shi'i political thought. In his following book, *Hokumat-e vela'i*, Kadivar went on to define the exact origin, basis and meaning of the guardianship of the jurist. Starting from the linguistic origins of the term *velāyat*, he discussed its meaning in the theological, philosophical and jurisprudential writings of religious scholars. In his highly complex study Kadivar came to the conclusion that, according to the scriptures and Islamic tradition, clerical guardianship is limited to widows and orphans, and its extension by Khomeini to cover an entire society is an innovation based on a fragile foundation. In Kadivar's view, the idea of political guardianship notably contradicts the idea of individual autonomy – and this is a central concept of Islam, as the entire religion is based on the idea that man can determine his own fate and is responsible for his own acts.

To better understand the meaning of *velāyat*, Kadivar went on
to compare it to the concept of *vekālat* (representation). In Islamic
jurisprudence this is a voluntary contract between two mature individuals,
by which one person makes another his or her representative in order to
execute his or her will. Unlike *velāyat*, it supposes the mutual consent and
satisfaction of both sides. While in *velāyat* the guardian (*vali*) is given a
lifelong mandate, which he can execute if necessary by force, in *vekālat* the
representative (*vakil*) is bound to respect the will of the represented and
the conditions set out in the contract. He is answerable to the represented,
and can be deposed if he violates the contract. All this shows, Kadivar
concluded, that *vekālat* and *velāyat* are irreconcilable opposites. Either
the ruler is given the guardianship over the people or he is chosen by
them as their representative.[48] In the constitution, however, the idea
of guardianship had been combined with the idea of representation
inherent in the republican system.

To resolve this contradiction, scholars had over the preceding decades
come up with three solutions. The first was to gradually strengthen the
powers of the *faqih* in order to replace the current system with the
absolute guardianship of the appointed jurist (*velāyat-e entezābi motlaq-e
faqih*). The second was to argue that a state can be considered a republic
if it respects Islam, as Islam is the will of the people, but this concept is
republican in name only. The third solution was to argue that in the time
of occultation, the *faqih* is not appointed but elected by the people. In
this last-named view, he does not directly exercise power but merely
supervises the government. He is bound to the constitution, which, as
the reflection of the will of the pious citizens, is based on the principles
of religion. Thus, both the respect of religion and the will of the people
are guaranteed. Once the people have elected a government and a
parliament, the *faqih*'s main task is to ensure the correct implementation
of religion in society. This was the solution proposed by Montazeri,
Motahhari and Salehi-Najafabadi.[49] Although Kadivar left it to his
readers to draw their own conclusions, it was clear that this was the
solution that he preferred. At the time of its publication, *Hokumat-e vela'i*
was considered the most severe criticism of the absolutist interpretation
of *velāyat-e faqih*. Kadivar not only questioned the religious legitimacy
of the concept, but also indirectly compared the current system to an
absolute monarchy. In the end, he not only openly acknowledged the
contradictory nature of the constitution but advocated as the sole

possible solution in the present situation the elective, limited and conditional version of *velāyat-e faqih* proposed by Montazeri.[50]

During this time, Montazeri did not remain inactive; eight months after his controversial speech he published an essay entitled 'Velayat-e faqih va qanun-e assasi' ('Velayat-e faqih and the Constitution'),[51] in which he sought to justify his speech and to elaborate the ideas he had raised therein. In the essay he took up many of the ideas first expressed in *Mabani feqhi-ye hokumat-e eslami* of 1988, but gave them a more radical twist. Where his book of 1988 was often ambivalent and at times contradictory, his 1998 essay clearly stated his main ideas. It was therewith testimony to the considerable radicalisation of his thought over the preceding decade. Montazeri reiterated that authority over the people belongs solely to God, but that in the time of occultation the right to exercise this authority was given to the jurists. As they cannot exercise power collectively, the people must elect from among them the most expert jurist. By this election, he is bound as by a contract to respect the people's will. He must enforce the laws of religion and the people must abide by them in all areas. However, the ruler himself must also abide by the laws and must respect the rights of the people. He can by no means claim absolute power over their lives, their property or their honour, as such power belongs only to God.

> Thus, the objective of *velāyat-e faqih* is the execution of the rulings of Islam and the administration of the affairs of Muslims on the basis of the principles of Islam, either under the guidance of the jurist himself or with his approval and under his supervision through the government elected by the people as set out in our constitution. In reality, *velāyat-e faqih* means *velāyat-e fiqh* (government of Islamic law), that is the orders of God for human society.[52]

To give absolute power to the *faqih* was contrary to religion and the constitution, Montazeri argued. The constitution set out that the State must be governed according to the will of the people (Article 6) and that man alone is the master of his own destiny (Article 56). It defined the *faqih*'s rights, which must be considered complete and cannot be extended at will (Article 111). Considering the complexity of the contemporary world, Montazeri asserted, the *faqih* must hear the opinion of all parties, consult with experts and only exceptionally intervene in the affairs of government. As the leader was elected by the people through the Expert Council he should be accountable to them, and during their yearly meeting they should point out his mistakes. Since, like all humans, he is fallible and prone to errors, it is irrational that he is not held responsible for his actions and does not respond to criticism. In view of the *faqih's* fallibility his mandate should be limited to a period of six to ten years, Montazeri advised.[53] He criticised the fact that the advocates of the absolute powers of the *faqih* ignored the articles pertaining to the rights of the people and the other organs of state. He recalled that the institution of the *faqih* was introduced to ensure the Islamic character of the State, but that at the same time the State was meant to have its origin and its objective in the people. When at the time of the revision of the constitution the word 'absolute' was added, Montazeri remarked, apparently nobody paid attention to the contradictions this provoked. By concentrating all power in the hands of the *faqih*, the system was transformed into an oppressive monarchy in the name of religion.

In a long interview in April 1999, Eshkevari critically discussed the ideas of Montazeri and Kadivar with the young journalist Mohammad Quchani in the reformist daily *Neshat*. Although Eshkevari agreed with their assertion that the *faqih's* role was originally meant to be one of supervision, he criticised the fact that they did not explain what form this supervision should take. Furthermore, he pointed out that by reducing his role to one of supervision they did not solve the fundamental problem that, by basing politics on Islamic law rather than on the general values and principles of Islam, *velāyat-e faqih* inevitably leads to a clerical government:

> [In a *fiqhi* government] all affairs, including decision-making in the executive, the legislative and the judicial powers, take place within the framework of *fiqh*. When everything is supposed to be done in accordance with *fiqh*, and when we approach legislation, the judiciary, the executive power and other matters from a *fiqh* perspective, then the result will be a clerical government. This is the inevitable result.[54]

Furthermore, Eshkevari pointed out that there is an inherent conflict between the system and the institution of *marja'iyat*. While the government tries to bring the *marja'iyat* under its control and cannot accept its spiritual, political and financial independence, the *marja'iyat* insists on preserving its independence and wants to subordinate the government to its authority. Both institutions claim supreme religious authority to define what is right and what is wrong in religious terms.

> [...] the government believes that all social, political and economic affairs of society [...] must come under government control, because it is a religious government [...]. On the basis of this theory, and because of the circumstances, the institution of *marja'iyat* must necessarily come under the government. Whereas, if the traditional *marja'iyat* wants to remain independent, the government will somehow be subordinated to it.[55]

Quchani asked whether the *maraje'-ye taqlid* could not enter the political field so that the people could choose one for a certain time as their ruler. Eshkevari answered that if the *maraje'* became the leaders of political parties, this would lead to irresolvable conflicts as they would all lay claim to the sacred truth. Also, because several different and possibly contradictory rulings cannot exist side by side in the political field, those *maraje'* not chosen as *faqih* would have to withdraw from the political field, while the *faqih* would have to withdraw from the religious field. This would lead to the separation of the two spheres.[56] Eshkevari criticised the fact that the reforms proposed by Montazeri and Kadivar did not resolve the conflict between the plurality of thought inherent in the religious field and the unity of action required by the political field. This certainly touched on a central problem of Montazeri's theory: for supervision to be meaningful, the *faqih* must be able to intervene in politics if it violates what he perceives as the Islamic precepts. He can apply a modern, liberal and permissive interpretation to give the government space for action, but in the end it remains his personal interpretation that determines policies. As these policies are binding on all citizens, the followers of *maraje'* with a different interpretation must necessarily come into conflict with the State.

Possibly in reaction to Eshkevari's criticism, Montazeri published a long text on 11 February 2000 in which he addressed the relationship of the ruling jurist and the *maraje'-ye taqlid*. The document was the extended version of a text he had sent to the US journalist Geneive Abdo one month earlier. Unable to personally interview him in his house in Qom, she had sent her questions by fax, whereupon he had faxed a long decree with his views on a reform of the system, excerpts of which were published in the form of an interview by Reuters and the UK *Guardian* as well as broadcast on the BBC. This decree then became the basis for his essay 'Hokumat-e mardomi va qanun-e assasi' ('Democracy and Constitution').[57] In the introduction to this text, which was later also translated into English, Montazeri admitted that he and the other authors of the constitution had 'lacked any experience with regard to lawmaking and the intricacies of that process'. To avoid the renewed emergence of despotism they had given all power to Khomeini, of whom a 'divine picture had been painted in the minds of people', while burdening the president with duties he lacked the power to fulfil.

> When it comes to the necessity of expanding ties with other countries and the extreme need for having economic and political relations with them, the president has to go to those countries with empty promises accompanied by anticlimactic remarks [...] The president talks about the rule of law and respecting civil rights of dissidents [...] and, in contrast, a military commander talks about cutting heads and tongues.[58]

Montazeri proposed that the president be given control over the security forces, that the independence of the judiciary be strengthened and that the freedom of elections be guaranteed. This notably concerned the right of the Guardian Council to approve candidates prior to elections, which was contrary to the original intention of the constitution. He also renewed his demand for the abolition of the unconstitutional and superfluous Special Court of the Clergy, the Revolutionary Courts and the Expediency Council, which in his view only weakened parliament and the Guardian Council. Finally, he proposed that the leader's mode of election and supervision be revised. The Expert Council, Montazeri asserted, had failed to fulfil its function of advising and controlling the leader, because the leader himself through the Guardian Council controlled the selection of its members. Montazeri therefore proposed that the council's tasks of electing, advising and controlling the leader be given to the *marāje'-ye taqlid*.

They should choose from among themselves a capable candidate who, under their collective supervision, should, for a limited period, guarantee the compatibility of politics with religion. Furthermore, they should, after consultation with the other clerics, also choose the members of the Guardian Council.[59] Montazeri thus meant to give the *marāje'-ye taqlid* a legal role in the political system. However, this was problematic not only because most *marāje'* would refuse such a political function, but also because it would hardly strengthen the democratic character of the system. After all, the *marāje'* are not elected by the people, but chosen in an informal and non-transparent process by their fellow clerics. The leader's election by the experts would actually be more democratic provided that they themselves were elected in a truly free election. Montazeri must have realised these problems and did not bring up this idea again.

In his text, Montazeri emphasised that the constitution is not sacred and that even the sacred laws may change according to time and place. Although he thought that the time was not yet right for such a step, he recognised the need for a revision of the constitution to resolve its contradictions. Furthermore, he evoked the possibility of a renewed referendum to confirm the system's legitimacy:

Although the majority of people voted for the current constitution, given the lapse of more than twenty years and the emergence of a new generation, a burgeoning of population, that majority no longer exists. The past generation cannot be considered as the representative of future generations. Therefore, their votes are not valid for future generations. On the whole, politics is constantly changing and political opinions of past generations cannot be accepted as the norm by their successors.[60]

In March 2001, Montazeri, in reply to a question on the legitimacy of a referendum, confirmed that the people are free to choose their political system just as they are free to choose their religion. He emphasised that in his view the only legitimate religion for Muslims is Islam and that Islam prescribes a certain social and political system that finds its best expression in the Islamic state. However, Montazeri also affirmed that should the people choose another system their choice must be accepted, as force has no place in religion or politics.[61] The idea of a referendum in the following years became one of the central demands of the opposition. In spring 2002, Ganji published a short book entitled *Manifest-e jomhuri-khahi* (*Republican Manifesto*), in which he took up the idea of a referendum to achieve a truly democratic system. Having been sentenced to six years prison in January 2001, he wrote the book in his cell in Evin prison. He was disillusioned with the reformers and their ability to achieve significant structural change. In his view they had failed because they had an erroneous perception of democracy and its relation to Islam and because they dared not challenge the constitution for fear of being excluded from politics. To change the constitution was legally and politically not possible as it required the *faqih* to initiate and validate any reform, he argued. In his view the only solution therefore was to hold a referendum on the future form of the system.[62]

Some months after the publication of his ideas on the reform of the constitution, Montazeri published another text that drew considerable attention. Largely isolated in his house and with his health increasingly weakened, Montazeri felt that it was time to present his version of history to future generations. During a long series of interviews with a group of unnamed students, Montazeri recounted the story of his life. On the basis of the transcripts of these interviews an autobiography with the unassuming title *Khaterat* (*Memoirs*) was composed. However, before the work could be completed the intelligence service arrested Montazeri's younger son Sa'id, who had been instrumental in editing the text, and seized the copies in his possession.[63] For fear that the other manuscripts might also be seized, Montazeri was forced to prematurely publish the text on 11 December 2000 on his London-based website. Despite the efforts of the regime to stop its publication, the text soon circulated in digital and printed form throughout Iran. The London weekly *Nimrooz* and other papers reported on it, and the following year it was even printed as a book by a publishing house in Europe. According to Montazeri, he had intended to also address the most common criticism of his own actions in his memoirs, but because of the arrest of Sa'id this work was left incomplete. It was only in *Enteqad az khod* (*Self-Criticism*), which was composed in 2006 and published in 2011, that he completed this work.

The publication of his memoirs, which for the first time provided the public with insight into crucial political episodes of the previous decades, caused considerable turmoil. Composed in the simple language characteristic of Montazeri, it was readily accessible even though in its internet version it numbered more than 600 pages of text as well as another 500 pages of annexes. These include 255 letters, speeches, interviews, fatwas, and other documents. It notably contained hitherto unknown documents on the Hashemi affair of 1986, the prison massacres of 1988 and the *marja'iyat* controversy of 1994 as well as on the conflict following his speech in 1997.[64] The book offered for the first time a complete and detailed account of the long-standing dispute between Montazeri and his former mentor, Khomeini. It challenged the idolisation of the 'Imam', presenting him as a man not only fallible but weak, who, in his later years, increasingly fell under the influence of his advisers. Montazeri left little doubt that he considered Khomeini's decisions to continue the war, to repress the opposition and to purge the prisons as major political errors. If he blamed Khomeini's advisers for having commanded the massacre of the Mojahedin, he nevertheless accused the leader of having been too weak to prevent it. As the book for the first time offered direct evidence that the prison massacres had been committed on the order of Khomeini, a group of British deputies in January 2001 called on the UN Human Rights Commission to conduct an investigation and to take legal action against those responsible. They cited an extensive report, which put the number of deaths at 30,000. However, as it had been drafted by the National Resistance Council controlled by the Mojahedin it lacked impartiality.[65] Although the complaint proceeded no further, Montazeri was criticised for having damaged the interests of the State.

At the time of the publication of his memoirs, Montazeri was aged 78. Suffering as he was from heart problems, diabetes and depression, his friends and family were increasingly concerned about his health. In January 2003, 100 deputies addressed an appeal to the president to end Montazeri's arrest, and the following week his close friend, Ayatollah Jalaleddin Taheri-Isfahani,[66] called upon the clergy to intervene. Fearing that Montazeri might become a martyr should he die under arrest, the conservatives agreed to his release. On 30 January, more than five years after his arrest, Montazeri was set free. When the following day he visited a mosque he looked weaker and frailer than before, but he assured his supporters that he had not accepted any conditions for his release and that he did not intend to remain silent. 'Just as I did during my

detention, I will continue to talk about issues and to act. It is my
religious duty.'[67]

## Silencing the Voices of Dissent

> People carried out the revolution so that they could make decisions
> not that decisions would be made for them [...] The revolution
> was about changing the system, but it appears that we have only
> changed its name and some particularities like the dependence
> from foreign powers and the reliance on repression. [This system]
> has no similarity with the Islamic republic we once imagined.
> (Kadivar, in an interview in Khordad in February 1999)[68]

Ever since the victory of the reformers, the conservatives had regarded
with rising concern their attempts to redraw the limits and redefine the
rules of the discourse. At first they had only criticised their endeavour to
open the discourse to new groups and ideas, but as the reformers' demands
became more radical they sought to put an end to the debate. This led to a
game of 'cat and mouse' between the conservative judiciary and the
reformist press, which each time a paper was closed launched a new one. It
also led to the prosecution of the leading voices of reform as well as their
physical elimination in what became known as the 'chain murders'. The
phrase was coined to designate a series of murders in autumn 1998 in
which six dissident intellectuals were killed by intelligence agents.
However, these assassinations are thought to have begun a decade earlier
and some count as many as 80 writers, journalist and politicians among
their victims. As most of the murders were reportedly disguised as car
accidents, criminal acts or heart attacks, it is impossible to draw up a
definitive list of the victims. It also remains unclear whether they were all
perpetrated by the same network, or whether different groups inside the
security and intelligence services were responsible. Several of the victims
had signed the 'Text of the 134' in October 1994, in which they
demanded the abolition of censorship and the permission to found a
writers association. In August 1995, a bus carrying 20 writers was almost
precipitated into a ravine in an apparent attempt to kill the passengers.[69]

The actual chain murders began on 22 November 1998 with the
brutal assassination of the veteran liberal politicians Dariush Forouhar

and his wife Parvaneh. The reports of the death of the elderly couple, who were found stabbed at their home in Tehran, shocked the public. The shock increased when their murders were followed by the disappearance and death of the translator and writer Majid Sharif, the poet and critic Mohammad Mokhtari and the essayist and translator Mohammad-Jafar Puyandeh. The publisher Parviz Davani, who had gone missing the previous August, was also counted among the victims.[70] Unlike during preceding years, when the press largely ignored the killings of dissidents, the murders provoked a public outcry. The reformist press not only published detailed accounts of the murders and pointed out similar incidents in the past, but also asked why the security services had not prevented the crimes. The minister of intelligence, Dori-Najafabadi, came under particular attack, as it was rumoured that a secret group in his ministry had perpetrated the murders and had established a list with the names of other dissidents. It was also rumoured that conservative clerics had issued fatwas that condoned the murders.[71]

One of the first to publicly condemn the murder of Forouhar was Montazeri, who knew the liberal politician from their time in Qazl Qale prison. Four days after his death, Montazeri paid tribute to him as a pious and persevering combatant against oppression, and pressed the President to do all in his might to bring the murderers to justice.[72] The Forouhars' funeral was attended by tens of thousands of people, among them numerous intellectuals who sang nationalist songs and chanted 'end tyranny'. Emboldened by the popular outcry, Khatami ordered an independent investigation into the murders, which quickly focused on the Intelligence Ministry. In a rare public outburst, Khatami warned of the danger of 'religious fascism' and accused the hardliners of having legitimised the murders. On 5 January 1999, the Intelligence Ministry was forced to make the unprecedented move of admitting that the murders had been perpetrated by rogue elements in its ranks. It was later declared that the Deputy Minister for Planning and Operations, Sa'id Emami, had led the group (and that he had unfortunately committed suicide in prison, thus taking any knowledge of the murders to his grave).[73] In what was a major victory for Khatami, the Minister of Intelligence, Dori-Najafabadi, was forced to resign and was replaced by the supreme military judge, Ali Yunesi, who had led the investigation into the murders.[74]

The reformist press, however, was not content with these moves but pressed for a more thorough probe into the killings. The charge was led by Ganji, who in a series of articles exposed what he claimed was the secret connection between the murderers and leading conservative clerics. In these pieces, which were later published in *Tarikhane-ye ashbah* (*The Dark Room of Ghosts*), he accused the former Minister of Intelligence, Fallahian, of having founded an assassination squad. He also claimed that Rafsanjani had known of this unit. Although Fallahian and other critics dismissed the allegations as fictitious, they considerably damaged the reputation of both men.[75] On 12 January, Kadivar also addressed the chain murders in a speech at an Isfahan mosque. He emphasised that in an Islamic state, nobody but the judiciary has the right to declare someone a fighter against God (*mohāreb*). Only those who take up arms against the State can be considered as such, and they must be tried and punished according to the official procedures. However, Kadivar regretted, today people 'who have no religious or jurisprudent eligibility issue the decree of apostasy'.[76]

Despite the scandal provoked by the chain murders, the conservatives were not subdued but pursued their efforts to silence the reformers. Their instrument of choice for prosecuting dissident clerics and other opponents was the Special Court of the Clergy. Established by Khomeini in 1987 for the trial of Mehdi Hashemi, it had been considerably extended in 1989 by Khamene'i. Separate courts were established in the country's main cities, and a separate prison system was created. Despite their extension, the courts were never legalised and remained outside the official justice system. Their sessions were held behind closed doors and the accused were denied the right to freely choose a lawyer.[77] From 1998 to 2005, Gholamhossein Mohseni-Ejei was the Prosecutor-General of the court. Like his predecessors, he had close links to the intelligence service and was suspected of being involved in at least one of the chain murders.[78] Beginning in June 1998 with the trial of Tehran's mayor, Gholam Hossein Karbastchi, who was accused of the use of public funds to finance Khatami's election campaign, Mohseni-Ejei set out to bring the most outspoken advocates of reform to court. With the trials of Khoa'iniha, Kadivar, Nuri and Eshkevari, the court became the focal point of the struggle for freedom of opinion as well as for a more progressive reading of religion.

In November 1998, Abdollah Nuri, who had been impeached by parliament as Minister of the Interior on 22 June, founded the daily *Khordad*. Named after the month of Khatami's victory, it was meant to replace *Jāme'eh*, which had been closed in July 1998 after the publication of Rahim-Safavi's controversial speech. *Khordad* soon gained a reputation as an outspoken voice of reform and, along with other papers, it pushed for a thorough probe into the chain murders. When, on the occasion of the 20th anniversary of the revolution, it published a series of interviews with Kadivar on 14, 15 and 16 February 1999, first Kadivar and then Nuri were arrested and sent to the Special Court of the Clergy. In the interview, Kadivar alleged that the republican element of the revolution was being neglected, the people excluded from decisions and the promise of justice and freedom left unfulfilled. Had it not been for the last two years since the elections, he declared, one could believe that there had been no progress at all. Rather than strengthen the people's faith, the regime alienated them by transforming religion into an ideology and an instrument to advance its own interests. Judging by the acts of certain officials, it appeared as if their interpretation of the system differed in name only from the previous monarchy:

Although we have been able to formally eliminate the monarchy, what remains in effect, and what we are still entangled with, is the regeneration of monarchic behaviour and relations [...]. the people carried out the revolution so that they could make decisions not that decisions would be made for them, even if they be taken by the most worthy person [...]. The revolution was about changing the system, but it appears that we have only changed its name and some particularities like the dependence from foreign powers and the reliance on repression, but not the structures. [This system] has no similarity with the Islamic republic we once imagined.[79]

Although not even the Imams claimed absolute power and absolute obedience, the leadership sought to impose its claim to absolute power with methods that differed little from those of the previous regime. Should the *faqih* only be accountable to God but not to the people, Kadivar warned, the regime would arrive at the same situation as in the past. 'If someone believes that in the Islamic republic the *faqih* can do whatever he wants, the name [of this system] can truly no longer be the Islamic republic.'[80] Asked about the main problems of the system, Kadivar mentioned three points. Firstly, he cited the false belief that religion contains answers to all questions, and the practice of certain people to present their own opinion as that of religion. Secondly, there was the practice of the State of enforcing the respect of the outer forms of religion but to neglect strengthening the belief in religious ethics. Thirdly, Kadivar highlighted the conflict between an autocratic and a democratic reading of the system, the latter of which was supported by Taleqani, Motahhari, Montazeri and the current government. Finally, there was also the question of the relationship between religion and politics. Politics was to follow the values of Islam, Kadivar argued, but instead of an Islamisation of politics there had been a politicisation of Islam. In the interest of both domains, the State should again be separated from religion. The clergy should supervise power but not exercise it itself, and politics should not intervene in the affairs of the clergy. 'In other words, religion shall not be become the state and the domain of religion must remain independent of the state.'[81]

During the proceedings from 14 to 21 April, the court charged Kadivar with undermining trust in the regime and spreading propaganda against the system. The accusations were based on the interviews in *Khordad* and his Isfahan speech. Only a few conservative journalists were allowed into the hearings, but after the trial Kadivar's defence was published by his wife Zahra Roudi under the title *Bahai azadi* (*The Price of Freedom*). This book was such a success that it went through several reprints.[82] In the first part of his defence, Kadivar challenged the right of the court to try him. Not only was it not responsible for offences of the press, he argued, but its entire existence was a violation of the constitution. Contrary to judicial practice, it also made no effort to prove the falsity of his remarks nor to prove his intention of undermining the system.[83] In the second part of his defence, Kadivar argued that the constitution guarantees the freedom of the press and does not allow it to be restricted under the pretext of preserving the interests of the country. Should all criticism be qualified as propaganda against the system, all debate would become impossible and society would not progress.[84] Propaganda against the system means rejecting the Islamic republic in favour of a different system, Kadivar argued. Yet, the system contains both an Islamic and a republican dimension, and since its inception there had existed two interpretations emphasising either one or the other dimension. Rather than reject the Islamic republic, Kadivar argued, he had defended it against attempts to transform it into an Islamic monarchy or a religious dictatorship. Emphasising his long commitment to religion and the revolution, Kadivar accused the court of monopolising religion and branding every view differing from its own as an attack on the system.

> Must all clerics think like the Special Court of the Clergy? Does a cleric not have the right to a different point of view to the prosecution? I am proud in this sacred gown to have made a step, however small, on the path of Na'ini, Taleqani, Motahhari and Beheshti [...]. Why is one accused whenever one critically analyses a certain interpretation of the Islamic Republic of conspiring against the faith of the people? [...] Is it not possible that someone does not approve your interpretation but is still a pious Muslim and a devoted supporter of the shari'a?[85]

When Kadivar was sentenced to 18 months' prison, the court removed him from the discourse but at the same time enhanced his prestige and prominence. In the eyes of the liberal public, his condemnation was a sign of distinction, which made him a martyr for the cause of reform. However, this did not prevent the court from pursuing its campaign. The next to be summoned was Khoa'iniha. As the Managing Director of the leftist daily *Salam*, he had for many years been an outspoken opponent of the conservatives. When *Salam* on 6 July 1999 with the publication of a letter by Sa'id Emami profoundly embarrassed the conservatives, the court intervened. In the letter in question, which was dated October 1998, Emami outlined a plan for the revision of the press code. Its content was almost identical to a draft scheduled for discussion the following day in the majles. This draft sought to make the prosecution of journalists easier, the granting of licences more difficult and to allow the Revolutionary Courts to hear press offences. As the letter made the draft appear to have been dictated by the man responsible for the chain murders, its publication was highly embarrassing for the conservatives.[86]

On 7 July, the judiciary ordered the closure of *Salam* and the arrest of its Editor in Chief, Abbas Abdi. This provoked the largest student unrest in the history of the Islamic Republic. Following peaceful protests in front of Tehran University – which were also directed against the imprisonment of the student leader Heshmatollah Tabarzadi, who had been arrested in late 1997 for having demanded the *faqih*'s election for a limited period[87] – Hezbollah thugs, backed by the police, stormed the men's dormitories in the early hours of 9 July. They beat the students in their sleep and threw several from the balconies. Officially one student was killed, but witnesses alleged that the death toll was considerably higher.[88] The attack triggered six days of mass protests in Tehran and other major cities throughout the country. As the demonstrations turned ever more violent and the slogans more radical, foreign media began to speak of a 'second revolution'. However, in the end the protests were brutally repressed. An unknown number of students were killed and wounded. More than 1,400 were arrested, many of whom were later condemned to long terms in prison. The students had not been prepared for the brutal attacks of the police and militias. However, if they failed to bring about change it was not only because of the violence but also because they were divided and lacked the support of the government. In a letter of 19 July, 24 commanders of the Revolutionary Guards had warned the President that they would take the law into their own hands should he not take action against the protesters.[89] Afraid of a further escalation, Khatami, instead of using the momentum created by the revolt to stand up to the hardliners, distanced himself from the students and blamed them for the riots. Instead of taking the public outrage at the violence as an opportunity to wrest control over the security services from the leader, he once more assured him of his loyalty. Thus, an opportunity was lost to shift the balance of power in favour of the reformers. As the suppression of the student protests made clear that Khatami was not willing to take up the fight with the conservative establishment, it marked a turning point for the reform movement. The reformers still won the parliamentary and presidential elections in 2000 and 2001, but the initial enthusiasm was lost.

Following the student protests, Khoa'iniha, the Managing Director of *Salam*, was summoned to the Special Court of the Clergy, and the following month sentenced to three years in prison for having spread lies and publishing classified documents. Although the sentence was later suspended, *Salam* was permanently closed down.[90] Next on the court's list was Nuri. The Vice-President and Editor of *Khordad* was extremely popular among students, who thronged in masses to his lectures and speeches. Moreover, he was also an able and ambitious politician who was determined to become the next speaker of parliament. With Nuri's trial, which opened on 30 October 1999, the court not only meant to silence his newspaper but also to prevent his candidature at the upcoming elections.[91] In the course of the trial Nuri was accused, among other points, of publishing the interview with Kadivar and propagating the ideas of Montazeri. This latter charge was based on the publication of Montazeri's statement on the chain murders and an article on relations with the USA in January 1999, in which he had written that the cessation of relations with the USA was a temporary measure and that it was legitimate to resume relations should it be judged in the interest of the State. Moreover, *Khordad* had published an editorial in April 1999 that described the public debate of Montazeri's ideas as a central event of the past year. As no law forbade the publication of Montazeri's articles, the court cited Khomeini's first letter of dismissal in which he forbade Montazeri to further intervene in politics. Though excerpts would have been sufficient to prove the point, the prosecution read out the entire letter. As Nuri later pointed out in his defence, the true reason to include this point was to discredit Montazeri.[92]

If the court had wished to silence Nuri, this hope was soon shattered. The proceedings were closely followed by the reformist press, and Nuri's defence was later published as a book under the title *Shukran-e eslah* (*Hemlock of Reform*), which rapidly became a bestseller. As in the case of Kadivar, the trial helped Nuri to greater prominence as he transformed the court case into a platform to propagate his views on reform. Accused of support for Montazeri, he used his defence to further expose and elaborate on his theories. He not only convincingly countered all arguments of the court but turned the accusations against the court and the regime itself. In the case of Kadivar's interview, Nuri followed much the same line as his friend's defence, insisting that the court was not authorised to judge offences of the press and that the passages in question had not only been deliberately misinterpreted but also could not be taken to be propaganda against the system. In the case of Montazeri's articles, Nuri argued that the field of emulation is limited to questions of religion and that Khomeini himself had insisted that the people act according to their own opinion and not blindly imitate others. Hence, nobody should be bound to abide by the opinions Khomeini expressed a decade earlier on Montazeri. Declaring the expression of opinions a crime when they differed from the opinions of Khomeini, Nuri argued, was contrary to public and religious law.

If someone from the point of view of religion, ethics and the analysis of history does not agree with the decisions of the *faqih*, does he not have the right to express his opinion in the press and to discuss it in society? Is it not the right and the obligation of the experts to discuss public policies and to analyse the course of history? Can one forbid the jurists, philosophers, historians and political scientists from exchanging their opinions? If the reply is positive, frame this as an official law and proclaim that whoever has an opinion contrary to the opinion of the *faqih* does not have the right to publish a newspaper, write a book or express an argument. And also inform all *marāje'-ye taqlid* that they no longer have the right to express an opinion or interpretation which diverges from the opinion of the *faqih*.[93]

Nuri used the opportunity to defend not only himself but also Montazeri. He reminded the court that Khomeini considered Montazeri an outstanding scholar and repeatedly delegated religious questions to him to decide. In his official letter of dismissal he had written: 'I am convinced that you are a scholar from whose advice both the system and the people can benefit.' As this contradicted the content of the earlier letter, Nuri argued, its authenticity had to be questioned. The court was not credible if it considered the first letter more authentic then the second, although it was not included in the official collection of Khomeini's statements and only published a decade later. As there was no reason to doubt the authenticity of the second letter, it had to be taken as Khomeini's will. Hence, there was no reason to exclude Montazeri from politics.[94] Those who insult Montazeri should be punished, Nuri declared, not *Khordad*, which only printed his statements as it printed those of other clerics:

Who now is the offender? Those who insult [Montazeri] or *Khordad* which refrains from insults but defends Ayatollah Montazeri's right to freely express his opinion in the limits officially set for any ordinary citizen, and which in the same way that it publishes the articles and messages of citizens and officials also publishes his? [...] Who said that everyone has the right to condemn the chain murders but not Ayatollah Montazeri?[95]

In its verdict of 27 November 1999, the court dropped the charge of apostasy and exonerated Nuri from the charges of opposing and insulting religion and Khomeini. But he was found guilty of propagating Montazeri's views and publishing material disturbing the public mind, and sentenced to five years in prison. Although in the short term the trial offered Nuri a platform to express his ideas, in the long term his imprisonment removed him from the political field and the public discourse. When, on 18 February 2000, parliamentary elections were held, Nuri was not allowed to present his candidature and also later did not regain his former position. These elections resulted in the victory of the reformers, who won 65 per cent of the mandates. To their own surprise, their candidates had not been barred by the Guardian Council as had been the case in previous elections. The reformers now had a comfortable majority in parliament and hopes were running high that they would be able to break the institutional deadlock that had prevented reforms. However, their position was weakened by the defection of the pragmatists, who after the elections again sided with the conservatives. One of the reasons for their defection was a press campaign against Rafsanjani led by Ganji, who in an article entitled 'The Red Eminence' on 19 January 2000 accused the former commander in chief of having unnecessarily prolonged the war with Iraq and of having, as president, ordered the murder of as many as 80 dissidents. As a result, Rafsanjani failed to secure one of the 30 mandates in Tehran. This was a humiliation he was not willing easily to forget or forgive.[96]

Despite the reformers' victory, the conservatives continued their crackdown on the leaders of the movement. On 12 March, Hajjarian was shot in the head in front of the Tehran city council building by an unknown assailant. The chief architect of the reformist victory survived the attack, but left hospital partially paralysed. The conservatives were determined to put an end to the debate on reform once and for all, and the Berlin Conference presented the necessary pretext to put their plans into action. This symposium, which was organised by the German Heinrich Böll Foundation from 7 to 9 April 2000 in the House of World Cultures in Berlin, was meant to offer religious and secular intellectuals from Iran the space to freely discuss the future of the reform movement.[97] However, on the first day the debates were disrupted by radical members of two leftist groups of the Iranian opposition in exile who held up banners and shouted slogans criticising the fact that they had not been invited to the podium.

Their protests culminated in a bikini-clad woman jumping onto the podium to protest against the oppression of women and a man partly undressing to show his torture marks.[98] Only on the second day could the conference go ahead under police protection with a lecture by Eshkevari on the question of 'Women's Rights and the Women's Movement'.[99] In this lecture he argued that social rulings concerning women's rights and corporal sanctions are not part of the immutable general principles of religion, but that these kind of rulings can be adapted to the changing conditions of time and place. Questioned on the veil, Eshkevari affirmed that this too falls into the domain of changeable social rulings and hence does not constitute a religious obligation.

Iranian state television broadcast a long feature on the conference, in which it was presented as having aimed at preparing the overthrow of the regime and in which the participants appeared to approve of the protests in the audience. When the participants, among them Ganji and Sahabi, returned to Iran they were arrested and sentenced to terms ranging from four months to ten years in prison. Eshkevari, who had stayed for a lecture tour in Europe, was arrested on his return and brought before the Special Court of the Clergy. In a trial behind closed doors he was accused of insulting Islam and waging war against God, and on 15 October sentenced to death. Only after prolonged protests inside and outside the country was this sentence reduced to seven years' imprisonment in a subsequent trial.[100] The scandal provoked by the conference offered the conservatives the necessary pretext for a crackdown on the reformist press. In a speech on 20 April 2000, Khamene'i accused the reformist newspapers of acting under the orders of foreign powers. In one of the last sessions of the outgoing parliament, the controversial revision of the press code was passed. Shortly afterwards, the judiciary closed down 12 reformist publications without trial in one sweeping move. Dozens more were shut down during the following months, among them *Kiyan*, *Iran-e Farda*, *Asr-e Azadegan* and *Sobh-e Emruz*, and numerous journalists and publishers were brought to court. Thus, the leading reformist journalist Emadeddin Baqi was sentenced to four years in prison for having questioned in *Neshat* the scriptural basis of capital punishment for apostasy and adultery. Among the closures was the Najafabad weekly *Ava*, whose publisher, Mostafa Izadi, was one of Montazeri's oldest and most outspoken supporters. He had written the latter's official biography in 1981, and had repeatedly defended him and his views in his newspaper. Following the closure of *Ava*, Izadi was summoned to the Special Court of the Clergy.[101]

When the new reformist parliament convened, its first project was to change the press code. However, before the debate could get under way, Khamene'i in an unprecedented move stepped in to stop the debate. On 6 August, he warned in a letter to the majles that 'should the enemies of Islam, the revolution and the Islamic system take over or infiltrate the press, a great danger would threaten the security, unity and the faith of the people and, therefore, I cannot allow myself and other officials to keep quiet in respect of this crucial issue'. As the current press law had been able to prevent the infiltration of the press, its amendment was not 'in the interest of the system'.[102] When the letter was read out in parliament it caused general consternation, then scuffles and protests. Never before had the *faqih* dared directly intervene in the work of the majles. However, the President of Parliament, Hojatoleslam Mehdi Karrubi, claimed that such interference was in line with the absolute powers given to the leader by the constitution. As the reformist majority shied away from openly challenging the *faqih's* will, the two men who had directed the press revolution, Burqani and Saharkhiz, resigned in protest. With their resignation and the parliament's submission, the efforts to change the rules and limits of the discourse were at an end.

## Conclusion

At the time of their victory, the reformers had promised to enforce the rule of law, to ensure respect for civil rights, and to enhance freedom of expression and political participation. Initially they were quite successful in opening up the political field and the public discourse to new groups and ideas, as they brought about an unprecedented boom in new associations, parties and publications. However, in the end they failed to realise the reform of the political structures that would have been necessary to consolidate their achievements, and remained powerless to prevent the conservatives from reversing the opening they had achieved. The elections in 1997, 1999, 2000 and 2001 proved that the political agenda of the reformers had broad popular support. The mass of the people were clearly tired of the restrictive cultural and religious policies of the conservatives, which were increasingly out of touch with the dreams and demands of society. With their vote, the people gave popular legitimacy to the reformers and their policies, and through their massive attendance at their rallies, speeches and lectures expressed their acceptance of their claim to political authority. The popularity of the reformist press further underlined the popular legitimacy of their views. The conservatives' reluctance to enter into a serious debate betrayed the weakness of their position. Rather than counter the reformist ideas with arguments, they denounced them as foreign and contrary to religion and the revolution. When this did not suffice, they resorted to the judiciary or outright violence to silence their critics. But even in court their arguments proved remarkably weak in the face of Kadivar's and Nuri's skilled defence, which highlighted the religious and legal illegitimacy of their indictment.

However, despite their popular legitimacy and their discursive superiority the reformers remained unable to put their agenda into action. Their support did not translate into political power as the conservatives refused to bend to the popular will. Consequently, the reformers remained unable to prevent the conservatives from using their legal and extra-legal means of coercion to remove their opponents from the political field and the public discourse. That their action was considered illegitimate by the public, and was constitutionally illegal, did not prevent the conservatives from forcefully suppressing and silencing the voices of dissent. The paradox of Khatami's rule of law was that the reformers were neither able to change those laws that legitimised the repression nor to enforce those that could have prevented it. Even after the reformers had gained control of parliament, the judiciary, the Guardian Council and the ruling jurist were still there to block unwelcome laws, prosecute unruly politicians and prevent a reform of the constitution. It was difficult to see how the structural deadlock could be broken by legal means. However, the failure to achieve substantial structural change was also due to Khatami's reluctance to risk a confrontation with the conservatives.

Neither at the time of the attack on Montazeri in 1997, of the chain murders in 1998, of the student revolts in 1999 nor of the closure of the reformist press in 2000 did Khatami step in to publicly denounce the violation of the law and to press for the prosecution of those responsible. The blatant illegality and immorality of these acts could have provided the opportunity to restrict the powers of the security services and the judiciary. However, rather than use the dynamic created by these events, Khatami shied away from a confrontation, silently accepted the repression of his supporters and assured the leader of his loyalty. Initially Khatami's silent acceptance of the obstacles laid in his way by his opponents won him the support of the people, in whose religious tradition sympathy lies with the innocent victim. However, when he failed to stand up to his opponents his supporters grew increasingly impatient, and finally lost interest in the continual conflict. Montazeri had warned Khatami in his letter of 27 June 1997 that if he did not prevent the leader from further interfering he would not be able to realise his reforms. In his speech of 14 November of that year, he once more urged Khatami to risk confrontation with Khamene'i lest he risk losing the support of the people.

Had Khatami really tried to restrict the role of the *faqih*, he would have needed to address the question of *velāyat-e faqih*. However, he shied away from this debate, hoping to change the regime's policies without tackling its ideological foundation. Hence, he refused to follow when Montazeri led the way by publicly proposing an alternative reading of *velāyat-e faqih*. This reading did not solve all problems, as Eshkevari correctly pointed out, but it offered the chance of restricting the *faqih*'s powers while maintaining the outer form of the system. As Montazeri and later Kadivar showed, it could lay claim to a religious legitimacy not easily dismissed. Of course, even with the support of Khatami it would have remained uncertain whether it would have been possible to change the structures of the system in accordance with this reading. What the reformers lacked was not legitimacy but power. In the end the reformist project did not fail because it was illegitimate but because it was against the interests of those in power. The members of the military, and the security and intelligence services, stood behind the leader because their political, economic and social position depended on him and they were not willing to put it at risk however legitimate the reformers' demands.

# CHAPTER 7

# THE GREEN MOVEMENT AND ITS FAILURE

## Populist Politics and the Return to a Nativist Discourse

Some people keep saying that our revolution is aimed at establishing democracy. No. Neither in the Imam's statements nor in the message of the martyrs nor in the words of the real pillars of the Islamic government has such an idea been considered.

(Ahmadinejad, in a speech on 10 May 2005)[1]

The submission of the reformers to the leader during the debate on the revision of the press law did not mark the end of their efforts at reform. However, it marked a turning point. During the following years ever more voters turned away from Khatami and his faction, disappointed by their inability to bring about substantial change. Fearing the complete loss of his support base, Khatami launched one last initiative to break the institutional deadlock. In an important speech on 28 August 2002, the President declared that as the legal guardian of the constitution he was determined to realise the religious democracy promised by the constitution. Three days later he introduced two bills which sought to abolish the Guardian Council's right to approve candidates for election, to reduce its right to review legislation and to strengthen the power of the president. The twin bills were passed by the majles in December 2002 but were predictably blocked by the Guardian Council in May 2003. After a prolonged debate, Khatami finally withdrew his attempt at curbing the approbatory powers of the council in April 2004.[2] This defeat once more confirmed to the public that the President and the reformist majority in parliament were unable to realise the promised reforms.

The disaffection of the voters with the reformers led to a low turnout in the elections for the local councils in 2003, for the parliament in 2004 and for the president in 2005. Surveys during these years showed that there was no general shift in attitudes or aspirations, and that a majority of the people still wanted more political, cultural and personal freedom.[3] However, as they lost hope of achieving it by political means, they withdrew to the private sphere. Their abstention during elections, as well as the disqualification of the reformist candidates by the Guardian Council, facilitated the victory of the conservatives in all three elections.[4] The new majles was once more dominated by the conservatives, but the composition of the deputies differed from previous parliaments. Many of the deputies had entered politics through the Pasdaran and the paramilitary volunteer corps of the Bassij, and were less pragmatic than their conservative predecessors. They saw themselves as defenders of the essential principles (*osul*) of the revolution, and hence called themselves 'principlists' (*osulgarān*). Their emphasis was not on Islamism or republicanism but on social justice, the third heritage of the revolution. This had lately been much neglected by both conservatives and reformers, who had privileged economic policies focused on liberalisation and privatisation.

In the presidential elections of June 2005, to the surprise of the political elite and the media, a man in a grey anorak sporting the dark stubbles characteristic of the Islamic revolutionaries who was previously practically unknown to the wider public, emerged as the victor. The hardliner Mahmud Ahmadinejad had only two years earlier emerged onto the national scene with his election as mayor of Tehran. He was considered by friends and foes alike a political lightweight, and even his own party supported another candidate. However, he not only defeated the reformer Mostafa Moin, the moderate Mehdi Karrubi and the conservatives Ali Larijani and Mohammad Baqer Qalibaf, but in the second round also won against the highly influential Rafsanjani.[5] Ahmadinejad's surprise victory was partly explained by his success in enlisting the support of the marginalised underclass. With his promise of bringing the oil revenues 'to the people's dinner table' he won many votes among the urban and rural poor, who had been neglected by the market-oriented policies of Rafsanjani and Khatami. Furthermore, Ahmadinejad's austere way of living and working contrasted sharply with the style of other politicians and gave credibility to his campaign against corruption. Notably compared to Rafsanjani, one of the richest men of the country, Ahmadinejad appeared as a man of the people.[6]

However, his victory was also the result of his success in mobilising the Pasdaran and the Bassij. They actively supported his campaign and mobilised their friends and families to give him their votes. Once in power, Ahmadinejad, who had himself been socialised in the militias, rewarded them for their support. He not only idealised their paternalist, traditionalist and religious culture as the true culture of Iran, but also helped them gain lucrative contracts. Since the revolution the Pasdaran had built up an economic empire reaching far beyond the defence sector. With Ahmadinejad's support they further extended their control into important industry and infrastructure projects.[7] He gave seven cabinet positions to former Pasdaran and replaced almost all 30 governors and hundreds of city and district administrators with men from the guards and militias.[8] As these men had no political or religious authority of their own, they depended on the support of the leader. Hence, their promotion to positions of power allowed Khamene'i to bolster his own position. Among the clergy, however, this shift of power led to considerable discontent as it meant their further marginalisation in the political field. Because Ahmadinejad also held some rather unorthodox beliefs, his relationship with the clergy was conflictual.[9]

Ahmadinejad was deeply influenced by the extremist and millenarian reading of Islam proffered by his spiritual mentor Mohammad-Taqi Mesbah-Yazdi. The head of the influential Haqqani seminary in Qom had actively engaged in politics after 1997 in order to counter what he perceived as a deviation from Islam. He rejected the idea of popular sovereignty, convinced that sovereignty belongs only to God. He perceived Islam as a closed system in which everything not explicitly allowed is forbidden. To enforce the rules and values of Islam, he considered violence as legitimate and was repeatedly accused of having issued fatwas to legitimise the murder of dissidents.[10] Notably, Ahmadinejad shared his belief in the imminent return of the Mahdi, who is said to usher in a rule of justice when he returns at the end of time, and declared that it was the duty of politics to prepare for his return. He also repeatedly claimed that the Mahdi appeared to him, and after his speech at the United Nations in September 2005 famously declared that the hidden Imam had opened the eyes and ears of the audience to his message. Although the story did not go down well with the public or the clergy, he continued to invoke the Mahdi. While it can be assumed that Ahmadinejad sincerely believed what he related, his claim to be in contact with the Mahdi also enabled him to dispense with the intermediation of the clergy, to compensate for his lacking religious authority, and to strengthen his position towards the leader.[11] Ahmadinejad, for all his profound piety and his conservative morals, had little interest in the clerical debates on hermeneutics that had marked the political discourse for the last quarter of a century. He certainly shared the Islamist conviction that Islam is the principal criterion of political legitimacy, but his Islam had its basis less in the Qur'an and the sunna than in the millenarian cult of the Mahdi. By basing his legitimacy not on his reading of the scriptures but on his proximity to the hidden Imam, Ahmadinejad transformed politics from a question of rational arguments to a question of belief.

In other aspects, the opening years of Ahmadinejad's presidency also saw a number of changes in the political and religious discourse in Iran, both in form and in content. While the reformers had sought a way to transform the system into an Islamic democracy respectful of civil liberties, political pluralism and the rule of law, the principlists called for a return to the original principles of the revolution. In their eyes, what was needed was not a reform of the system but the completion of the revolution, which notably meant a return to a populist and nativist discourse. For the principlists, the West was the ultimate 'other' against which the 'self' is defined. Where the reformists had recognised the need for and the benefit of a dialogue with the West, the principlists rejected the idea of any exchange − both in the field of politics and of science. Their ideal was not only political and economic autonomy, but autarchy and ideological and cultural authenticity. They opposed liberal values not only because they perceived them as a threat to their claim to absolute power but also because they perceived them as foreign and incompatible with the true Iranian culture.

For the principlists the revolution had been left incomplete. Not only had the regime failed to deliver on its promise of social justice, but it had also failed to eradicate Western influence. In their view, Khomeini's objective had never been an Islamic republic, but an Islamic state. If they recognised the necessity to maintain the impression of popular legitimacy, they did not seek the participation of the people. They did not see the need for political pluralism to represent the ethnic, religious and cultural diversity of society as, for them, the only true Iranian culture is the culture of the Bassij. The populism and nativism of the principlists gave their discourse a strongly anti-intellectual and anti-elitist tint. For them, social justice did not simply mean the redistribution of wealth from the rich to the poor, but also implied the redistribution of power from the 'foreignised' upper to the 'authentic' lower class. They were deeply mistrustful of intellectualism, which they associated with modernism, secularism and liberalism. Rather than critical inquiry and technical ability, they valorised faith and commitment. This disdain for intellectualism and expert knowledge led them not only to disregard the position of the clergy but also to ignore the advice of economic experts.

In their quest to realise the original principles of the revolution the principlists turned on the universities, which were one of the last bastions of the reformers. Ahmadinejad as a student had actively participated in the cultural revolution, and felt that the endeavour to purge the universities of 'foreignised' intellectuals had yet to be completed. In summer 2006, the government sent about 200 professors perceived as ideologically unreliable into forced retirement.[12] At the same time the cautious opening of the cultural field was reversed and Islamic values were once more made the guiding principle in arts, film, theatre and literature. Censorship of the press was once more increased, and new licences were only rarely issued. One of the last reformist newspapers, *Sharq*, was temporarily closed down in September 2006 after publishing a cartoon on the nuclear negotiations showing a chessboard with a knight and a donkey with a halo around his head. The media supervisory board considered this as an insult to the President.[13]

However, the principlists only partially succeeded in changing society. The changes in cultural values, gender relations and family models which had given rise to the reform movement were too profound to be easily reversed. The endeavour of the principlists to establish their cultural and political hegemony was also considerably hindered by the arrival of the internet in 2001. Attracted by the initially uncensored access to information and the possibility to freely express oneself, millions joined the web, making Iran the most rapidly growing internet community in the Middle East and opening up a new discursive sphere in society. The regime and the clergy were also quick to grasp the threat posed by the internet, as well as the opportunities it offered to reach the public and to spread religious and political propaganda. Just months after the introduction of the internet in Iran, the seminaries in Qom and Mashhad opened large computer centres for their students and numerous *marāje'-ye taqlid* set up multilingual websites.[14] The internet also helped keep alive the discourse on reform, which had lost much of its intensity since its main journals had been closed down and its leading voices thrown into prison or forced into exile. Even before Ahmadinejad's victory, many reformers had lost hope of transforming society and the system on the basis of a progressive interpretation of Islam.

Yet, not all reformist clerics and intellectuals abandoned their efforts to develop a reading of the scriptures in line with the needs and demands of modern society. Montazeri during these years notably drew attention with two fatwas on apostasy and the rights of the Baha'i. In the first decree, issued on 30 January 2005 in response to a question from one of his followers in Europe, he declared that the Qur'an does not command the execution of apostates. Where this was mentioned in other scriptures, it referred to the case of newly converted Muslims who returned to their former religion in order to inflict damage to Islam. However, Muslims who, after serious scrutiny, convert to another religion may not be executed.[15] In the second decree, issued on 14 May 2008 in response to a question on the civil rights of the Baha'i, Montazeri declared that even though they are not a recognised religious minority they should have the same civil rights as other citizens. As this fatwa caused considerable debate and was read by some Baha'i as a religious recognition of their creed, Montazeri one month later in a second decree explained that he still regarded Baha'ism as a misled creed whose adherents should be shunned and whose propagation should be forbidden. However, their human rights should be respected, Montazeri asserted.[16] This was certainly not an endorsement of Baha'ism, but it did mean the religious recognition of the legal equality of the Baha'i.

Apart from Grand Ayatollah Yussef Sane'i, who had gained notoriety by some liberal fatwas on women's rights, Montazeri was the only *marja'-e taqlid* to openly advocate a progressive interpretation of Islam. Among the younger generation, however, a growing number of clerics recognised the need to adapt Islam to the changing world in order to maintain its relevance in society. Like Montazeri, these clerics did not approve of the radical theories proposed by Soroush or the far-reaching demands of Ganji, but they were ready to revise the most controversial religious precepts and to adapt the traditional reading of the shari'a where it contradicted human rights, modern customs and common reason. The main organisation of these reformist clerics was the Majma'e Mohaqqeqin va Modarresin-e Houze Elmiye Qom (Assembly of Teachers and Researchers of Qom), which had been founded in 2001 by the ayatollahs Hossein Mussavi-Tabrizi, Assadollah Bayat-Zanjani, Abayi-Khorasani, Taqi Fazel-Meybodi and others. Many of its members had studied under Montazeri, and some had actively participated in the reform movement.

However, the most far-reaching project to develop a progressive reading of the scriptures was undertaken by Ahmad Qabel. Born in 1954 as the son of the Friday prayer leader of Fariman near Mashhad, Qabel had studied with Montazeri and received the degree of *ejtehad* from him in 1998. Although he had shed the robes of the clergy in 1991, he continued to work as a religious scholar and in 2002 he was authorised by Montazeri to answer religious questions in his stead. In June 1997, he was briefly arrested for publishing Montazeri's letter to Khatami, and after the attack on Montazeri's house in November he was once more arrested and given a suspended prison sentence. In December 2001, Qabel was imprisoned for insulting the leader and spent four months in solitary confinement. In September 2004, due to constant pressure, he was forced into exile in Tajikistan. In May 2005, shortly before the presidential elections, he published a highly critical letter to Khamene'i, in which he held the leader responsible for the oppression of Montazeri and other dissident clerics, as well as a long list of murders, executions and other violations of rights.[17] In August 2005, when he temporarily returned to Iran for medical treatment, his passport was confiscated and he was forbidden from leaving the country.

Qabel was convinced that all religious law must be based on reason in order to be valid and acceptable. In his most important project, *shari'at-e aqlan*i (rational shari'a), he sought to develop a progressive reinterpretation of the entire shari'a based solely on reason and logic. In the introduction to his book *Mabani-ye shari'at* (*The Basis of the Shari'a*) – which was published in the last months of his life with the help of his friend, Kadivar – he declared that the sole truly authentic source is the Qur'an.[18] All other religious texts should be treated with caution as they had been indirectly transmitted, and in the process repeatedly altered or falsified. As many of the ethical and theological beliefs, as well as most laws of the shari'a, were deduced from these texts, they should be submitted to rational scrutiny, Qabel argued. Moreover, the laws inferred from the Qur'an by religious jurists could not be taken as God's word, but should be treated just like any other product of human scholarship. Unfortunately, his ambitious project to do away with outdated and obsolete laws was left incomplete because of his premature death: when travelling to Montazeri's funeral in December 2009, Qabel was arrested and imprisoned for six months before being put on a show trial in May 2010. Having subsequently published his spirited defence in court, he was again arrested in September 2010 for several months before being sentenced in December 2011 to 20 months in custody. Denied proper treatment in prison, he died of a brain tumour on 22 October 2012.[19] To judge whether Qabel's efforts for a rational reinterpretation of the shari'a were consistent and convincing is beyond the scope of this book. However, his example shows that Montazeri's teachings were not lost upon his students but led them to continue his quest for a progressive reading of the scriptures in a more radical form.

## The Electoral Coup d'État

We have received evidence of the interference of some of the officials and commanders of the Pasdaran and Bassij in the elections. Should these reports be verified, this action would not only be a violation of the law but it would also deepen the rift between the commanders and officials and the true and healthy body of the forces.

(Mussavi, in his letter to Khamene'i on the eve of the elections)[20]

The tenth presidential election, scheduled for June 2009, was initially viewed with little interest by the Iranian people. Several months ahead of the poll, little indicated that either the reformers or the principlists would be able to mobilise the electorate for their cause. Many voters had still not forgiven the reformers for their failure to realise the promised reforms and doubted that they would have more success if re-elected. The prospect of another four years under the presidency of Ahmadinejad, however, also raised little enthusiasm. Even many conservatives were frustrated with his erratic policies, his eccentric beliefs, his extremist rhetoric and his blatant disrespect for parliament and the clergy. As president, Ahmadinejad had remained true to his promise of improving the lot of the poor, yet several of his projects were ill-conceived and some badly backfired. While some policies, such as petrol rationing, were so unpopular that the President was quickly forced to back down, others, such as wage increases and the reduction of the interest rate, were well meant but in the end created more problems than they solved.[21] On his extended tours through the provinces, he also made numerous promises that were a strain to the budget. His spending spree resulted in a sharp increase in inflation, notably affecting the cost of food and housing. Although the President's generous distribution of the oil revenues certainly won him support, in the end few people reaped its benefits while all had to bear the inflation it provoked. As his critics remarked, Ahmadinejad brought the oil revenues to the people but, with the increase in prices, there was hardly more on the dinner tables.[22]

Apart from these economic problems, the President was confronted with an increasing number of political conflicts. Although parliament was dominated by his own faction, his relationship with the deputies was difficult from the start and only worsened as he refused to abide by their decisions. Many deputies were also critical of the President's attacks on Israel and his denial of the Holocaust. In October 2005, Ahmadinejad caused international outrage when he quoted Khomeini as saying that 'the regime occupying Jerusalem must disappear from the pages of time'. Incorrectly translated as 'Israel must be wiped off the map', it appeared as if Iran was set to actively intervene against Israel. But rather than correct the translation Ahmadinejad continued on this course, and, in December 2005, questioned the reality of the Holocaust. Ignoring the damage to Iran's image in the world, he asked the Foreign Ministry to organise a conference on the 'myth' of the Holocaust.[23] While parliament harshly criticised the conference, held in December 2006 in Tehran, many ordinary Iranians simply wondered about the pointlessness of the entire exercise.

By the time of the 2009 elections, support for Ahmadinejad among his own faction had considerably eroded and several prominent members publicly expressed their frustration. Among the reformers this limited and lukewarm support for Ahmadinejad raised the hope that Khamene'i would allow a free and fair election. Initially Khatami considered running for the reformists, but in March 2009 Mussavi also announced his candidacy. To avoid a split in the reformist vote, and possibly also because the leader had opposed his candidacy, Khatami withdrew from the race and threw in his support behind Mussavi. On 20 May, the Guardian Council approved his candidacy as well as that of Karrubi, while on the conservative side Ahmadinejad and Reza'i were registered for the elections. Initially, enthusiasm for the uncharismatic painter and architect Mussavi was limited among both the reformers and the public. As Prime Minister in the 1980s, he had won himself respect for his handling of the economic crisis triggered by the war with Iraq, but in the 1990s he had only played a limited role in politics. By 2009, he was largely unknown to the public and widely considered a colourless man of the past. However, those who knew him respected him as an honest, unassuming man of integrity, and the reformist parties Mosharekat, Mojahedin-e Enqelab and the small Mardomsalari party quickly expressed their support for his candidacy. Thanks to his wife, Zahra Rahnavard, a renowned artist, scholar and former Chancellor of Tehran's Al-Zahra University, who actively participated in his campaign, he also won the backing of large parts of the women's movement.

As in the past, Mussavi and Karrubi mainly catered to the interests of the urban middle class, focusing on issues of social and political freedom while largely neglecting popular concerns such as inflation, corruption and unemployment. However, after four years of his ill-conceived economic policies Ahmadinejad's promise of social justice rang hollow, and many voters were willing to forgive the reformers their elitist focus and lack of regard for 'bread and butter' issues. While interest in the election was initially limited, the situation changed with the series of televised debates among the candidates. It was the first time in Iran's history that such debates were held, and they were closely followed by the electorate. They not only established Mussavi as a serious contender for the presidency but also triggered a wave of support, unforeseen both by himself and his opponents. In the last week before the poll the atmosphere at his campaign rallies and the spontaneous gatherings in the streets was exuberant. The carnival-like celebrations, with crowds dressed in green dancing and singing until late at night, surprised the authorities as much as the participants themselves.

As usual, Khamene'i did not endorse any candidate but Ahmadinejad was generally considered his first choice. Montazeri also declined to endorse a candidate, but in a thinly veiled hint declared that he was confident that the people would elect a 'man of reform' (*fard-e eslāh*). In the face of rumours of an impending intervention by the Pasdaran to prevent a 'velvet revolution', Montazeri issued a fatwa declaring any interference contrary to Islam.[24] Mussavi, in a letter to Khamene'i, also warned of a manipulation of the election by the Revolutionary Guards, and called upon him to intervene.[25] Since the 1997 presidential elections, voter participation had constantly fallen to reach a low of 60 per cent in the second round of 2005. However, the exuberant campaign in 2009 prompted even the exiled communities to come in masses to the ballot box. In view of the long queues in front of polling stations, polling was extended for four hours until 10 o'clock in the evening of Friday 12 June 2009. According to the Interior Ministry, in the end 39 of the 46 million eligible voters cast their vote: the turnout of 85 per cent was the highest in the history of the Islamic Republic.

However, while all candidates welcomed the record level of participation, there was less agreement on the allocation of the votes. Late in the evening reformist officials from the Interior Ministry reportedly told Mussavi that he had won, but while Mussavi prepared a press conference his campaign headquarters and associated institutions were raided. At the conference Mussavi claimed that he had won 54 per cent of the votes and appealed to Khamene'i to intervene against the fraud. Thereupon, the Election Commission announced, just two hours after polls had closed, that Ahmadinejad had won by a wide margin. This uncommonly early announcement of results, when only 10 per cent of the votes had been counted, raised suspicions, and during the night tensions increased. On Saturday afternoon, the Election Commission confirmed that Ahmadinejad had won and was far ahead of Mussavi. According to the final results Ahmadinejad received 63.6 per cent of the votes while Mussavi came second with 33.7 per cent, Reza'i obtained 1.7 per cent and Karrubi 0.8 per cent. Reports of inconsistencies and irregularities quickly emerged, and the sheer number of votes with which Ahmadinejad was credited gave further cause for doubt.[26] Nevertheless, Khamene'i quickly congratulated Ahmadinejad on his victory, denied the occurrence of irregularities and urged the other candidates to accept the outcome. However, Karrubi rejected the leader's invocation and denounced the results as 'ridiculous' and 'unbelievable'.[27] Mussavi in a message to the people declared: 'I will not submit to these dangerous manipulations. Such actions by dishonest officials will shake the pillars of the Islamic Republic and result in the establishment of tyranny.' In a second message to the clergy he decried 'an extent of vote rigging in front of the eyes of the astonished world by a government which claims to be committed to religious justice' and warned the clerics that the 'silence of the *olemā* and the *marāje'* [...] may cause more damage than any manipulation of the vote'.[28] Although it appeared that the regime had expected protests after the elections, it was clearly not prepared for their extent. The people's anger at what they perceived to be the blatant disrespect of their vote far exceeded anything anticipated by the regime.

## The Protests and their Repression

A regime based on violence, repression and the violation of rights, which illegally seizes votes and falsifies results, which murders, detains and imprisons [...], which censures the press and disturbs communication, which imprisons the educated elite under empty pretexts and extracts false confessions, is, according to religious law and human reason, to be condemned and without value.

(From Montazeri's declaration on the legitimacy of the regime)[29]

Following the announcement of the results on Saturday 13 June 2009, people in Tehran and other cities spontaneously poured out onto the streets to voice their protest. Under the slogan 'Where is my vote', 10,000 people assembled at the capital's central Vanak Square to denounce the manipulations and to demand a recount of the votes or a new election. Many were stunned and shocked by the results, and convinced that the regime had stolen their victory. While the protesters assembled at Vanak Square, Ahmadinejad held a rally in celebration of his re-election at the nearby Valiasr Square. In his speech he compared the protesters to dissatisfied soccer fans, and scorned them as 'dust and dirt'. As the air buzzed with calls for protests, the regime cut mobile phone services. Facebook, YouTube, Twitter and other social networks were blocked, and the websites of domestic and foreign media were filtered. Foreign journalists were forbidden from covering the protests, and were told to leave the country upon expiry of their visas.[30] While the regular uniformed police on this day, as on later occasions, hardly participated in the violence, the riot police, which are part of the Pasdaran, played an active role in the repression, employing batons, tear gas and rubber bullets against the protesters. The most violent however, were the plain-clothes men on motorcycles who, armed with chains, batons, knives and guns, attacked the protesters as well as uninvolved onlookers. They were reported to have particularly targeted women and were widely believed to be members of the Bassij, though they may also have belonged to other security and intelligence services.[31] On the second night of the protests, security and Bassij forces attacked the student dormitories of Tehran University. They beat students in their rooms and arrested several hundred, many of whom were taken to Kahrizak prison in the south of Tehran. At least six students were killed during the raid, and many more severely injured. Similar attacks were reported from universities in Shiraz, Isfahan, Tabriz, Mashhad, Babol and Zahedan.[32]

After a meeting with Mussavi to hear his complaints, Khamene'i reversed his former position and on 15 June charged the Guardian Council with investigating the allegations of irregularities. However, this concession failed to calm the situation. Denied permission by the Interior Ministry and threatened with repression by the hardliners, Mussavi and Karrubi called off the planned protests in Tehran but the rally went ahead anyway. In the afternoon, hundreds of thousands of protesters silently marched from Enqelab Square to the vast Azadi Square west of the city centre, where they were joined by more protesters. When Khatami and Mussavi joined the crowd, the people started shouting 'Ya Hossein, Mir Hossein' and 'Death to the dictator'. In his first speech since the elections, Mussavi called on the people to remain calm but unwavering while his allegation of fraud was being investigated. Never, he assured them, would he abandon the fight for their rights. In the end, the entire Azadi Square was submerged by people with green scarves, flags and ribbons. With the total number possibly reaching three million, it was the largest protest since the revolution. However, after the end of the rally clashes broke out. At least eight people were killed in Tehran, while more deaths were reported from Isfahan, Mashhad and Kermanshah.[33]

After the elections none of the *maraje'-ye taqlid* endorsed Ahmadinejad's victory, yet the only ones to respond to Mussavi's call for support and to condemn the fraud and the ensuing violence were Sane'i and Montazeri. On 15 June, Sane'i wrote that he would pray for the success of Mussavi's endeavour to realise the 'sacred objectives of the system of Imam Khomeini', which was an 'Islam respectful of individual rights and dignity'. Two days later he offered his sympathy to the families of the victims, mentioning especially the students who were hurt while exercising their legitimate right to defend their vote.[34] Montazeri for his part, in a sharply worded message to the 'honoured and oppressed nation of Iran' on 16 June, rejected the results and condemned the violence. The enthusiastic mobilisation for the election would have been a good occasion for the system to renew its relationship with the country's youth, but 'unhappily the worst use was made of this good occasion', he wrote.

> In the face of the protests following the announcement of the results, which nobody in his right mind could accept, considering the credible reports of numerous modifications of the people's votes, [...] [the regime] before the eyes of the world and the cameras of domestic and foreign journalists has attacked the children of this oppressed nation, and with force and utter brutality repressed, beaten and arrested defenceless men, women and students. In a settling of political accounts, it has, without reason, detained numerous activists, scholars and intellectuals some of whom have been high-ranking officials of the Islamic Republic.[35]

The regime must seek the participation of all classes, even if they do not share its own views, Montazeri asserted, adding, 'I have stated time and again that the votes of the nation belong to God and the people and that a government based on the falsification of votes has no sacred or political legitimacy.' Montazeri called on the young to desist from all violence in order to not provide the regime with any pretext for the repression of their protests. The officials should not believe that at the present time the truth could be kept hidden, Montazeri warned: sooner or later their crimes would be exposed and they would be punished for their deeds, both in this world and in the hereafter.

On 19 June, amid continuing protests, Khamene'i held the Friday prayer in Tehran. Mussavi and Karrubi did not attend. In his sermon the leader called the high turnout a sign of the people's maturity and an expression of their allegiance to the system. The election, Khamene'i claimed, was a victory for 'religious democracy', which he called a 'third way' between dictatorship and secular democracy. In an attempt to calm the situation he downplayed the differences between the candidates. Although he did not approve of all their ideas, he said, all candidates were supporters of the system and their conflict was not one for or against the revolution. Significantly Khamene'i neither then nor subsequently denied the relevance of elections for the legitimacy of the regime. Not once did he challenge the reformist paradigm that the regime depended on the approval of the people. Not once did he refer to the idea, defended by the more radical conservative thinkers, that the president receives his legitimacy from the *faqih* as the representative of God. This showed to what extent the reformists had, over the previous few years, succeeded in imposing their reading of *velāyat-e faqih*. The debate was not about whether the regime needed the people's approval, but only about whether it had received this approval or not. However, Khamene'i left little doubt that he was not willing to accept further protests. The political leaders should be conscious of the risks of further protests, he warned, pointing to the civil wars in Iraq and Afghanistan. 'If the political elites violate the law [. . .] they will be responsible for the bloodshed, the violence and the chaos which will ensue', Khamene'i warned. If the opposition let terrorists infiltrate their protests, it would be to blame for the response of the security forces. 'I want all to end these ways [the protests]. It is not right. If they do not end this, the responsibility lies on their shoulders.'[36]

His warning that the opposition would bear responsibility for the bloodshed should they not heed his order to end the protests, was perceived as a green light for the crushing of the opposition. Mussavi and Karrubi had once more demanded permission for a rally the following day – but, again, this permission was denied. Despite the massive presence of the police and the militias several thousand protesters managed to assemble on Enqelab Square, although many more were prevented by barriers and the security forces from joining the crowd. The following repression was the most violent since the election. Unidentified gunmen were reported to have shot at protesters and uninvolved onlookers from rooftops, windows and motorcycles. At least 20 people were reported killed that day in Tehran. A 26-year-old student, Neda Agha-Soltan, became the most prominent victim of the violence when she was fatally shot in the chest in Kargar Street. The moment blood gushed out of her mouth and nose was captured on a camcorder, and the scene was posted online and spread through the internet. As she rapidly became the icon of the protest, her family was pressured and prevented from holding a public funeral service.[37]

In a bid to calm the situation the Guardian Council conceded to a recount of 10 per cent of the vote, but Mussavi and Karrubi refused to attend the meeting. In a letter to the council Mussavi insisted that the elections be annulled, and accused the regime of having prepared the manipulation in advance. In a statement to his supporters he rejected Khamene'i's claim that the protests were part of a foreign conspiracy to foment a velvet revolution. In reality, he declared, the country's youth were seeking to defend the original principles of the revolution: freedom, justice and democracy. If the fraud were accepted, the republican side of the system would be defeated, he warned and 'the idea of the incompatibility of Islam and republicanism will be confirmed'. It was not the protesters but those who ordered their repression who were responsible for the bloodshed.

> The authorities of the country by endorsing the results and by limiting the investigations so that the election will not be annulled and the results will not be changed, have accepted the responsibility of what has happened during the elections, though in more than 170 constituencies the number of votes cast exceeded the number of registered voters,

he declared. Rather than continue the violent repression of the protests and blame the opposition for the ensuing bloodshed, the government should allow a fair and free debate to avoid a repetition of scenes that 'break the heart of anyone who loves the revolution and the country'. Mussavi admitted that in many ways it was not him but the people who led the way. However, he assured his supporters that he would stand with them regardless of what happened.[38] On this and later occasions, Mussavi and Karrubi were careful to remain inside the official discourse and to emphasise their respect for the constitution. In all their speeches they insisted that by calling for the freedom of elections they were defending the republican heritage of Khomeini. Thus, they not only denied the regime the possibility to denounce them as Western-inspired secularists and liberals, but also reached out to the more conservative sections of the electorate. While their expression of faith in the system was genuine, it can be assumed that many of their supporters actually preferred a more secular system but dared not publicly express this.

After the bloodshed on 20 June, Montazeri called for a three-day period of mourning, and on 24 June he expressed his sorrow, anger and shame in the face of the crimes committed in the name of Islam. The regime, he wrote, had transformed Tehran and other cities into vast garrisons and sent plain-clothes agents resembling the thugs of the Shah to beat up innocent people. Calling on the people to remain calm but unrelenting, Montazeri warned officials that if 'the honoured people today cannot calmly express their demand for justice and are forcefully repressed, the problems will take on a form that even the strongest basis of government may be shaken'.[39] The violent repression of the protests on 20 June temporarily brought to a halt the demonstrations that had continued uninterrupted for a week, but other forms of protest, such as shouting 'Allah-o akbar' from the rooftops at night, continued. Despite the bloody crackdown, the regime remained on the defensive and failed to regain the initiative throughout the summer. Its blatant disrespect for the law and its excessive and often indiscriminate use of force led to a public outcry, which repeatedly forced it to back down. The regime's attempts to cover up its crimes by blaming foreign agents did not convince the public, and only further contributed to their anger. When the Guardian Council confirmed the election results in its final verdict on 26 June, Mussavi remained defiant. In possibly his most important statement, on 4 July, he called the council's review of the complaints a show which convinced nobody. The regime had lost the people's trust, Mussavi affirmed, and it should not believe that military force could replace popular legitimacy.[40] In a language testifying to his revolutionary roots he warned that should the regime continue in its path the Islamic Republic would be transformed into a military regime.

> It is our historic responsibility to continue our protests and not lessen our efforts to realise the people's rights. It is our religious responsibility to not permit the revolution and the system to be transformed in a way contrary to Islam. It is our revolutionary duty to not allow the blood of the hundreds of thousands of

martyrs to be degraded by a military regime [. . .]. I appeal to all government officials not to act like the Guardian Council and not to block the channels for the correction of errors, because if this path is closed the only alternative is repression.[41]

With every sentence, Mussavi emphasised that his struggle was to realise the revolution's original principles. It was not those who called for the respect of the will of the people and defended its rights who deviated from the revolution, he affirmed, but those who violated these rights. His statement once again made clear that the struggle was about the authority of interpretation:

Islam is not the coat turned inside out which your opponents wear. Their way is to transform the sacred and the sublime to suit their own needs [. . .]. The true Islam has no relation with their hypocrisy and wickedness but is a religion of salvation, which if we reach its truth and its light, will cure all our personal and social pains.[42]

Despite three weeks of violence and threats, Mussavi remained resolved to continue the struggle. Unlike Khatami, who during similar conflicts had backed down, Mussavi stayed firm in the face of pressure. In his struggle he had the full support of Sane'i and Montazeri. In early July, Sane'i issued a fatwa in which he openly questioned the regime's legitimacy. 'From a political and legal perspective the legitimacy of the government has come into question', he wrote, warning that the people's doubts about the election could lead to 'the government's inability to function while its persistence may become the reason for legal and social problems'.[43] Some days later, Montazeri went one step further, issuing the harshest condemnation of the regime any cleric had yet dared to publish: in response to questions on the conditions of political legitimacy addressed to him by Kadivar, he declared on 10 July in a historic fatwa that a regime based on force which systematically violates the people's rights has no religious or legal value. The people, and especially the clergy, have the religious duty to seek the restoration of justice. In other words, he declared that in view of the violence committed since the election injustice had reached such a point that the regime had lost its legitimacy and must be replaced. Responding to Kadivar's question as to whether the preservation of the system justified the violation of the people's rights as well as the transgression of ethical and religious principles, Montazeri declared that 'the protection of the system is neither essential nor in itself obligatory, especially if "system" actually means a person'. The necessity for the preservation of the system is dependent on its respect for the people's rights and its fulfilment of its other duties. 'With oppressive and unislamic deeds it is clearly impossible to protect and preserve an Islamic system,' he asserted.

> A regime based on violence, repression and the violation of rights, which illegally seizes votes and falsifies results, which murders, detains and imprisons and employs medieval and Stalinist tortures, which censures the press and disturbs communication, which imprisons the educated elite under empty pretexts and extracts false confessions, is, according to religious law and human reason, to be condemned and without value.[44]

Montazeri stressed that the country belongs to the people, that they must make the decisions and officials must serve their will. The Shah, Montazeri reminded his readers, only heard the voice of the people when it was too late. Now, it is incumbent upon the independent clerical and intellectual elite, as well as the general people, to recognise injustice and to act against tyranny:

> The justice or injustice of the rulers is clear to society and its consequences are obvious: its face is not hidden behind a veil. Everybody has, according to his knowledge and abilities, the duty to fight against injustice and the oppression of people's rights and to alert others to the present condition so that they too can 'enjoin good and prohibit evil' and seek a solution [to the present crisis].[45]

The fatwa immediately found a resounding echo in the domestic and foreign press. None of Montazeri's earlier declarations had been so widely published, and none had had such a profound effect. The text was not only printed by numerous Iranian websites, but also translated into several foreign languages. It was even chosen for a 'worldwide reading for democracy and freedom' on 16 September. The fatwa not only confirmed his position as the regime's most outspoken clerical critic but also established him as the spiritual guide of the Green Movement. The regime was well aware of the importance of the fatwa, but rather than attack its author it questioned its authenticity. Pointing to Montazeri's health problems, the principlist website *Rajanews* claimed that the fatwa was written by Kadivar and published with the help of Montazeri's sons. The old man, the website claimed, suffered from such severe amnesia that he could not even recognise his closest family members. Montazeri thereupon issued a handwritten declaration confirming the authenticity of the fatwa.[46] He was certainly weakened by his illness, but there was no evidence that he was no longer master of his wits.

On 17 July, Rafsanjani gave his only Friday prayer sermon after the election. Contrary to the usual practice, the sermon, which was attended both by Mussavi and Karrubi, was not broadcast live on television. Although the surrounding streets were crowded with followers of the Green Movement, the hall of Tehran University was filled with supporters of the regime. When Rafsanjani stepped onto the podium the hostile crowd in the hall prevented him from speaking for several minutes and repeatedly interrupted his sermon. The people, Rafsanjani asserted, had always been the basis of the system and today so they remained:

> You know that, according to the constitution, everything in this country is based on the vote of the people. Even in the case of the leader the people must elect the experts, hence he too is the product of the people's vote [. . .]. All those who occupy a post, do so thanks to the people's vote. There is the people and this is a religious government: Islamic Republic is not an empty word. It is both 'Republic' and 'Islamic' [. . .]. It is certain that if one of these two is violated this revolution ceases to exist.[47]

The past events were bitter, Rafsanjani said, and many had legitimate doubts about the election that should be addressed. He regretted that the Guardian Council did not follow the leader's order to investigate the complaints and thus win back the people's confidence. The government should encourage dialogue, television should permit all groups to present their views and newspapers should be allowed to be published. It was wrong, he said, that protesters were imprisoned. They should be freed and the regime should apologise to those who had suffered during the past events. Following the end of the prayer, clashes erupted.[48]

Apart from Montazeri and Sane'i, of the high-ranking clergy initially only the former Friday prayer leader of Isfahan, Taheri-Isfahani, who had resigned from his post in June 2003 in protest against the repression of renewed student protests and the instrumentalisation of religion by the regime, openly supported the Green Movement. In a public statement he criticised Khamene'i for having openly taken sides in the political conflict and disputed the principlists' claim to the heritage of Khomeini. Most other high-ranking clerics were careful not to take sides in the conflict. Bayat-Zanjani, Musavi-Ardebili, Makarem-Shirazi, Javadi-Amoli and Mussavi-Tabrizi all expressed doubts about the legality of the election and concern about the violations of the law, but when their remarks were harshly criticised by the hardline faction they lapsed into defiant silence.[49] In the face of the continuing silence of the clergy, Montazeri urged the *maraje'-ye taqlid* and the other clerics to stand up against the abuses committed in the name of religion. Although the aim of the revolution had 'not simply been to change the names and slogans [of the system], the crimes and the violations of rights committed by the former regime are continued in another form under the name of religious government and the rule of the jurist', he declared in his message of 13 September. Considering that he had fought for this system, Montazeri wrote, he felt shame for the blood spilled in its name. Should the clergy not intervene, he warned, the people's faith would still further decrease:

> The people ask: If this oppression, this violation of rights and these deviations [*be'yat*] are contrary to Islam why do the honoured *maraje'* and religious scholars, whose responsibility is the protection and strengthening of religion and its rules, as well as the defence of the people's rights [...] not speak out against these acts which are committed in the name of Islam? [...] The respected *maraje'* are aware of the power and the influence of their words on the government and know well that the government depends on them for the preservation of its legitimacy [...] and that it takes advantage of their silence regarding the violations.[50]

Following the publication of this message three of his grandchildren, as well as the children of several other clerics, were detained on the order of the Special Court of the Clergy.[51] However, Montazeri's appeal did not remain without response: on 28 September, more than 300 people

THE GREEN MOVEMENT AND ITS FAILURE      229

published an open letter to express their support for Montazeri and to urge the clergy to raise their voice.[52] On 2 October, the society of the teachers of the seminary and university of Isfahan published another letter, emphasising the need for the clergy to stand up against injustice.[53] Later, Taheri-Isfahani also sent a letter of support. Moreover, on 22 September, Ayatollah Ali-Mohammad Dastgheib in a speech to the Expert Council called on its members to intervene against the attacks on loyal supporters of Khomeini and the repression of dissent. Mussavi and Karrubi should be allowed to speak in the Expert Council, Dastgheib demanded, and the delegates should decide 'whether or not there has been a breach of the constitution'.[54]

Protests continued throughout the autumn, and official rallies on 18 September (Al Quds Day), 4 November (US Embassy occupation anniversary) and 7 December (International Student Day) were used to stage protests in Tehran and other cities. However, the regime slowly regained the upper hand. Although its brutality hardly helped it win back legitimacy, it did manage to break the protests. By the end of summer the movement was severely weakened by several waves of arrests. In addition to thousands of ordinary protesters detained on the street, hundreds of reformist politicians, journalists, students leaders, human rights defenders and women's rights activists had been arrested.[55] Many of those detained were never officially charged or brought to court. While some were released within days others remained for months in prison, where they were often placed in solitary confinement and subjected to various other forms of torture. Students not protected by their age or position were especially badly mistreated. During interrogations they were submitted to insults, threats, mock executions and hour-long beatings. The situation in the secret prisons of the Bassij, Pasdaran and other security services was often worse than in the official detention facilities. Even the judiciary was often not informed of these prisons and their inmates.[56]

Some of the worst human rights violations took place in Kahrizak prison in the south of Tehran. The judiciary had ordered its closure two years earlier due to its disrespect for even the most basic standards, but it had remained in operation. Many of those arrested during the student protests of 9 July were brought there. Numerous detainees were sexually abused and raped. Officially, three prisoners died in Kahrizak, but reports indicate that the actual number of dead was considerably higher.

In the face of the public outcry caused by these reports, Khamene'i on 27 July ordered the closure of the facility, but it appeared that the prison remained in operation after this date.[57] A letter by Karrubi on the rape of male and female detainees in Kahrizak caused further outrage. Even conservative deputies demanded that action be taken to prevent a recurrence of such abuses, and Larijani set up a parliamentary committee to investigate the situation in Kahrizak. The committee rapidly dismissed the reports of rape, a position later echoed by the investigation committee set up by the judiciary, but it confirmed reports about the systematic torture of detainees. It also rejected the authorities' claim that the deaths had been caused by meningitis, and made Tehran's Prosecutor-General, Sa'id Mortezavi, who for many years had been notorious for his role in the persecution of the opposition, personally responsible for the crimes.[58]

On 1 August 2009, the first of a series of five mass show trials against reformist politicians, journalists and activists was opened at the Revolutionary Court of Tehran.[59] These trials, which were meant to substantiate the claim that the protests were part of a 'velvet revolution' organised by foreign powers, violated the most basic requirements of due process. The accused were denied the right to a defence counsel, and the often vaguely worded accusations did not amount to crimes punishable under Iranian law. Many of the accused appeared in pyjama-like prison uniforms and seemed to have been drugged, and some also bore traces of torture. The first two of the show trials were broadcast on television, but as they failed to reach their intended effect with the public the later hearings were held behind closed doors. In all trials, the indictment relied heavily on forced confessions. Why the court again resorted to public recantations, which had been largely abandoned since the 1990s, remained a mystery, as they had long ceased to achieve their aim and it was highly doubtful that they would now fool the public. Even before the opening of the trials, the use of forced confessions and their publishing in the press was criticised by reformist groups and parties as well as some clerics like Bayat-Zanjani. In a sharply worded fatwa on 4 August, Montazeri also condemned the show trials and declared the confessions used in court to be invalid. According to his fatwa, to force the accused 'to testify in show trials according to the wishes of the judges against their own beliefs and convictions and to confess to crimes they did not commit' leads the people 'to compare their courts with those of

Stalin, Saddam and other dictators'. Referring to passages from the Qur'an and the hadith, he formally declared:

> Confessions which are taken in illegal prisons under irregular circumstances by deceiving and intimidating the prisoners, interrupting their contact with society and exerting mental and physical pressure on them, which regrettably have become common in the Islamic Republic in recent years, have no legal or religious legitimacy and count among the worst sins and crimes [...]. Those responsible [for these confessions] must be condemned and no regular court can sentence someone on the basis of such confession and interviews.[60]

The following day Sane'i too, in no uncertain terms, condemned both the show trials and the taking of forced confessions as legally and religiously invalid.[61] As the controversy continued, Khamene'i declared on 20 September that while confessions against others were religiously and legally not admissible in court, confessions against oneself were totally acceptable.[62] The verdicts, which were passed in autumn 2009 and often based on nothing more than the confessions of the accused, hardly convinced any impartial observer, but they had their intended effect: although they did not immediately bring the protests to an end, they did break the back of the Green Movement.[63]

## A Challenge even after his Death

> Ayatollah Montazeri continuously updated his legal-religious views. If, in the beginning, the doctrine of velāyat-e faqih played a prominent role in his religious philosophy, in the end, he reformed his philosophy and prioritised citizenship rights. His end was another beginning. His passing gave him new life [...]. If the Green Movement achieves its goals, he has won in reality.
> (Ganji on the death of Montazeri; 22 December 2009)[64]

On 19 December 2009, at the age of 87, Montazeri passed away in his sleep. The news of his death spread like wildfire among the opposition, and his funeral led to one of the last major protests of the Green

Movement. Hundreds of thousands of people from Qom, Tehran, Isfahan, Najafabad and other cities joined the funeral procession to pay their last tribute to the man who in the past months had become the spiritual guide of the reformist movement. With the crowd sporting green scarves and shouting slogans in support of the opposition, the procession from Montazeri's house to the shrine of Hazrat Masumeh was transformed into a vast protest march. Mussavi, Karrubi and many other reformist clerics, politicians and intellectuals, such as Abdollah Nuri, Jalaleddin Taheri-Isfahani, Ezatollah Sahabi, Habibollah Peyman, Mostafa Moin, Mohammad-Reza Khatami, Emadeddin Baqi,[65] Ali-Akbar Mohtashemi and Hadi Khamene'i, attended the ceremony. Significantly, conservative figures like the Friday prayer leader of Qom, Ebrahim Amini, Mahmud Hashemi-Shahrudi, and Qorban'ali Dori-Najafabadi were also present. While foreign journalists were forbidden to cover the ceremony, the official media reported on the funeral but did not show pictures of the extent of the crowd.[66] When Khamene'i's message of condolence was read out in the shrine's courtyard, the crowd shouted 'Death to the dictator'. Montazeri was laid to rest in the inner complex of the shrine where some of Iran's most renown clerics lie. In accordance with his wishes he was buried in a simple tomb beneath the floor of the hall, next to his son Mohammad. The prayers at his grave were read by his old friend Ayatollah Mussa Shabairi-Zanjani, a quietist and rather reclusive cleric, who regularly led the prayers in the Great Mosque and who had only once broken with his usual restraint to protest against Montazeri's house arrest. During the funeral procession, regime supporters and students of Mesbah-Yazdi tried to drown out the opposition slogans with loudspeakers and repeatedly clashed with the crowd. After the end of the ceremony, they occupied the courtyard of the Great Mosque. To avoid further violence, Ahmad Montazeri, who as the eldest son of the deceased led the ceremony, was forced to call off the planned prayers. Regime supporters then assembled outside the offices of Montazeri and Sane'i and tore down banners, posters and photographs while the police looked on. When Mussavi left the ceremony, plain-clothes agents attacked his car.[67]

At the news of Montazeri's death, a flood of condolence messages from clerics, politicians and intellectuals poured into his office. Almost all senior Shi'ite clerics and practically all the major figures, groups and parties of the reform movement sent letters of sympathy or published obituaries in the press. Mussavi, Karrubi, Khatami, Kadivar, Nuri and many more paid tribute to Montazeri as an outstanding scholar of religious law and ethics, and a courageous, unrelenting and unbending defender of the fundamental rights of the people and of political prisoners.[68] The head of the Sunnite clergy of Sistan and Baluchistan praised Montazeri's commitment to the reconciliation of the confessions. Ganji emphasised his courage when he alone stood up against Khomeini to criticise the prison massacres. Soroush highlighted the oppression he had suffered because he dared question the authority of Khamene'i. Shirin Ebadi called him the 'father of human rights' in Iran, and a model for the peaceful defence of the oppressed. Several international human rights organisations and foreign governments also paid tribute to his commitment to freedom of speech and the defence of prisoner's rights.[69] Abdol'ali Bazargan, Ganji, Soroush, Kadivar and Mohajerani on 3 January 2010 in a joint statement on the objectives of the opposition paid tribute to Montazeri as the 'spiritual leader of the movement' who had, during the past six months of his life, fought unrelentingly for the defence of the people's rights and thus given the movement new life.[70] With the notable exception of Ahmadinejad and Jannati, the heads of the principal institutions of the country also expressed their condolence. Khamene'i published a short message in which he paid tribute to 'Ayatollah' Montazeri as an experienced jurist and a prominent teacher, who for many years had served the clerical movement against the Shah irrespective of the hardships that he had to bear on this path. However, Khamene'i wrote, in the last period of Khomeini's life Montazeri had to pass a 'difficult and important test', an event for which he asked God's pardon and forgiveness, therewith implying that Montazeri failed this test.[71]

In the days following Montazeri's death, mourning ceremonies in his memory were banned in all cities except Qom and Najafabad. Attempts in Isfahan and Zanjan to hold prayers were forcefully repressed by the security services. On the eve of Ashura' a prayer in the Great Mosque in Isfahan was called off when the crowd outside started shouting slogans against the regime. Subsequent protests were forcefully repressed. Similarly, a sermon by Khatami in the *hosseiniye* of Jamaran next to Khomeini's house was stormed by regime supporters. Thereupon, protesters assembled in the adjacent streets until the crowd reached down to Niavaran and Tajrish. Ashura' in this year coincided with the tenth day after Montazeri's death. The rallies organised for this occasion in Tehran, Isfahan, Najafabad and other cities became the largest opposition protests since June, and the last major demonstration of the Green Movement. In the heated atmosphere after Montazeri's death the opposition slogans and demands had become more radical, but the regime was no longer prepared to tolerate any challenge to its power. The repression on this day was extremely brutal. Several dozen people were reportedly killed throughout the country, but the exact number of deaths remains unknown.[72] The violent repression of the Ashura' rallies marked the end of the post-election protests in Iran. The Green Movement was certainly not yet dead, but the repression had left its mark. Many of its key leaders, speakers and activists had been placed in prison and many of its central parties, platforms and newspapers had been shut down. After months of violence, arrests and trials all knew the price of continuing protest, and many shrank back from further confrontation.

Nevertheless, the Green Movement remained a thorn in the side of the regime. Its existence and its support by the people was a constant challenge to the regime's legitimacy. Nobody had represented this challenge more than Montazeri. Even after his death he remained a source of concern to the regime and its leader. His sons, Ahmad and Sa'id, who were respected clerics in their own right and had long played an active part in drafting declarations and distributing the writings of their father, did their best to keep his memory alive and, despite complaints of several *marāje'-ye taqlid*, refused to close his office. Sa'id repeatedly used his position as the guardian of his father's legacy to sharply criticise the regime. However, over the ensuing months the pressure to close his office increased. On 28 March 2010, less than 100 days after their father's death, their mother, Khadija, who had aided him both morally and physically in his studies and his religious and political activities and had shared with him the long years of exile, imprisonment and house arrest, passed away.[73] This left their house empty. When on the first anniversary of the presidential elections in June 2010, Khamene'i paid an informal visit to the shrine in Qom, he ordered that the embroidered cloth on Montazeri's tomb be removed. When on the following afternoon the offices of Sane'i[74] and Montazeri were attacked, it was difficult not to see a connection to the leader's visit. As the mob of plain-clothes agents and conservative students rampaged through the house and office of Sane'i they shouted slogans against him, Karrubi, Mussavi and Hassan Khomeini, who the previous week, during a speech at his grandfather's tomb in Tehran, had been shouted down by supporters of the regime for having sided with the Green Movement.[75] Having vandalised the office, the mob moved on to Montazeri's house situated in a nearby alley. As on similar occasions in the past, the security forces only stepped in once the work was done. The following day, on the order of the Special Court of the Clergy intelligence agents officially closed the office and sealed its doors. Thus, what the regime had failed to achieve during Montazeri's lifetime, it accomplished after his death.

# CONCLUSION

When, after Montazeri's death, the regime sealed the doors of his office and removed the sign from his tomb, it sought to eliminate the last physical traces of his existence. As a *lieu de mémoire*, his tomb and his office had represented a symbolic challenge to the regime. Since it could not remove his thoughts and theories from the discourse, it sought to at least remove from sight what remained of his physical presence. Its power was not enough to break his discursive authority, but it did manage to close his office. Although this did not diminish the influence of his ideas, it did limit the possibility of their propagation. For the conservatives, the ideas of religious reformers like Montazeri, Soroush and Khatami were dangerous not only because they had popular support but also because their religious and political authority could not easily be refuted. They were not Westernised liberals whose ideas could be dismissed as foreign, secular and thus illegitimate, as they had participated in the revolution and helped construct the system. The conservatives' reluctance to challenge their ideas in a free and fair debate betrayed their lack of confidence in the persuasiveness of their own ideas. Rather than respond to arguments with counter-arguments, they sought to undermine the position of their opponents. Where defamation did not suffice to break their authority, the conservatives resorted to force to limit their means of expression and to exclude them from the discourse.

Never was the discursive weakness of the conservatives more apparent than after the elections of 2009. At no time did they question the importance of elections or invoke the approval of the *faqih* to bolster the legitimacy of the president. With their recognition that his legitimacy depended on his election by the people and not on the approval of the leader, they accepted the republican reading of *velāyat-e faqih*. However, although the reformers successfully asserted their interpretation of the system they could not prevent the manipulation of the elections – the central element of the republican system. Just as in the years after 1997, the conservatives' control of the security forces prevented the reformers from attaining the positions of power necessary to realise their programme. With the prosecution of critical journalists, politicians and clerics as well as the beating, torture and murder of protesters, the conservatives persuaded no one of the legitimacy of their ideas, but they did manage to at least temporarily silence their opponents. After 2009, the conservatives redrew the limits of the discursive field to exclude their rivals. In the years following the election, the principal reformers were thrown into prison, forced into exile or placed under house arrest. Soroush, Ganji, Eshkevari and Kadivar all left the country, and although the election of the moderate cleric Hojatoleslam Hassan Ruhani as president in June 2013 brought some hope for an easing of tensions, Karrubi, Mussavi and Rahnavard remained under house arrest, while Khatami and even Rafsanjani remained largely marginalised. After the death of Montazeri, neither Sane'i nor any other cleric was able to fill his place. Several years after his demise, the question of Montazeri's legacy remains. In many ways Montazeri was a tragic figure who spent much of his later years trying to correct what he had himself helped to frame. Having fought throughout much of his adult life to establish an Islamic state, it was bitter for him to realise that this state was not only just as ruthless, repressive and authoritarian as its predecessor but that it also threatened to undermine the very values it had set out to protect. It was even more bitter to realise that it was precisely the post of *vali-ye faqih*, which he had so strongly pushed for inclusion in the constitution, which opened the doors to despotism and led to irreconcilable contradictions within the system. To resolve these contradictions he sought since 1985 to develop a revised reading of *velāyat-e faqih*, which allowed for greater freedom, pluralism and popular participation. In this reading, the *faqih* was not considered the people's guardian but their representative who was held to recognise their rights and respect their will. He was not considered to be appointed by God, but elected by the people from among the eligible jurists. The people rather than the *faqih* were viewed as the primary source of political legitimacy. In his later writings, Montazeri also argued that the *faqih*'s mandate should be limited and that he should not exercise power himself, but rather supervise the political institutions to ensure respect of Islamic precepts. As only a *marja'* can fulfil this function, Montazeri argued, the separation of *velāyat* and *marja'iyat* was wrong.

Even though his revised version of *velāyat-e faqih* still presented a number of inconsistencies, most notably regarding the *faqih*'s relationship with the other *marāje*, it did open up the perspective of a democratic reform of the system. However, the tragedy for Montazeri was that his propositions remained largely without response and that the reformers mostly refused to embrace his ideas. This was notably due to the fact that adopting his ideas would not only have obliged them to tackle the contentious issue of the *faqih*'s powers, but also to break the taboo surrounding Montazeri. This, however, the reformers failed to do. While they succeeded in introducing new ideas and concepts to the discourse, they did not manage to once more make Montazeri a recognised source of discursive legitimacy. However, in his later years, Montazeri's ideas were also increasingly out of touch with both the political realities and the desires of the people. In the face of the gradual shift of power from the clergy to the military his proposition for limiting the powers of the *faqih* lost its relevance, as it no longer sufficed to solve the problems. In summary one can therefore conclude that his revision of *velāyat-e faqih* was in theory of considerable importance, but in practice it failed to significantly influence the debate.

If the people nevertheless flocked to his funeral, it was to pay tribute to an outspoken critic of oppression and an unbending advocate of the people's rights. Many who did not share his views on *velāyat-e faqih* readily recognised the perseverance, pertinacity and courage with which he had called for pluralism, participation and the respect of human rights, persistently condemning the use of torture in prison and of forced confessions in court. Although Montazeri was not a charismatic figure, an able political tactician or a very impressive orator, his willingness to listen to others and his readiness to speak his mind had made him a voice of the people. Unlike other clerics he never completely gave in to the attraction of power, seeing his role rather as one of supervision and advice. When he realised that his advice was not accepted, he withdrew to the traditional role of the clergy as a critical corrective to the State. While some saw him as naive, and considered it a tactical blunder that he had criticised the repression before he had the power to end it, many respected him precisely because he had stood up against such aberrations as the prison purges, even if it cost him his post and power.

The experience that led Montazeri from the belief that Islamic law under the guardianship of a just jurist can assure the reign of justice to the realisation that the sacred law alone is not sufficient to govern a modern state – and that even a just jurist, without the control of the people, tends to abuse his powers – was shared by an entire generation of revolutionary clerics, activists and intellectuals. As in Montazeri's case, the inefficiency and injustice of the regime, as well as its blatant disrespect of citizen's rights, led them to question the structures of the system and its underlying ideology. Harking back to the religious sources, they sought to develop an alternative reading of Islam which prioritised freedom, equality, pluralism and popular participation. In many ways, Montazeri and the other reformers in Iran were in the situation of those communist dissidents in the socialist countries of Eastern Europe, who, despite all doubts, retained their faith in communist ideology but advocated an opening up of the system in the hope of thus both preserving the system and realising its original values. In Eastern Europe, even though history passed over these reformers, their ideas played a central role in paving the way for democracy. In Iran this transition remains still to be achieved, but the reformers have undoubtedly made some important steps in the right direction.

# NOTES

## Introduction

1. Hossein-Ali Montazeri, *Enteqad az khod* (Qom, 1390 SH), p. 188.
2. Mohsen Kadivar, 'Sir-e tahavol-e andishe siasi Ayatollah Montazeri' (1390 SH). Available at http://kadivar.com/?p=5568.
3. Pierre Bourdieu, *Propos sur le champs politique* (Lyons, 2000), p. 6.
4. Achim Landwehr, 'Das Sichtbare sichtbar machen. Annäherung an "Wissen" als Kategorie historischer Forschung', in Achim Landwehr (ed.), *Geschichte(n) der Wirklichkeit, Beiträge zur Sozial- und Kulturgeschichte des Wissens* (Augsburg, 2002), p. 76.
5. Michel Foucault, *Archäologie des Wissens* (Frankfurt am Main, 1994), pp. 42, 100.
6. Ibid., pp. 75, 92.
7. Bourdieu, *Propos sur le champs politique*, p. 52.
8. Rainer Diaz-Bone, *Kulturwelt, Diskurs und Lebensstil: Eine diskurstheoretische Erweiterung der bourdieuschen Distinktionstheorie* (Opladen, 2002), p. 55.
9. Landwehr, 'Das Sichtbare sichtbar machen', p. 85.
10. Ibid., p. 84.
11. In Iran, the term *roushanfekran* (literally: enlightened thinkers) was traditionally used as a substitute for the term 'intellectual' to designate professionals with a modern education, such as journalists, researchers, lawyers, doctors or engineers. In the 1980s, the term *roushanfekran-e dini* (religious intellectuals) was introduced to designate socially and politically engaged clerical and lay thinkers who sought to redefine the meaning of religion and its relation to politics, and this soon became a synonym for religious reformers (Mehrzad Boroujerdi, *Iranian Itellectuals and the West: The Tormented Triumph of Nativism* (Syracuse, 1996), p. 22).
12. The term clergy (*ruhaniyat*) is used here as a synonym for religious scholars (*olamā*). It is employed to designate those scholars who have followed the classical curriculum in a religious seminary (*madresse*) and thus does not include such figures as religious storytellers (*rouze khans*). Although the Shi'i clergy is

not as hierarchically and centrally organised as its Christian equivalent, it can, in its present form, be understood as a group which by its function, education and identity constitutes a class separate from the rest of the religious community.

13. Labelling the different political factions in Iran is difficult. It has rightly been alleged that designations such as right and left, moderate and radical, as well as conservative, pragmatist and reformist do not truly apply or do not fully reflect the factions' views. Nevertheless, I have retained these designations because they do at least partly reflect those views and because they are used by the factions themselves.

# Chapter 1    Montazeri's Path into Politics

1. Hossein-Ali Montazeri, *Matn-e kamel-e khaterat Ayatollah Hossein-Ali Montazeri* (Essen, 2001), p. 27.

2. Roy Mottahedeh, *Der Mantel des Propheten. Das Leben eines persischen Mullah zwischen Religion und Politik* (Munich, 1987), pp. 201–3.

3. Ibid., p. 200; Ervand Abrahamian, *Tortured Confessions: Prisons and Public Recantations in Modern Iran* (Berkeley, 1999), p. 26.

4. Mottahedeh, *Der Mantel des Propheten*, p. 208.

5. Ibid., p. 206.

6. When in 1928 a cleric dared admonish the Shah's mother (or wife, according to another version), who had briefly bared her head during a visit to the shrine in Qom, the Shah came to the city accompanied by an army detachment, entered the shrine in riding boots and beat (or kicked) the cleric who had reprimanded his mother. When in 1935 a crowd assembled in the shrine in Mashhad to listen to preachers criticising the regime, the army opened fire from the roofs, killing an unknown number of people (ibid., pp. 200, 54).

7. Ibid., p. 204.

8. Montazeri, *Khaterat*, p. 15.

9. Ibid., pp. 18, 27.

10. Mottahedeh, *Der Mantel des Propheten*, p. 203.

11. In the osuli school of Shi'ism each believer (*moqalled*) is required to choose from among the clerics a source of emulation (*marja'-e taqlid*) who acts as his guide and guardian in religious matters. The *moqalled* is required to respect the religious decrees (fatwas) issued by his *marja'* and to pay him his religious tax (*khoms*). The *maraje'-ye taqlid* are designated by their fellow clerics in an informal procedure. Any *mojtahed*, e.g. a cleric able to practise *ejtehād* (interpretation), who has published a religious treatise (*resāle-ye amali-ye*) in one of the major religious centres is eligible.

12. Montazeri, *Khaterat*, p. 36

13. Daniel Brumberg, *Reinventing Khomeini: The Struggle for Reform in Iran* (Chicago, 2001), p. 52.

14. Montazeri, *Khaterat*, p. 106.
15. Ibid., p. 109.
16. Montazeri like many traditional Muslims believed in randomly consulting the Qur'an for advice. In other aspects he also adhered to traditional beliefs and superstitions. Thus, he writes in his memoirs of several occasions when he found advice in his dreams. He also recounted having during a severe drought participated in a prayer for rain in Qom. As it actually rained over the followings days, he later advised other clerics to follow this practice (ibid., p. 166).
17. Ibid., p. 36.
18. Yann Richard, 'Hoseyn-'Ali Montazeri', *Orient,* September 1985, p. 303.
19. 'Gahshomar zendegi hazrat Ayatollah al-ozma Montazeri'. Available at www.am ontazeri.com/farsi/frame2.asp; Personal Email from Office of Ayatollah Montazeri (4 May 2014).
20. The concept of *marja'iyat* developed during the nineteenth century in the osuli school of Shi'ism. In the mid-nineteenth century for the first time a *marja'*, Sheikh Morteza Ansari (1800–64), was recognised by all clerics as the absolute authority (*marja'-e taqlid-e 'āmme*), whose rulings were binding on all other *marāje'-ye taqlid*. Since then this position has been only temporarily occupied, because mostly the clergy could not agree on one supreme authority.
21. Montazeri, *Khaterat*, p. 68.
22. Mottahedeh, *Der Mantel des Propheten*, p. 210.
23. Montazeri, *Khaterat*, p. 94.
24. Ibid., p. 83.
25. Ibid., p. 77.
26. Seyyed Mohammad Ali Taghavi, *The Flourishing of Islamic Reformism in Iran: Political Islamic Groups in Iran (1941–1961)* (New York, 2005), pp. 113–32.
27. Montazeri, *Khaterat*, p. 70.
28. Ibid., p. 74.
29. Ibid., p. 70.
30. Ibid., p. 80.
31. Ibid., p. 422.
32. A practical religious treatise (*resāle-ye amali-ye*) is a compilation of answers issued by a jurisprudent (*mojtahed*) in response to the questions posed to him by his followers (*moqaledin*). These answers touch on the practical aspects of religious principles and are designed to guide the pious in their daily conduct. The publication of a *resāle-ye amali-ye* is one of the preconditions for becoming a *marja'-e taqlid* (Katajun Amirpur, *Die Entpolitisierung des Islam: Abdolkarim Sorushs Denken und Wirkung in der Islamischen Republik Iran* (Würzburg, 2003), p. 61).
33. Montazeri, *Khaterat*, pp. 102–10.
34. Ibid., p. 113.
35. Nikki R. Keddie, *Modern Iran: Roots and Results of Revolution* (New Haven, 1981), p. 156.
36. Montazeri, *Khaterat*, p. 114.
37. Ibid., p. 115.

38. Ibid., p. 118.
39. Mehrzad Boroujerdi, *Iranian Intellectuals and the West: The Tormented Triumph of Nativism* (Syracuse, 1996), p. 81.
40. Ibid., p. 82.
41. Montazeri, *Khaterat*, p. 118.
42. Ibid., p. 114.
43. Brumberg, *Reinventing Khomeini,* p. 74.
44. Keddie, *Modern Iran*, p. 158.
45. Montazeri, *Khaterat*, p. 126.
46. Ibid., p. 129.
47. Montazeri, *Khaterat*, p. 139; Mottahedeh, *Der Mantel des Propheten*, p. 217.
48. Keddie, *Modern Iran*, p. 158.
49. Said Amir Arjomand, 'Constitution-Making in Islamic Iran: The Impact of Theocracy on the Legal Order of a Nation-State', in June Starr and Jane Collier (eds), *History and Power in the Study of Law, New Directions in Legal Anthropology* (New York, 1989), p. 121.
50. Seyyed Ruhollah Khomeini, *Islamic Government: The Guardianship of the Jurisprudent (Hokumat-e eslami: Velayat-e faqih)* (Tehran, 2002), p. 16.
51. At the time of its publication, the book seems to have received only limited attention as Khomeini was still a fairly young cleric, little known outside the clerical circles of Qom. Today the book is no longer published in Iran and can only be bought second-hand. The reason is probably that many of the ideas exposed therein were not consistent with his later writings, notably *Velayat-e faqih*. The only copy I was able to obtain did not contain a date of publication, and is therefore cited as 'no date'.
52. In the book, Khomeini called on the public to act against these 'heretics'. In March 1946, Kasravi was murdered by Navab Safavi on the way to a trial for blasphemy. Safavi possibly acted on the inspiration of '*Kashf al-Asrar*' and had reportedly received religious approval and financial support from several senior clerics.
53. Seyyed Ruhollah Khomeini, *Kashf al-asrar* (Qom, no date), pp. 223, 224.
54. Ibid., pp. 181–5.
55. Ibid., pp. 232–3.
56. Ibid., p. 222.
57. Mohsen Kadivar, 'Sir-e tahavol-e andishe siasi Ayatollah Montazeri' (1390 SH). Available at http://kadivar.com/?p=5568.
58. Taghavi, *Flourishing of Islamic Reformism*, pp. 113–32; Sohrab Behdad, 'Utopia of Assassins: Navvab Safavi and the Fadaiyan-e Islam in Prerevolutionary Iran', in Ramin Jahanbegloo (ed.), *Iran: Between Tradition and Modernity* (Oxford, 2004), p. 77.
59. Kadivar, 'Sir-e tahavol'.
60. Boroujerdi, *Iranian Intellectuals*, pp. 14, 24.
61. Brumberg, *Reinventing Khomeini*, p. 64.
62. Jalal Al-e Ahmad, 'The Outline of a Disease', in Lloyd Ridgeon (ed.), *Religion and Politics in Modern Iran: A Reader* (New York, 2005).

63. Khomeini, *Islamic Government*, p. 19.
64. Ibid., p. 29.
65. Ibid., p. 42.
66. Ibid., p. 45.
67. Ibid., p. 64.
68. Ibid., p. 136
69. Mottahedeh, *Der Mantel des Propheten*, p. 308.
70. Montazeri, *Khaterat*, p. 423.
71. Ibid., p. 142.
72. Ibid., p. 423.
73. Ibid., p. 144.
74. Yann Richard, 'L'islam politique en Iran', *Politique Etrangère*, Spring (2005), pp. 61–72.
75. Azadeh Kian-Thiebaut, *Secularization of Iran a Doomed Failure? The New Middle Class and the Making of Modern Iran* (Paris, 1998).
76. Abrahamian, *Tortured Confessions*, p. 89.
77. Kian-Thiebaut, *Secularization of Iran*, pp. 152–69.
78. Asghar Schirazi, *The Constitution of Iran, Politics and the State in the Islamic Republic* (New York, 1997), p. 129.
79. Wilfried Buchta, *Who rules Iran? The Structure of Power in the Islamic Republic* (Washington DC, 2000), pp. 111–16.
80. Forough Jahanbakhsh, *Islam, Democracy and Religious Modernism in Iran (1953– 2000): From Bazargan to Soroush* (Leiden, 2001), pp. 119–26.
81. Vanessa Martin, *Creating an Islamic State: Khomeini and the Making of a New Iran* (London, 2000), p. 92.
82. Abrahamian, *Tortured Confessions*, p. 102.
83. Montazeri, *Khaterat*, p. 188
84. Ibid., p. 191.
85. Ibid., p. 155.
86. Ibid., p. 161.
87. Hossein-Ali Montazeri, 'Nazari bar zendegi kutah amma por az jehad va mobareze ostad shahid Mohammad Montazeri'. Available at www.amontazeri.com/Farsi/article_read.asp?id=338.
88. Montazeri, *Khaterat*, p. 172.
89. Since the publication of Salehi's work in 1969, more than a dozen books have been written in refutation of his theories (Buchta, *Who rules Iran?* pp. 93, 100). Ahmad Khomeini claimed that in 1989 parts of the clergy had still not forgiven Montazeri for his defence of the book (Seyyed Ahmad Khomeini, 'Ranjname', *Majmu'e azar-e yadgar-e imam*, Vol. 2 (Tehran 1375/1996), p. 147). Salehi later wrote a book on the conspiracy of the Savak against Khomeini. Montazeri's critique was printed in Montazeri, *Enteqad az khod*, p. 14.
90. Montazeri, *Khaterat*, p. 167.
91. Ibid., p. 169.
92. Ibid., p. 175.

93. Mottahedeh, *Der Mantel des Propheten*, p. 291.
94. Ervand Abrahamian, 'The Structural Causes of the Iranian Revolution', *Merip Reports 87: Iran's Revolution: The Rural Dimension*, May (1980), p. 25.
95. Montazeri, *Khaterat*, p. 211.
96. Ibid., p. 215.

## Chapter 2   The Invention of a New System

1. Hossein-Ali Montazeri, *Matn-e kamel-e khaterat Ayatollah Hossein-Ali Montazeri* (Essen, 2001), p. 436.
2. Azadeh Kian-Thiebaut, *Secularization of Iran a Doomed Failure? The New Middle Class and the Making of Modern Iran* (Paris, 1998), p. 158.
3. Ibid., p. 158.
4. Mohsen Kadivar, *Hokumat-e vela'i* (Tehran 1377/1998), p. 174.
5. Ibid., p. 176.
6. Montazeri, *Khaterat*, p. 233.
7. Ibid., p. 233.
8. Ibid., p. 240.
9. Ibid., p. 451.
10. Arjomand distinguishes two phases in the debate on the constitutional role of Islam in the Muslim world: in the first phase, up to the 1950s - and thus also in the Iranian constitution of 1906 – the shari'a was perceived as a *limitation* to legislation and government, while in the second phase it was increasingly viewed as the *basis* of the constitution and the state. The draft of 1979 appears in line with the former concept as it considered the shari'a as a *limitation* rather than as the *basis* of legislation (Said Amir Arjomand, 'Islam and Constitutionalism since the Nineteenth Century: The Significance and Pecularities of Iran', in Arjomand (ed.), *Constitutional Politics in the Middle East* (Oxford, 2007), p. 33).
11. Siavush Randjbar-Daemi, 'Building the Islamic State: The Draft Constitution of 1979 Reconsidered', *Iranian Studies*, 64.4 (2013), p. 647.
12. Different notions are employed in the official and scholarly discourse to designate the ruling jurist. In Iran both *vali-ye faqih* (ruling jurist, literally 'ruler-jurist') or *rahbar-e enqelāb* (revolutionary leader) are employed as official designation. While the first emphasises the religious aspect the second refers more to the political function. In the West the designation 'supreme leader' or 'supreme jurist' is also used, but shall not be employed here.
13. Randjbar-Daemi, 'Building the Islamic State', p. 652.
14. Said Amir Arjomand, 'Constitution-Making in Islamic Iran: The Impact of Theocracy on the Legal Order of a Nation-State', in June Starr and Jane Collier (eds), *History and Power in the Study of Law, New Directions in Legal Anthropology* (New York, 1989), p. 121.
15. Randjbar-Daemi, 'Building the Islamic State', p. 653.

16. Said Saffari, 'The Legitimation of the Clergy's Right to Rule in the Iranian Constitution of 1979 ', *British Journal of Middle Eastern Studies*, Vol. 20, No. 1 (1993), p. 66.

17. Kadivar, *Hokumat-e vela'i*, p. 176.

18. Montazeri, *Khaterat*, p. 256.

19. Brumberg, *Reinventing Khomeini: The Struggle for Reform in Iran* (Chicago, 2001), p. 101.

20. After the revolution Khomeini was officially addressed as 'Imam'. At first he rejected this title and insisted that he be called 'representative of the Imam'. He rightly feared that the title, which in Shi'ism is traditionally reserved for the 12 Imams, would be perceived as a presumption by other clerics, as it conjured up the impression, that he was the expected Mahdi. However, he soon abandoned resistance to being addressed with this title.

21. Montazeri, *Khaterat*, p. 238.

22. Tawfiq Alsaif, *Islamic Democracy and its Limits: The Iranian Experience since 1979* (Beirut, 2007), p. 145; Baqer Moin, *Khomeini: Life of the Ayatollah* (London, 1999), p. 210.

23. In the referendum the questions were phrased in such a way that rejecting the Islamic republic meant supporting the monarchical regime. Furthermore, the card for the yes-vote was green, the colour of Islam, while the card for the no-vote was red, the colour of Yazid. Officially, the turnout was 75 per cent and the rate of approval 98.2 per cent.

24. 'Ayatollah Montazeri: Imam Khomeini riasat-e jomhuri nakhahand paziraft', *Etela'at*, 26 Khordad 1358 SH.

25. Hossein-Ali Montazeri, 'Khastar tajdid-e nazar dar asl 8 qanun-e assassi shod', *Keyhan*, 3 Tir 1358 SH.

26. Montazeri, *Khaterat*, p. 451.

27. Ibid., p. 452.

28. Ibid., p. 253.

29. Asghar Schirazi, *The Constitution of Iran, Politics and the State in the Islamic Republic* (London, 1997), p. 31.

30. Ervand Abrahamian, *Tortured Confessions: Prisons and Public Recantations in Modern Iran* (Berkeley, 1999), p. 125.

31. Saffari, 'The Legitimation of the Clergy's Right to Rule', p. 67.

32. Behrooz Ghamari-Tabrizi, *Islam and Dissent in Postrevolutionary Iran: Abdolkarim Soroush, Religious Politics and Democratic Reform* (London, 2008), p. 69.

33. Seyyed Ruhollah Khomeini, 'Payam-e tarikhi Imam Khomeini be majles barrasi-ye qanun-e assassi', *Etela'at*, 28 Mordad 1358 SH.

34. Ibid.

35. Montazeri, *Khaterat*, p. 256.

36. Ibid., p. 251.

37. Saffari, 'The Legitimation of the Clergy's Right to Rule', p. 68.

38. 'Ejlas emruz majles-e khabregan', *Keyhan*, 2 Sharivar 1358 SH.

39. Ghamari-Tabrizi, *Islam and Dissent in Postrevolutionary Iran*, p. 65.

40. Montazeri, *Khaterat*, p. 254.
41. Schirazi, *The Constitution of Iran*, p. 46.
42. Saffari, 'The Legitimation of the Clergy's Right to Rule', p. 72.
43. Ibid.
44. Ghamari-Tabrizi, *Islam and Dissent in Postrevolutionary Iran*, pp. 68–9.
45. Ibid.
46. Arjomand, 'Constitution-Making in Islamic Iran', p. 122.
47. Saffari, 'The Legitimation of the Clergy's Right to Rule', p. 74.
48. Ibid.
49. Arjomand, 'Constitution-Making in Islamic Iran', p. 122.
50. Although Ahmad Khomeini had little political or religious capital of his own, he pursued a political line independent of his father. After the revolution he was part of the 'Third Line', which was critical of both the provisional government and the Islamic Republican Party. He was close to the Mojahedin-e Khalq and advocated their inclusion in the political field. This was opposed by his father and other members of the 'Third Line' (Anonymous).
51. Ghamari-Tabrizi, *Islam and Dissent in Postrevolutionary Iran*, p. 62.
52. Brumberg, *Reinventing Khomeini*, p. 106.
53. Ghamari-Tabrizi, *Islam and Dissent in Postrevolutionary Iran*, p. 62.
54. Mohsen Kadivar, 'Sir-e tahavol-e andishe siasi Ayatollah Montazeri', 1390 SH, Available at http://kadivar.com/?p=5568.
55. 'Ayatollah Montazeri: Aza-ye shura-ha ra az qashr-ha-ye mokhtalef entkehab konid', *Etela'at*, 31 Sharivar 1358 SH.
56. Moin, *Khomeini*, p. 218.
57. Nikki R. Keddie, *Modern Iran: Roots and Results of Revolution* (New Haven, 1981), p. 194.
58. Saffari, 'The Legitimation of the Clergy's Right to Rule', p. 78.
59. 'Bozorgtarin namaz jom'eh tarikh bar mezar-e shohada', *Keyhan,* 24 Sharivar 1358 SH.
60. 'Ayatollah Montazeri: Aza-ye shura-ha', *Etela'at*, 31 Sharivar 1358 SH.
61. Kadivar, 'Sir-e tahavol'.
62. Saffari, 'The Legitimation of the Clergy's Right to Rule', p. 80.
63. In 1981, Shariatmadari was accused of backing a military coup by Qotbzadeh against the regime. While Qotbzadeh was executed, Shariatmadari was forced to confess and repent in a public show trial. In an unprecedented move, a clerical assembly stripped him of his title and status as *marja'-e taqlid*. When he died in 1985 he was refused an official funeral, a step which shocked many clerics (Moin, *Khomeini*, p. 252; Abrahamian, *Tortured Confessions*, p. 157; Montazeri, *Khaterat*, p. 276).
64. Hossein-Ali Montazeri, *Enteqad az khod* (Qom, 2011), pp. 26, 30, 164–8.

## Chapter 3    The Difficult Consolidation of the Regime

1. Asghar Schirazi, *The Constitution of Iran: Politics and the State in the Islamic Republic* (London, 1997), p. 188.
2. Homa Omid, *Islam and the Post-Revolutionary State in Iran* (London, 1994), pp. 98–101.
3. According to Abrahamian, between June and November 1981 a total of 2,665 political prisoners were executed. The number of victims of the armed internal conflict had climbed to 5,000 by August 1983, and 12,500 by June 1985. Of the 7,943 executed by this date, 6,472 were from the Mojahedin, 350 from the Fedaiyan-e Khalq, 255 from Peykar (a Marxist offshoot of the Mojahedin) and 171 from Kurdish parties (Ervand Abrahamian, *Tortured Confessions: Prisons and Public Recantations in Modern Iran* (Berkeley, 1999), p. 129; Baqer Moin, *Khomeini: Life of the Ayatollah* (London, 1999), p. 233).
4. Abrahamian, *Tortured Confessions*.
5. Schirazi, *The Constitution of Iran*, pp. 161–221.
6. Hossein-Ali Montazeri, *Matn-e kamel-e khaterat Ayatollah Hossein-Ali Montazeri* (Essen, 2001), p. 292.
7. Schirazi, *The Constitution of Iran,* pp. 172, 200.
8. Mehdi Moslem, *Factional Politics in Post-Khomeini Iran* (New York, 2002), p. 73.
9. Daniel Brumberg, *Reinventing Khomeini: The Struggle for Reform in Iran* (Chicago, 2001), p. 135.
10. Montazeri, *Khaterat*, p. 459.
11. Ibid., p. 247.
12. Omid, *Islam and the Post-Revolutionary State*, p. 96.
13. Montazeri, *Khaterat*, p. 257.
14. Ibid., p. 271.
15. Ibid., p. 273.
16. On Montazeri's recommendation Taleqani was appointed the first Friday Imam in Tehran. On Taleqani's death in September 1979, Montazeri assumed the function himself until November, when he returned to Qom. On his recommendation Khamene'i was appointed his successor. Since the prayer leader in Qom had become too old, Montazeri also briefly assumed the post in Qom, but withdrew to his studies at the end of the year (ibid., p. 246).
17. Ibid., p. 459; Mohammad Mohammadi Reyshahri, *Khaterat, jeld-e chaharom* (Tehran, 1388 SH), p. 29.
18. Montazeri, *Khaterat*, p. 459.
19. Ibid., p. 265.
20. Ibid., p. 266. Sadeq Ruhani remained, with some interruptions, under arrest in his house in Qom and was not permitted to give courses, lead prayers or publish any works. Grand Ayatollah Hassan Tabatabai-Qomi in Mashhad also voiced his opposition to Montazeri's designation. He had already been placed under house arrest in 1984 for having criticised the system. He remained there until his death in 2007 (Miriam Künkler, 'The Special Court of the Clergy

(*Dadgah-e Vizheh-ye Ruhaniyat*) and the Repression of Dissident Clergy in Iran,'
in Said Amir Arjomand and Nathan Brown (eds), *Constitutionalism, the Rule of
Law and the Politics of Administration in Egypt and Iran* (New York, 2012), p. 3).

21. Wilfried Buchta, 'Die Islamische Republik Iran und die religiös-politische
Kontroverse um die marja'iyat', *Orient*, September (1995), p. 463.

22. Montazeri, *Khaterat*, p. 508.

23. Ibid., p. 270.

24. Ibid., p. 248

25. Moin, *Khomeini*, p. 228.

26. Montazeri, *Khaterat*, p. 508.

27. Ibid., p. 457. The unlawful confiscation of agricultural and industrial property
much alarmed Montazeri, and he repeatedly complained about it to Khomeini.
When he heard that huge estates seized for the Bonyad-e Mostaz'afin
(Foundation of the Deprived) had dried up, he bitterly remarked to the leader
that they were acting in the name of the deprived but in reality did nothing for
them (ibid., p. 248).

28. Omid, *Islam and the Post-Revolutionary State*, pp. 97, 102.

29. Montazeri, *Khaterat*, p. 491.

30. Ibid., p. 508.

31. Hossein-Ali Montazeri, *Enteqad az khod* (Qom, 1390 SH), pp. 92–4.

32. Abrahamian, *Tortured Confessions*, p. 136; Maziar Behrooz, 'Reflections on Iran's
Prison System during the Montazeri Years (1985–88)', *Iran Analysis Quaterly*,
Winter (2005), p. 17.

33. Montazeri, *Khaterat*, p. 284.

34. Ibid., p. 285.

35. Ibid., p. 285.

36. Ibid., p. 174; Iran Human Rights Documentation Centre, *Deadly Fatwa: Iran's
1988 Prison Massacre*, September (2009), p. 10.

37. Montazeri, *Khaterat*, pp. 286, 510; Kambiz Behi, 'The "Real" in Resistance:
Transgression of Law as Ethical Act', *Unbound*, 30 (2008), p. 36.

38. Behrooz, 'Reflections on Iran's Prison System', p. 19; Geoffrey Robertson,
*The Massacre of Political Prisoners in Iran, 1988* (London, 2011), p. 35.

39. Montazeri, *Khaterat*, p. 510.

40. Hossein-Ali Montazeri, *Mabani-e fehqi-ye hokumat-e eslami, Vol. I: Doulat va
hokumat* (Tehran, 1368 SH), p. 204.

41. Ibid., pp. 74–5.

42. Hossein-Ali Montazeri, *Az aqaz ta anjam: Goftogu-ye do daneshju* (Qom,
1388 SH).

43. Montazeri, *Mabani-e fehqi, Vol. I*, p. 88.

44. Hossein-Ali Montazeri, *Mabani-e fehqi-ye hokumat-e eslami Vol. II: Emamat va
rahbari* (Tehran, 1369 SH), pp. 295–303.

45. Ibid., p. 287.

46. Ibid., p. 200.

47. Ibid., pp. 366–90.

48. Montazeri, *Mabani-e fehqi, Vol. I*, p. 93.
49. Montazeri, *Khaterat*, p. 109.
50. Mohsen Kadivar, 'Sir-e tahavol-e andishe siasi Ayatollah Montazeri', 1390 SH. Available at http://kadivar.com/?p=5568.
51. Montazeri, *Enteqad az khod*, pp. 26, 30; Kadivar, 'Sir-e tahavol'.
52. Farhang Rajaee, *Islamism and Modernism: The Changing Discourse in Iran* (Austin, 2007), pp. 173–8.
53. Thomas Fourquet, 'Le chiisme élitiste de l'ayatollah Mesbah Yazdi', *Maghreb-Machrek*, Winter (2006/2007).

## Chapter 4   An Inconvenient Successor

1. Hossein-Ali Montazeri, *Matn-e kamel-e khaterat Ayatollah Hossein-Ali Montazeri* (Essen, 2001), p. 508.
2. Mustafa Izadi, *A Glance at the Life Ayatullah Montazeri* (Tehran, 1984), p. 26.
3. Eric Hooglund (ed.), 'In Search for Iran's Moderates', *Merip Reports*, No. 144, January/February (1987), p. 6.
4. 'Dustan-e Mohammad Montazeri pas az khal'-e selah afrad forudgah, u ra ba khod bordand', *Keyhan*, 24 Sharivar 1358 SH; 'Ayatollah Montazeri khastar bazdasht va mo'aleje-ye Mohammad Montazeri shod', *Keyhan*, 30 Sharivar 1358 SH.
5. 'Montazeri Jr to Send 17.000 Youths to Help Lebanese Struggle', *Tehran Times*, 6 December 1979; 'Montazeri's Teenage Army Occupies Airport Lounge', *Tehran Times*, 13 December 1979.
6. Samuel Segev, *The Iranian Triangle: The Untold Story of Israel's Role in the Iran-Contra Affair* (New York, 1988), p. 124.
7. Hossein-Ali Montazeri, *Enteqad az khod* (Qom, 1390 SH), p. 70.
8. Montazeri, *Khaterat*, p. 510.
9. Wilfried Buchta, *Die iranische Schia und die islamische Einheit 1979–1996* (Hamburg, 1997), pp. 137–47; Anonymous, *Vaq'iyat-ha va qezavat-ha* (no date). The latter available at www.amontazeri.com/farsi/frame4.asp.
10. Segev, *The Iranian Triangle*, pp. 125–8.
11. Magnus Ranstorp, *Hizb'allah in Lebanon: The Politics of the Western Hostage Crisis* (Basingstoke, 1997), p. 34.
12. Ibid., pp. 81–5.
13. Ibid., p. 90.
14. Ibid., pp. 91–3.
15. Montazeri, *Khaterat*, p. 333.
16. Baqer Moin, *Khomeini: Life of the Ayatollah* (London, 1988), p. 199.
17. Wilfried Buchta, 'Mehdi Hashemi's Fall: An Episode of Intra Elite Struggle for Power under Khomeini', in Mohammad M. Ansari (ed.), *Iran Today: Twenty Five Years after the Revolution* (New Delhi, 2005), p. 216; Anonymous, *Vaq'iyat-ha va qezavat-ha*.

18. Montazeri claimed that he had been in favour of accepting a ceasefire in 1982, but that he had decided to remain silent because an open dispute in the leadership would have weakened the regime. However, there is no written proof for this claim. According to Rafsanjani, Montazeri advocated carrying the war into Iraq. In light of his former fervour for the export of the revolution, this latter account has some credibility (Montazeri, *Enteqad*, pp. 104–11).

19. Segev, *The Iranian Triangle*, pp. 141–6

20. Since 1980, rumours about secret arms deals between Iran and the USA and Israel had repeatedly appeared in the Western press. In 1980, the delivery of weapons had reputedly been part of the deal to end the hostage crisis in the US Embassy (Edward Said, 'Irangate: A Many-Sided Crisis', *Journal of Palestine Studies*, Summer (1987), p. 38).

21. Theodore Draper, *A Very Thin Line: The Iran-Contra Affairs* (New York, 1991), pp. 155–202.

22. Ibid., pp. 315–30.

23. Montazeri, *Khaterat*, pp. 320, 335, 493–9.

24. The intervention was possibly also in response to another affair: on 9 August, passengers of an Iran Air flight from Isfahan on their way to the Hajj were arrested by Saudi authorities upon arrival in Jiddah with explosives hidden in their baggage. Hashemi was accused of having smuggled the explosives aboard the plane to stage attacks in Mecca in order to disrupt a tentative rapprochement with Riyadh (Jacob Goldberg, 'The Saudi Arabian Kingdom', in Itamar Rabinovich and Haim Shaked (eds), *Middle East Contemporary Survey, Volume X: 1986* (London, 1988), p. 556; Montazeri, *Khaterat*, p. 510). While there are doubts that Hashemi was truly responsible, the affair possibly persuaded his rivals to finally intervene against his group.

25. Mohammad Mohammadi Reyshahri, *Khatere-ha*, Vol. IV (Tehran, 1388 SH), p. 73.

26. Ibid., p. 85.

27. Montazeri, *Khaterat*, p. 508.

28. Ibid., p. 509.

29. Ibid., p. 510.

30. Ibid.

31. Draper, *A Very Thin Line*, p. 452.

32. Segev, *The Iranian Triangle*, p. 283.

33. Reyshahri, *Khatere-ha*, p. 184.

34. Ibid., p. 189.

35. Ibid., p. 167; Montazeri, *Khaterat*, p. 338.

36. Montazeri, *Khaterat*, p. 332; Anonymous, *Vaq'iyat-ha va qezavat-ha*; Hashemi possibly acted on the inspiration of Khomeini, who had written in *Velayat-e faqih* that the court clergy should be punished: 'Our youths must strip them of their turbans. The turbans of the akhunds, who cause corruption in Muslim society while claiming to be *foqahā* and *olamā*, must be removed. [...] They do not need to be beaten much; just take off their turbans and do not permit them

to appear in public wearing turbans' (Seyyed Ruhollah Khomeini, *Islamic Government: The Guardianship of the Jurisprudent (Hokumat-e eslami: Velayat-e faqih)* (Tehran, 2003), p. 135).

37. Reyshahri, *Khatere-ha*, p. 131.
38. Ibid., p. 233.
39. Ibid.
40. Wilfried Buchta, 'Die Inquisition in der Islamischen Republik Iran. Einige Anmerkungen zum Sondergericht für die Geistlichkeit', in Rainer Brunner (ed.), *Islamstudien ohne Ende* (Würzburg, 2002), p. 72; for the complete text of the verdict see Reyshahri, *Khatere-ha*, p. 269.
41. Montazeri, *Khaterat*, p. 519.
42. Ibid., p. 519.
43. In his memoirs Montazeri refers to an article in *al-Shira* from 21 April 1997 in which Reyshahri is quoted as having said that in spite of a telephone call from Ahmad Khomeini he had Mehdi Hashemi executed. In his own memoirs Reyshahri denounced this account as false and baseless (Reyshahri, *Khatere-ha*, p. 279).
44. Montazeri, *Khaterat*, p. 340; Buchta, *Die Inquisition*, p. 72.
45. Reyshahri, *Khatere-ha*, p. 126.
46. Montazeri, *Khaterat*, p. 500; Anonymous, *Vaq'iyat-ha va qezavat-ha*.
47. Montazeri, *Khaterat*, p. 337.
48. Homa Omid, *Islam and the Post-Revolutionary State in Iran* (London, 1994), p. 138.
49. Montazeri, *Khaterat*, p. 520.
50. Iran Human Rights Documentation Centre, *Deadly Fatwa: Iran's 1988 Prison Massacre*, September (2009), p. 10; Montazeri and others indicate that a purge of the prisons had long been discussed among hardliners, but there is no evidence that the massacres had actually been planned in advance (Geoffrey Robertson, *The Massacre of Political Prisoners in Iran, 1988* (London, 2011), p. 90. Available at www.iranrights.org/library/document/1380/the-massacre-of-political-pris oners-in-iran-1988-report-of-an-inquiry).
51. Khomeini and the regime commonly referred to the Mojahedin-e Khalq because of their heterodox religious beliefs with the Koranic term '*monafeqin*', i.e. the hypocrites.
52. Montazeri, *Khaterat*, p. 519.
53. Ibid., p. 346.
54. Ibid., p. 519.
55. Ibid.
56. Ibid., p. 350.
57. Iran Human Rights Documentation Centre, *Deadly Fatwa*.
58. Montazeri, *Khaterat*, p. 520.
59. Ahmadi sent Montazeri a copy of a letter he had written to Khomeini, in which he pointed out that a prisoner's refusal to go to the front is no proof for his opposition and no reason for his execution, as many Iranians were unwilling to participate in the war. In this letter he mentioned the case of one Mohammad

Reza Ashouq. This Mojahedin member later managed to escape on the way to the firing squad (Montazeri, *Khaterat*, p. 522; Robertson, *The Massacre of Political Prisoners*, pp. 54, 61).

60. Montazeri, *Khaterat*, p. 521.
61. Ibid., p. 521,
62. Ibid., p. 347.
63. Ibid., p. 346.
64. Ibid., p. 521.
65. Ibid., p. 347.
66. Ervand Abrahamian, *Tortured Confessions: Prisons and Public Recantations in Modern Iran* (Berkeley, 1999), p. 215.
67. Montazeri, *Khaterat*, p. 345.
68. Iran Human Rights Documentation Centre, *Deadly Fatwa*, p. 3.
69. Ibid, p. 49; Robertson, *The Massacre of Political Prisoners*, p. 6
70. Moin, *Khomeini*, p. 281.
71. Montazeri, *Khaterat*, p. 477.
72. Ibid., p. 525.
73. Moin, *Khomeini*, p. 280.
74. Ibid., p. 281.
75. Ibid., p. 283.
76. Ibid., p. 284.
77. Ibid., p. 285; for the full text see Reyshahri, *Khatere-ha*, p. 296.
78. Montazeri, *Khaterat*, p. 538.
79. Ibid., p. 528.
80. In February 1989, the Tehran representative of the BBC Farsi service reportedly came to Montazeri's house in Qom. During a meeting with Hadi Hashemi, he asked to be given Montazeri's letter of protest against the prison purges, of which he had learnt through a member of the judiciary. According to this account, it later became known that the BBC representative acted on behalf of the Intelligence Ministry (Anonymous, *Vaq'iyat-ha va qezavat-ha*).
81. Montazeri, *Khaterat*, p. 538.
82. Ibid., p. 362.
83. Ibid., p. 539; in his memoirs Montazeri insists that he never employed the word *este'fā'* (resignation) in his letter. He argued that the Expert Council had not elected him, but only confirmed his 'election' by the people. Because he had never been appointed or elected as deputy leader, he could not resign, and much less be deposed, from this post.
84. Khomeini's letter of 26 March 1989 was only published after Montazeri's controversial speech in November 1997 – by his opponents, who therewith hoped to discredit Montazeri.
85. Montazeri, *Khaterat*, p. 367.
86. Ibid., p. 540
87. Moin, *Khomeini*, p. 290.
88. Ibid., p. 293.

89. Seyyed Ahmad Khomeini, 'Ranjname', in *Majmu'e azar-e yadgar-e imam. Vol. II* (Tehran, 1375 SH), p. 178.
90. Ibid., p. 201.
91. Ibid., p. 184.
92. Moin, *Khomeini*, p. 291.
93. Ibid., p. 289.
94. In early 1980, Banisadr had proposed nominating Ahmad as his prime minister, but Khomeini had refused to give his consent. He reportedly also later refused to allow his son to enter politics as long as he was alive. When his father's death was imminent, Ahmad apparently saw his chance. In an interview published in 1994, he claimed that he had pushed for the removal of Montazeri after Khamene'i and Rafsanjani had promised to help him in his bid for the succession (Anonymous, *Vaq'iyat-ha va qezavat-ha;* Katajun Amirpur, *Die Entpolitisierung des Islam: Abdolkarim Sorushs Denken und Wirkung in der Islamischen Republik Iran* (Würzburg, 2003), p. 76). In the end Ahmad Khomeini not only lost the race for the leadership but also much of his power, and only played a minor role until his death in March 1995. Officially, he died of a heart attack, but it was rumoured that he was poisoned by the intelligence service, as, one month prior to his death, he had attacked Khamene'i in a public speech, holding him responsible for the failures of the regime. Reportedly, Ahmad also regretted the publication of *Ranjname* (Montazeri, *Khaterat*, p. 394; 'How Did Haj Ahmad Khomeini die?' (English translation), *Aftab-e Yazd*, 25 September 2000. Available at www.netnative.com/news/00/sep/1113.html).
95. Moin, *Khomeini*, p. 299.
96. Ibid., p. 309.
97. Ibid., p. 310.
98. Wilfried Buchta, *Who rules Iran? The Structure of Power in the Islamic Republic* (Washington DC, 2000), p. 127.
99. Daniel Brumberg, *Reinventing Khomeini: The Struggle for Reform in Iran* (Chicago, 2001), p. 143; Henner Fürtig, *Liberalisierung als Herausforderung: Wie stabil ist die Islamische Republik Iran?* (Berlin, 1996), p. 24.
100. Asghar Schirazi, *The Constitution of Iran, Politics and the State in the Islamic Republic* (New York, 1997), p. 110.
101. Brumberg, *Reinventing Khomeini*, p. 147.
102. Montazeri, *Khaterat*, p. 273.
103. Ibid., p. 583.
104. Ibid., p. 585.
105. Brumberg, *Reinventing Khomeini*, p. 172.

## Chapter 5    Political Crisis and the Debate on Reform

1. Mehdi Moslem, *Factional Politics in Post-Khomeini Iran* (New York, 2002), p. 146.
2. Rainer Hermann, 'Von der Wirtschafts- zur Legitimationskrise: Die Ära Khamenei/Rafsanjani in der Islamischen Republik Iran', *Orient*, 4 (1994), p. 550.

3. Ibid., p. 552.
4. Farzin Sarabi, 'The Post-Khomeini Era in Iran: The Elections of the Fourth Islamic Majlis', *Middle East Journal*, Winter (1994), p. 93.
5. Moslem, *Factional Politics*, p. 171.
6. Katajun Amirpur, *Die Entpolitisierung des Islam: Abdolkarim Sorushs Denken und Wirkung in der Islamischen Republik Iran* (Würzburg, 2003), p. 140.
7. Ziba Mir-Hosseini and Richard Tapper, *Islam and Democracy in Iran: Eshkevari and the Quest for Reform* (London, 2006), pp. 74–95.
8. Sarabi, 'The Post-Khomeini Era', pp. 92–6.
9. Moslem, *Factional Politics*, p. 186.
10. Ibid., pp. 215–18.
11. Geneive Abdo and Jonathan Lyons, *Answering only to God: Faith and Freedom in Twenty-First-Century Iran* (New York, 2003), p. 108.
12. Ali Mirsepassi, *Democracy in modern Iran: Islam, Culture and Political Change* (New York, 2010), pp. 145, 135.
13. Ahmad Sadri and Mahmud Sadri (eds), *Reason, Freedom and Democracy in Islam: Essential Writings of Abdolkarim Soroush* (Oxford, 2002), p. 28.
14. Iran's religious reformers of the 1980s and 1990s can be understood as the heirs to modernists such as the Indian scholar and politician Seyyed Ahmad Khan or the Pakistani poet and philosopher Mohammad Iqbal, and as direct descendants of progressive Iranian intellectuals such as Naini, Kasravi, Motahhari, Shari'ati and Bazargan.
15. Amirpur, *Abdolkarim Sorushs Denken*, p. 10.
16. Sadri and Sadri, *Essential Writings*, pp. 3–25.
17. Behrooz Ghamari-Tabrizi, *Islam and Dissent in Postrevolutionary Iran: Abdolkarim Soroush, Religious Politics and Democratic Reform* (London, 2008), p. 36.
18. Sadri and Sadri, *Essential Writings*, p. 31.
19. Ibid., p. 37.
20. Amirpur, *Abdolkarim Sorushs Denken*, p. 89.
21. Sadri and Sadri, *Essential Writings*, p. 102.
22. Amirpur, *Abdolkarim Sorushs Denken*, p. 183.
23. Ibid., p. 179.
24. Ibid., p. 183.
25. Mohammad Mojtahed Shabestari, 'Tchera bayad andishe-ye dini ra naqd kard?', *Kiyan*, No. 18 (1373 SH), p. 16.
26. Ibid., p. 18.
27. Mohammad Mojtahed Shabestari, 'Motun-e dini va jahanbini-ye naqd-e tarikhi', *Kiyan*, No. 26 (1374 SH), p. 24.
28. Mir-Hosseini and Tapper, *Islam and Democracy*, pp. 41–8.
29. Hassan Yussefi Eshkevari, 'Kasrat gerā'i dar nazar va vahdat gerā'i dar amal', *Kiyan*, No. 39, (1377 SH), p. 32.
30. Ibid., p. 33.
31. Hossein-Ali Montazeri, *Safir-e haq va safir-e vahi* (Tehran, 1387 SH).
32. Sadri and Sadri, *Essential Writings*, p. 61.

33. Akbar Ganji, 'Mashru'iyat, velayat va vekalat', *Kiyan*, No. 13 (1372 SH), pp. 22–30.
34. Sadri and Sadri, *Essential Writings*, p. 61.
35. Mir-Hosseini and Tapper, *Islam and Democracy*, pp. 65–70.
36. Sadri and Sadri, *Essential Writings*, p. 128.
37. Hamid Peydar, 'Paradoks-e eslām va demokrasi', *Kiyan*, No. 20 (1373 SH), pp. 23–6.
38. Hassan Yussefi Eshkevari, 'Paradoks-e eslām va demokrasi?', *Kiyan*, No. 21 (1373 SH), p. 25.
39. Ibid., p. 26.
40. Sadri and Sadri, *Essential Writings*, p. 132.
41. Abdo and Lyons, *Answering only to God*, pp. 56–89.
42. Seyyed Mohammad Khatami, *Bim-e mouj* (Tehran, 1371 SH), p. 136
43. Farhang Rajaee, *Islamism and Modernism: The Changing Discourse in Iran* (Austin, 2007), p. 213.
44. Ebrahim Towfigh, 'Islamische Demokratie und "Restauration" der Theokratie: Diskursanalytische Betrachtung des Reformprozesses in der Islamischen Republik Iran', *Orient*, December (2004), p. 532.
45. Jahangir Salahpur, 'Din-e demokratik-e hokumati', *Kiyan*, No. 20 (1373 SH), p. 11.
46. Hossein-Ali Montazeri, *Matn-e kamel-e khaterat Ayatollah Hossein-Ali Montazeri* (Essen, 2001), p. 628.
47. Olivier Roy, 'The Crisis of Religious Legitimacy in Iran', *Middle East Journal*, Spring (1999), p. 205.
48. Ibid., p. 207.
49. Daniel Brumberg, *Reinventing Khomeini: The Struggle for Reform in Iran* (Chicago, 2001), p. 174; William Millward, 'Leadership in the Islamic Republic and the Hierarchy of Shia Islam', *Commentary*, January (1994), p. 6.
50. Montazeri, *Khaterat*, p. 386.
51. Henner Fürtig, *Liberalisierung als Herausforderung: Wie stabil ist die Islamische Republik Iran?* (Berlin, 1996), p. 30; Wilfried Buchta, 'Die Islamische Republik Iran und die religiös-politische Kontroverse um die marja'iyat', *Orient*, September (1995), p. 465.
52. Hossein-Ali Montazeri, *Enteqad az khod* (Qom, 1390 SH), p. 137; many of Montazeri's friends and allies paid dearly for their support for him. Political and clerical leaders such as the Friday Imam of Najafabad, Hojatoleslam Azadi were arrested, others were banned and excluded from taking part in elections (Hermann, 'Die Ära Khamenei/Rafsanjani', p. 557). According to some sources, as many as 600 of his supporters and students were executed by the Special Court of the Clergy after 1989 (Buchta, 'Kontroverse um die marja'iyat', p. 473).
53. Montazeri, *Khaterat*, pp. 329, 374, 388, 590–622.
54. Sharough Akhavi, 'The Thought and Role of Ayatollah Hossein Ali Montazeri in the Politics of Post-1979 Iran', in *Iranian Studies*, December (2008), p. 648; Amirpur, *Abdolkarim Sorushs Denken*, p. 53.

55. Buchta, 'Kontroverse um die marja'iyat', p. 454.
56. Traditionally the scholastic method of teaching was employed in the seminaries. In lectures and debates, teachers and students exchanged arguments drawn from the scriptures and other religious sources to test their validity. Possibly the best account of the seminary debates in Qom can be found in the semi-fictitious book by Roy Mottahedeh, *Der Mantel des Propheten. Das Leben eines persischen Mullah zwischen Religion und Politik* (Munich, 1987).
57. Millward, 'Leadership', p. 10.
58. Literally meaning 'circle' or 'field of science', the houze elmiye Qom designates the entirety of the religious seminaries in Qom. These seminaries are traditionally interconnected but administratively and financially independent, each one having its own scholarly focus and religious identity.
59. Katajun Amirpur, 'Reformen an theologischen Hochschulen in Iran: Revolutionäres Establishment contra religiöse Aufklärer', *Orient*, 09 (1997), p. 1,997.
60. Montazeri, *Khaterat*, p. 406.
61. Maziar Behrooz, 'The Islamic state and the Crisis of the Marja'iyat in Iran', *Comparative Studies of South Asia, Africa and the Middle East*, Vol. XVI, No. 2 (1996); Buchta, 'Kontroverse um die marja'iyat', p. 460.
62. Ibid., p. 456.
63. Ibid., p. 466; Behrooz, 'Crisis of the Marja'iyat', p. 6.
64. Montazeri, *Khaterat*, p. 401.
65. Ibid., p. 624.
66. Ibid., p. 407; Behrooz, 'Crisis of the Marja'iyat'; Hermann, 'Die Ära Khamenei/ Rafsanjani', p. 562.
67. Buchta, 'Kontroverse um die marja'iyat', p. 357.
68. Montazeri, *Enteqad*, pp. 155–6.
69. Behrooz, 'Crisis of the Marja'iyat', p. 7.
70. Buchta, 'Kontroverse um die marja'iyat', p. 472.
71. Montazeri, *Khaterat*, pp. 398, 615–19.
72. Pierre Bourdieu, *Das religiöse Feld: Texte zur Ökonomie des Heilsgeschehens* (Konstanz, 2000), p. 73.

## Chapter 6   Power and Impotence of the Reform Movement

1. Said Amir Arjomand, 'Civil Society and the Rule of Law in the Constitutional Politics of Iran Under Khatami', *Social Research*, 3 (2000).
2. Mehran Kamrava, *Iran's Intellectual Revolution* (Cambridge, 2008), pp. 21–4.
3. Farhad Khosrokhavar, 'L'Iran, la democratie et la nouvelle citoyennete', *Cahiers internationaux de sociologie*, No. 111 (2001/02), p. 304.
4. Ibid., p. 308.
5. Mehdi Moslem, *Factional Politics in Post-Khomeini Iran* (New York, 2002), p. 240.

6. Geneive Abdo and Jonathan Lyons, *Answering only to God: Faith and Freedom in Twenty-First-Century Iran* (New York, 2003), p. 61.

7. Ibid., pp. 59, 64.

8. Ibid., p. 70.

9. Ibid., p. 71.

10. Hossein-Ali Montazeri, *Matn-e kamel-e khaterat Ayatollah Hossein-Ali Montazeri* (Essen, 2001), p. 421.

11. Abdo and Lyons, *Answering only to God*, pp. 60, 73–5.

12. Ibid., p. 82.

13. Arjomand, 'Civil Society'

14. Navid Kermani, *Iran: Die Revolution der Kinder* (Munich, 2005), pp. 162–78.

15. Montazeri, *Khaterat*, p. 622.

16. Ibid., p. 624.

17. Wilfried Buchta, *Who rules Iran? The Structure of Power in the Islamic Republic* (Washington DC, 2000), pp. 46, 163.

18. Tawfiq Alsaif, *Islamic Democracy and its Limits: The Iranian Experience since 1979* (Beirut, 2007), p. 81.

19. Ibid., pp. 82, 165.

20. Abdo and Lyons, *Answering only to God*, pp. 151–71, 190.

21. Kermani, *Revolution der Kinder*, p. 80.

22. Golbarg Bashi, 'Eyewitness History: Ayatollah Montazeri', 3 August 2006. Available at http://www.payvand.com/news/06/mar/1067.html.

23. Montazeri, *Khaterat*, p. 628.

24. Ibid., p. 409.

25. Wilfried Buchta, 'Die Islamische Republik Iran und die religiös-politische Kontroverse um die marja'iyat', *Orient*, September (1995), p. 464; Miriam Künkler, 'The Special Court of the Clergy (Dadgah-e Vizheh-ye Ruhaniyat) and the Repression of Dissident Clergy in Iran,' in Said Arjomand and Nathan Brown (eds), *Constitutionalism, the Rule of Law and the Politics of Administration in Egypt and Iran* (New York, 2012), p. 6.

26. Tabarzadi, Heshmatollah, 'Ekhtiarat-e vali-ye faqih bayad be osul qanun-e assassi makhdud shavad', *Nimrooz*, 9 Aban 1376; 'Tazahorat vazi' zed velayat-e faqih dar Teheran', *Nimrooz*, 9 Aban 1376.

27. Mohsen Kadivar, 'Tchera Azari mahzur shod?' (09.03.1392 SH). Available at http://kadivar.com/?p=13174.

28. Ibid.

29. 'Azari-Qomi az jame'eh modaressin houze elmi-ye Qom ejrah shod', *Nimrooz*, 23 Aban 1376.

30. Montazeri, *Khaterat*, pp. 624–9.

31. Ibid.

32. Ibid.

33. 'Mikhahand Montazeri ra be etteham tu'te aliye hokumat mohakeme konand', *Nimrooz*, 7 Azar 1376.

34. Ibid., Montazeri, *Khaterat*, p. 411.

35. Katajun Amirpur, *Die Entpolitisierung des Islam: Abdolkarim Sorushs Denken und Wirkung in der Islamischen Republik Iran* (Würzburg, 2003), p. 77.

36. Sharough Akhavi, 'The Thought and Role of Ayatollah Hossein Ali Montazeri in the Politics of Post-1979 Iran', *Iranian Studies*, December (2008), p. 651.

37. Douglas Jehl, 'Iranian Clerics hint at Treason Trial for Critic', *New York Times*, 16 December 1997. Available at www.nytimes.com/1997/12/16/world/iranian-clerics-hint-at-treason-trial-for-a-critic.html.

38. Montazeri, *Khaterat*, p. 413.

39. Montazeri and Azari-Qomi were not the only *maraje'-ye taqlid* to live under house arrest. The quietist Hassan Tabatabai-Qomi in Mashhad was under arrest since 1984 for having criticised the regime. The orthodox Sadeq Ruhani had been placed under arrest in Qom after he had publicly criticised Montazeri's choice as deputy leader in 1985. His brother, Mohammad Ruhani, was forbidden from giving courses or receiving visitors after having called for the separation of religion and politics in 1994. Mohammad Shirazi was under arrest in Qom because he had advocated a clerical council to lead the country instead of a single *faqih* (Künkler, 'Special Court', p. 7).

40. Montazeri, *Enteqad*, p. 148.

41. Olivier Roy, 'The Crisis of Religious Legitimacy in Iran', *Middle East Journal*, Spring (1999).

42. Ziba Mir-Hosseini and Richard Tapper, *Islam and democracy in Iran: Eshkevari and the quest for reform* (London, 2006), p. 135.

43. The text of the speech of 21 June 1997 was published in *Kiyan* shortly before his trial in December 1997. The following year, it was included in Ganji's book *Talaqi fashisti az din va hokumat (The Fascist Interpretation of Religion and Government)*.

44. Amirpur, *Abdolkarim Sorushs Denken*, p. 151.

45. Ibid., p. 150.

46. *Velāyat* can mean rule, power, governance or guardianship. In the religious context it traditionally designated the guardianship of a jurist over widows and orphans. Khomeini, with his concept *velāyat-e faqih*, extended this guardianship to include the entire people. The system which is the result of this concept is therefore called *hokumat-e velā'i*, e.g. the government/state of the guardian/guide.

47. Mohsen Kadivar and Zahra Roudi (eds), *Bahai azadi: Defa'yat-e Mohsen Kadivar dar dadgah-e vize ruhaniyat* (Tehran, 1378 SH), pp. 17–19.

48. Mohsen Kadivar, *Hokumat-e vela'i* (Tehran, 1377 SH), pp. 151–7.

49. Ibid., pp. 204–14.

50. In his later writings, Kadivar rejected not only the appointed, absolute guardianship of the jurist but also the elective, conditional version developed by Montazeri, because it only allows for a limited democracy. In 'Wilayat al-faqih and democracy', he argued that the theory not only lacks a sound religious basis but also that the execution of Islamic law by the jurists offers no adequate response to the problems of modern society (Mohsen Kadivar, 'Wilayat al-faqih

and Democracy', in Asma Afsaruddin (ed.), *Islam, the State, and Political Authority: Medieval Issues and Modern Concerns* (New York, 2011)).

51. The text of the essay, dated 28 July 1998, is largely identical to two articles published in *Rah-e Nou* on 21 and 30 August 1998. The essay itself is included in *Didgah-ha*, from which these quotes are taken.

52. Hossein-Ali Montazeri, *Didgah-ha: Payam-ha-ye va nazariat-e montashere-ye faqih aliqadr Ayatollah al-ozma Montazeri. Vol. I* (Qom, 1382 SH), p. 38. Available at http://www.amontazeri.com/farsi/frame10.asp.

53. Ibid., p. 56.

54. Mir-Hosseini and Tapper, *Islam and democracy*, p. 115.

55. Ibid., p. 123.

56. Ibid., pp. 125–8.

57. Geneive Abdo, 'Rethinking the Islamic Republic: A "Conversation" with Ayatollah Hossein Ali Montazeri', *Middle East Journal*, Winter (2001); Hossein-Ali Montazeri, *Democracy and Constitution* (11 February 2001). Available at www.amontazeri.com/farsi/f1.asp.

58. Montazeri, *Democracy and Constitution*, p. 13. In late April 1998, the head of the Pasdaran, Rahim Safavi, accused the Minister of the Interior, Abdollah Nuri, of tolerating the protests of Montazeri's supporters: 'We must behead some and cut out the tongues of others. [...] The Interior Ministry is behind Montazeri's mayhem' (Moslem, *Factional Politics*, p. 262).

59. Montazeri, *Democracy and Constitution*, p. 19.

60. Ibid., p. 12.

61. Montazeri, *Didgah-ha, Vol. I*, p. 387.

62. Akbar Ganji, *Manifest-e jomhuri-khahi* (1381 SH). Formerly available at www.4shared.com/document/ly6sAmig/510- Akbar_Ganji-Manifest_Jomho.html.

63. Hossein-Ali Montazeri, *Enteqad az khod* (Qom, 1390 SH), p. 158.

64. Reyshahri felt prompted by Montazeri's account of the Hashemi affair to publish a revised edition of his own memoirs to counter his allegations. In the fourth volume of these memoirs he quoted long passages from Montazeri's memoirs, to which he juxtaposed his own version of the facts (Mohammad Mohammadi Reyshahri, *Khatere-ha, Vol. IV* (Tehran, 1388 SH)).

65. Geoffrey Robertson, *The Massacre of Political Prisoners in Iran, 1988* (London, 2011), p. 8. Available at www.iranrights.org/library/document/1380/the-massacre-of-political-prisoners-in-iran-1988-report-of-an-inquiry.

66. Amirpur, *Abdolkarim Sorushs Denken*, p. 6; Frederique Tellier, 'La république islamique dans l'impasse', *Revues internationales et strategiques*, No. 49 (2003), p. 48.

67. 'Freed Iran cleric vows to continue to fight for justice', *New York Times*, 31 January 2003. Available at http://www.nytimes.com/2003/01/31/world/freed-iran-cleric-vows-to-continue-to-fight-for-justice.html.

68. Kadivar and Roudi, *Bahai azadi*, p. 147.

69. Farhang Rajaee, *Islamism and Modernism: The Changing Discourse in Iran* (Austin, 2007), p. 170; Kermani, *Revolution der Kinder*, pp. 24, 108.

70. Kermani, *Revolution der Kinder*, p. 113.
71. Abdo and Lyons, *Answering only to God*, p. 180.
72. Montazeri, *Khaterat*, p. 67.
73. Kermani, *Revolution der Kinder*, pp. 118–23, 221.
74. Wilfried Buchta, *Who rules Iran? The Structure of Power in the Islamic Republic* (Washington DC, 2000), pp. 156, 169.
75. Amirpur, *Abdolkarim Sorushs Denken*, p. 137.
76. Kadivar and Roudi, *Bahai azadi*, p. 173.
77. Miriam Künkler, 'The Special Court of the Clergy (Dadgah-e Vizheh-ye Ruhaniyat) and the Repression of Dissident Clergy in Iran,' in Said Arjomand and Nathan Brown (eds), *Constitutionalism, the Rule of Law and the Politics of Administration in Egypt and Iran* (New York, 2012).
78. Human Rights Watch, *Ministers of Murders: Iran's New Security Cabinet* (2005), p. 11.
79. Kadivar and Roudi, *Bahai azadi*, p. 147.
80. Ibid., p. 149.
81. Ibid., p. 158.
82. Ibid., pp. 11–31.
83. Ibid., pp. 40–53.
84. Ibid., pp. 79–85.
85. Ibid., p. 94.
86. William Samii, 'Sisyphus' Newsstand: The Iranian Press under Khatami', *Middle East Review of International Affairs*, September (2001), pp. 3, 10.
87. Ibid., p. 4.
88. Abdo and Lyons, *Answering only to God*, pp. 196–207.
89. Samii, 'Sisyphus' Newsstand', p. 3.
90. Ibid.
91. Abdo and Lyons, *Answering only to God*, p. 51.
92. Abdollah Nuri, *Shukran-e eslah: Defa'yat-e Abdollah Nuri dar dadgah-e vize ruhaniyat* (Tehran, 1378 SH), p. 180.
93. Ibid., p. 181.
94. Ibid., p. 189.
95. Ibid., p. 195.
96. Amirpur, *Abdolkarim Sorushs Denken*, p. 138.
97. Heinrich Böll Stiftung, *Iran nach den Wahlen: Eine Konferenz und ihre Folgen* (Münster, 2001).
98. Mir-Hosseini and Tapper, *Islam and Democracy*, p. 148.
99. Ibid., pp. 164–9.
100. Eshkevari was released in February 2005; Ganji in March 2006. The journalist Khalil Rostamkhani, who had helped organise the conference, and the translator Sa'id Sadr were accused of waging war against God, but later sentenced to nine and ten years in prison respectively. Apart from Sahabi and Lahiji, all others left the country after their release.

101. Abdo and Lyons, *Answering only to God*, p. 134; Samii, 'Sisyphus' Newsstand', p. 7.
102. Ibid., p. 6.


## Chapter 7     The Green Movement and its Failure

1. Kasra Naji, *Ahmadinejad: The secret history of Iran's radical leader* (Los Angeles, 2008), p. 70.
2. Said Amir Arjomand, *After Khomeini: Iran under his Successors* (Oxford, 2009), p. 103.
3. Mansoor Moaddel, 'The Iranian Revolution and its Nemesis: The Rise of Liberal Values among Iranians', *Comparative Studies of South Asia, Africa and the Middle East*, No. 1 (2009).
4. Arjomand, *After Khomeini*, p. 196.
5. In the first round on 17 June, with a turnout of 63 per cent, Ahmadinejad came in second with 5.7 million votes after Rafsanjani with 6.1 million. Karrubi was placed third with just over 5 million votes, coming before the reformer Moin and the conservatives Larijani and Qalibaf. In the second round, with a turnout of 60 per cent, Ahmadinejad won 62 per cent of the votes, well in front of Rafsanjani with just 36 per cent (Naji, *Ahmadinejad*, p. 73).
6. Tawfiq Alsaif, *Islamic Democracy and its Limits: The Iranian Experience since 1979* (Beirut, 2007), p. 170.
7. International Crisis Group, 'Iran: Ahmadi-Nejad's Tumultous Presidency', Middle East Briefing, No. 21, 6 February 2007, p. 12. Available at www.crisis group.org/en/regions/middle-east-north-africa/iraq-iran-gulf/iran/B021-iran-ahmadi-nejads-tumultuous-presidency.aspx.
8. Naji, *Ahmadinejad*, p. 118.
9. Alsaif, *Islamic Democracy*, p. 173.
10. Arjomand, *After Khomeini*, p. 162.
11. Ibid., p. 156.
12. Naji, *Ahmadinejad*, p. 238.
13. International Crisis Group, 'Tumultous Presidency', p. 14; Naji, *Ahmadinejad*, p. 248.
14. Amir-Ebrahimi Masserat, 'Blogging from Qom: Behind Walls and Veils', *Comparative Studies of South Asia, Africa and the Middle East*, 2 (2008), p. 235; Annabelle Sreberny and Gholam Khiabani, 'Becoming Intellectual: The Blogestan and Public Political Space in the Islamic Republic', *British Journal of Middle Eastern Studies*, December (2007).
15. Hossein-Ali Montazeri, *Didgah-ha: Payam-ha-ye va nazariat-e montashere-ye fagih aliqadr Ayatollah al-ozma Montazeri. Vol. II* (Qom, 1385 SH), p. 393. Available at http://www.amontazeri.com/farsi/frame10.asp.
16. Hossein-Ali Montazeri, 'Piravan-e ferqe baha'iyat va hoquq-e sharvandi' (25.03.1387 SH). Available at www.amontazeri.com/farsi/fhome.asp.

17. Ahmad Qabel, 'Name be rahbar-e jomhuri-ye eslami-ye Iran' (10.03.1384 SH). Available at www.bbc.co.uk/persian/iran/story/2005/06/050601_ahmad-qabel-letter.shtml.

18. Ahmad Qabel, *Mabani-ye shar'iat* (1391 SH), p. 6. Available at www.ghabel.net/shariat/books.

19. Mohsen Kadivar, 'Payam-e taslit be monasebet-e dargozasht-e Ahmad Qabel' (05.08.1391 SH). Available at http://kadivar.com/? P=9791.

20. Mir-Hossein Mussavi, 'Matn-e kamel-e name Mir-Hossein Mussavi be Ayatollah Khamene'i' (11 June 2009). Available at www.bbc.co.uk/persian/iran/2009/06/090611_op_ir88_mousavi_khamenei_letter_text.shtml.

21. Naji, *Ahmadinejad*, pp. 225, 231.

22. Ibid., p. 235.

23. Ibid., pp. 139, 156–75.

24. Hossein-Ali Montazeri, 'Pasokh-e Ayatollah al-ozma Montazeri be do porsesh piramun-e re'ayat-e qanun-e entekhabat' (12 and 13.03.1388 SH). Available at www.amontazeri.com/farsi/fhome.asp.

25. Mussavi, 'Matn-e kamel-e name'.

26. With an official score of 63.6 per cent on a turnout of 85 per cent, Ahmadinejad had received 24.5 million votes. Yet, in the 2005 second round he had obtained only 62 per cent on a turnout of 60 per cent. Given the dismal results of his economic policies, it appeared unlikely that he would have increased his share by 7.2 million. Karrubi, by contrast, had won more than 5 million votes in 2005 but was only credited with 333,000 votes four years later (Iran Human Rights Documentation Centre, *Violent Aftermath: The 2009 Election and Suppression of Dissent in Iran* (2010). Available at www.iranhrdc.org/english/publications/reports/3161-violent-aftermath-the-2009-election-and-suppression-of-dissent-in-iran.html#.U0J9taYidKA.)

27. Robert F. Worth and Nazila Fathi, 'Protests Flare in Tehran as Opposition Disputes Vote', *New York Times*, 14 June 2009. Available at www.nytimes.com/2009/06/14/world/middleeast/14iran.html?_r=2&.

28. Mir-Hossein Mussavi, 'Matn-e kamel-e name Mir-Hossein Mussavi be olema va maraje'-ye Qom' (13 June 2009). Available at www.bbc.co.uk/persian/iran/2009/06/090613_bd_ir88_mousavi_letter_qom.shtml; Mir-Hossein Mussavi, 'Matn-e bianiye Mir-Hossein Mussavi dar eteraz be natayej-e elam shode entekhabat' (13 June 2009). Available at www.bbc.co.uk/persian/iran/2009/06/090613_bd_ir88_mousavi_statement.shtml.

29. Hossein-Ali Montazeri, 'Pasokh-e feqhi-siasi Ayatollah al-ozma Montazeri be porsesh-ha-ye hojatoleslam va al-moslemin doktor Mohsen Kadivar' (19.04.1388 SH). Available at www.amontazeri.com/farsi/fhome.asp.

30. Amnesty International, *Iran: Election amid repression of dissent and unrest* (9 June 2009), p. 22. Available at www.amnesty.org/en/library/info/MDE13/053/2009.

31. Iran Human Rights Documentation Centre, *Violent Aftermath*, p. 33.

32. Ibid., p. 14.

33. Ibid., p. 20.

34. Yussef Sane'i, 'Javabi-ye Ayatollah al-ozma Sane'i dar pasokh be Mohandes Mir Hossein Mussavi' (25.03.1388 SH). Available at http://1saanei.org/?view =01,01,01,61,60; Yussef Sane'i, 'Ebraz hamdardi Hazrat Ayatollah al-ozma Sane'i ba khanevade qorbanian-e fejai' akheir' (27.03.1388 SH). Available at http://1saanei.org/?view=01,00,00,00,0#01,01,01,62,60.

35. Hossein-Ali Montazeri, 'Payam-e Ayatollah al-ozma Montazeri piramun-e natayej-e entekhabat-e riasat-e jomhuri-ye eslami va havadez-e pas az an' (26.03.1388 SH). Available at www.amontazeri.com/farsi/fhome.asp.

36. Seyyed Ali Khamene'i, 'Khatbe-ha-ye namaz jom'e Tehran' (29.03.1388 SH). Available at http://farsi.khamenei.ir/speech-content?id=7190.

37. Iran Human Rights Documentation Centre, *Violent Aftermath*, p. 26.

38. Mir-Hossein Mussavi, 'Biyani-ye shomare 5 Mohandes Mir Hossein Mussavi' (30.03.1388 SH). Formerly available at http://www.rahesabz.net/section/archi ve/1388/3/30.

39. Hossein-Ali Montazeri, 'Payam-e Ayatollah al-ozma Montazeri dar eteraz be amalkard namonaseb-e ma'sulan va sarkub-e mardom' (03.04.1388 SH). Available at www.amontazeri.com/farsi/fhome.asp.

40. Mir-Hossein Mussavi, 'Matn kamel-e bianiye Mussavi pas az ta'yyid entekhabat tavassot-e shura-ye neghaban' (13.04.1388 SH). Available at http://www.bbc.co. uk/persian/iran/2009/07/090701_op_ir88_mousavi9_text.shtml.

41. Ibid.

42. Ibid.

43. Yussef Sane'i, 'Bianiye marja'-e aliqadr Hazrat Ayatollah al-ozma Sane'i dar ertebat ba masa'el-e jari keshvar' (14.04.1388 SH). Available at http://1saanei. org/?view=01,00,00,00,0#01,01,01,63,60.

44. Montazeri, 'Pasokh-e feqhi-siasi'.

45. Ibid.

46. Hossein-Ali Montazeri, 'Dastkhat-e Ayatollah al-ozma Montazeri dar takzib shaye porakani-ha va dorugh afkani-ha-ye sait rajanews' (24.04.1388 SH). Available at www.amontazeri.com/farsi/fhome.asp.

47. Ali-Abkar Hashemi Rafsanjani, 'Khatbe-ha-ye namaz jom'e' (26.04.1388 SH). Available at www.hashemirafsanjani.ir/news_archive/1388.

48. Iran Human Rights Documentation Centre, *Violent Aftermath*, p. 30.

49. Muhammad Sahimi, 'The Widening Divide among Iranian Clerics', *Tehran Bureau*, 30 June 2009. Available at www.pbs.org/wgbh/pages/frontline/ tehranbureau/2009/07/the-widening-divide-among-irans-clerics.html.

50. Hossein-Ali Montazeri, 'Payam-e Ayatollah al-ozma Montazeri be maraj'e azam-e taqlid, olama' va huze-ha-ye elmi-ye' (22.06.1388 SH). Available at www.am ontazeri.com/farsi/fhome.asp.

51. Amnesty International, *Iran: Election Contested, Repression Compounded* (10 December 2009), p. 29. Available at www.amnesty.org/en/library/info/MDE13/123/2009.

52. Hamid Asafi et al., 'Hemayat 310 nafar az fe'alan siasi va madani az farakhan Ayatollah al-ozma Montazeri' (06.07.1388 SH). Available at www.amontazeri. com/farsi/article_read.asp?id=102.

53. Ahmad Abdini et al., 'Hemayat jam'e-i az osatid-e houze va daneshgah Esfahan az payam Ayatollah al-ozma Montazeri khetab be maraj'e-ye taqlid, olema va houze-ha-ye elmiye' (10.07.1388 SH). Available at www.amontazeri.com/farsi/ article_read.asp?id=105.

54. Ali-Mohammad Dastgheib, 'Ayatollah Dastgheib's Speech in the Assembly of Experts' (22.09.2009). Available at http://khordaad88.com/?p=660.

55. Human Rights Watch, *The Islamic Republic at 31: Post-election Abuses Show Serious Human Rights Crisis*, February (2010), p. 5. Available at www.hrw.org/reports/ 2010/02/11/islamic-republic-31-0.

56. Iran Human Rights Documentation Centre, *Violent Aftermath*, p. 61.

57. Amnesty International, *Election Contested*, p. 46.

58. Ibid, pp. 48, 54; in the face of public criticism Mortezavi was transferred to the less influential post of Iran's Deputy Prosecutor-General. It was only in February 2013 that he was finally arrested and charged for the murders in Kahrizak. In June of that year he was acquitted of this charge and only condemned for minor charges.

59. Iran Human Rights Documentation Centre, *Violent Aftermath*, pp. 75–87; among the accused were the reformist politicians Abtahi, Hajjarian, Mirdamadi and Nabavi, and Mussavi's election campaign manager, Shahaboddin Tabatabai, as well as the American-Iranian scholar Kian Tajbakhsh and the Canadian-Iranian journalist Maziar Bahari. Several Iranian staff members of the British and French embassies, as well as the young French university lecturer Clotilde Reiss, also appeared in the trials (Amnesty International, *Election Contested*, pp. 29, 55).

60. Hossein-Ali Montazeri, 'Payam-e Ayatollah al-ozma Montazeri dar eteraz be bargozari-ye dadgah-ha-ye farmayeshi' (13.05.1388 SH). Available at www.am ontazeri.com/farsi/fhome.asp.

61. Yussef Sane'i, 'Bianiye marja'-e aliqadr Hazrat Ayatollah al-ozma Sane'i dar pi bargozari dadgah-ha-ye pas az entekhabat dahomin dure riasat jomhuri' (14.05.1388 SH). Available at http://1saanei.org/?view=01,01,01,67,50.

62. Amnesty International, *Election Contested*, p. 54.

63. The first verdicts were announced on 5 October, and by December almost all of the accused had been condemned – most to long prison sentences, and some to lashing and exile. Six alleged members of the Mojahedin and the little known Royalist Society were condemned to death (Iran Human Rights Documentation Centre, *Violent Aftermath*, pp. 75, 83, 86).

64. Akbar Ganji, 'Historians and the History-Maker Ayatollah Montazeri', *Rooz*, 22 December 2009. Formerly available at www.roozonline.com/english/ opinion/opinion-article/article/2009/december/22//historians-and-the-history-maker-ayatollah-montazeri.html.

65. In September 2006, Baqi had in a long interview with Montazeri questioned him on crucial episodes of his life. When parts of this interview were broadcast on the day of Montazeri's death, Baqi was arrested and after five months in solitary confinement sentenced to six years' prison (Hossein-Ali Montazeri,

*Didgah-ha: Payam-ha-ye va nazariat-e montashere-ye fagih aliqadr Ayatollah al-ozma Montazeri. Vol. III* (Qom, 1389 SH), p. 205. Available at http://www. amontazeri.com/farsi/frame10.asp).

66. 'Qodrat nemai million mardom', *Rooz*, 22 December 2009. Available at www. roozonline.com/persian/archive/archivenews/news/archive/2009/december/22/article/-d48f41cc22.html.

67. Ibid.

68. After Montazeri's death his office published two volumes of the reactions to his passing. The first volume, with messages of condolence by prominent clerics, politicians and institutions, numbered 100 pages; the second, with obituaries, was 300 pages long (Beit-e Hazrat Ayatollah al-ozma Montazeri, *Sugname*, 2 Vols (Qom, 1388 SH)).

69. Fereshte Qazi, 'Ta'zim-e donya be pedar-e ma'nvai jonbesh-e sabz', *Rooz*, 22 December 2009. Available at www.roozonline.com/persian/archive/archivenews/news/archive/2009/december/22/article/br-br.html.

70. Abdol'ali Bazargan, Abdolkarim Soroush, Akbar Ganji, Mohsen Kadivar and Ataollah Mohajerani, 'Khāste-hā- ye hadāqali jonbesh sabz dar biāniye panj rushanfekrān' (13.10.1388 SH). Available at http://news.gooya.com/politics/archives/2010/01/098533.php.

71. Seyyed Ali Khamene'i, 'Payam-e taslit dar pi dargozasht faqih bozorgvar Ayatollah Montazeri' (19.09.1388 SH). Available at http://farsi.khamenei.ir/message-content?id=8534.

72. Iran Human Rights Documentation Centre, *Violent Aftermath*, p. 38.

73. Mohsen Kadivar, 'Banu-ye moqavemat, hamsar-e marja'iyat, madar-e shohadat' (08.01.1389 SH). Available at http://kadivar.com/?p=8280.

74. After Montazeri's death Sane'i was the highest-ranking cleric to support the Green Movement. On 2 January 2010, the Jāme'e Modaressin in Qom issued a decree on the initiative of Mesbah-Yazdi stipulating that Sane'i did not fulfil the conditions of a *marja'-e taqlid*. The decision was highly controversial, and numerous clerics questioned the authority of the Jāme'e Modaressin to make this decision.

75. Mohammad-Reza Yazdan-Panah, 'Daftar-e Montazeri va Sanei takhrib va plomb shod', *Rooz*, 14 June 2010. Available at www.roozonline.com/persian/archive/archivenews/news/archive/2010/june/14/article/-d6a1efa9e9.html; 'Sokhanrani Seyyed Hassan na-tamam mand', *Sharq*, 16 Khordad 1389.

# BIBLIOGRAPHY

## Primary Sources

Abdini, Ahmad et al., 'Hemayat jam'e-i az osatid-e houze va daneshgah Esfahan az payam Ayatollah al-ozma Montazeri khetab be maraj'e-ye taqlid, olema va houze-ha-ye elmiye' (10.07.1388 SH). Available at www.amontazeri.com/farsi/article_read.asp?id=105.

Afshari, Ali et al., 'A Popular Appeal in Support of a Referendum for a New Constitution' (November 2004). Available at www.iranrights.org/english/document-213.php.

Alavitabar, Ali-Reza, 'Ide'olozi va totalitarism', *Kiyan*, No. 20 (1373 SH), pp. 12–14.

Al-e Ahmad, Jalal, 'The Outline of a Disease', in Lloyd Ridgeon (ed.), *Religion and Politics in Modern Iran: A Reader* (New York, 2005).

Anonymous, *Vaq'iyat-ha va qezavat-ha* (No date). Available at www.amontazeri.com/farsi/frame4.asp.

Asafi, Hamid et al., 'Hemayat 310 nafar az fe'alan siasi va madani az farakhan Ayatollah al-ozma Montazeri' (06.071388 SH). Available at www.amontazeri.com/farsi/article_read.asp?id=102.

Bazargan, Abdol'ali, Abdolkarim Soroush, Akbar Ganji, Moshen Kadivar and Ata'ollah Mohajerani, 'Khāste-hā-ye hadāqali jonbesh sabz dar biāniye panj rushanfekrān' (13.10.1388 SH). Available at http://news.gooya.com/politics/archives/2010/01/098533.php.

Beit-e Hazrat Ayatollah al-ozma Montazeri, *Sugname*, 2 Vols (Qom, 1388 SH).

Dastgheib, Ali-Mohammad, 'Ayatollah Dastgheib's Speech in the Assembly of Experts' (22 September 2009). Available at http://khordaad88.com/?p=660.

Eshkevari, Hassan Yussefi, 'Paradoks-e eslām va demokrasi?', *Kiyan*, No. 21 (1373 SH), pp. 24–9.

———, 'Kasrat gerā'i dar nazar va vahdat gerā'i dar amal', *Kiyan*, No. 39, (1377 SH), pp. 30–5.

Ganji, Akbar, 'Mashru'iyat, velayat va vekalat', *Kiyan*, No. 13 (1372 SH), pp. 22–30.

———, *Talaqi fashisti az din va hokumat* (Tehran, 1378 SH).

———, *Manifest-e jomhuri-khahi* (1381). Formerly available at www.4shared.com/document/ly6sAmig/510-Akbar_Ganji-Manifest_Jomho.html.

————, 'Historians and the History-Maker Ayatollah Montazeri', *Rooz*, 22 December 2009. Formerly vailable at www.roozonline.com/english/opini on/opinion-article/article/2009/december/22//historians-and-the-history-m aker-ayatollah-montazeri.html.

Kadivar, Mohsen, *Hokumat-e vela'i* (Tehran, 1377 SH).

———— and Zahra Roudi (eds), *Bahai azadi: Defa'yat-e Mohsen Kadivar dar dadgah-e vize ruhaniyat* (Tehran, 1378).

————, 'Banu-ye moqavemat, hamsar-e marja'iyat, madar-e shohadat' (08.01.1389 SH). Available at http://kadivar.com/?p=8280.

————, 'Sir-e tahavol-e andishe siasi Ayatollah Montazeri' (1390 SH). Available at http://kadivar.com/?p=5568.

————, 'Payam-e taslit be monasebet-e dargozasht-e Ahmad Qabel' (05.08.1391 SH). Available at http://kadivar.com/?p=9791.

————, 'Tchera Azari mahzur shod?' (09.03.1392 SH). Available at http://kadivar.com/?p=13174.

————, 'Wilayat al-faqih and Democracy', in Asma Afsaruddin (ed.), *Islam, the State, and Political Authority: Medieval Issues and Modern Concerns* (New York, 2011).

Khamene'i, Seyyed Ali, 'Khatbe-ha-ye namaz jom'e Tehran' (29.03.1388 SH). Available at http://farsi.khamenei.ir/speech-content?id=7190.

————, 'Payam-e taslit dar pi dargozasht faqih bozorgvar Ayatollah Montazeri' (19.09.1388 SH). Available at http://farsi.khamenei.ir/message-content?id=8534.

Khatami, Seyyed Mohammad, *Bim-e mouj* (Tehran, 1371 SH).

————, *Eslam, ruhaniyat va enqelab-e eslami* (Tehran, 1379 SH).

Khomeini, Seyyed Ahmad, 'Ranjname', *Majmu'e azar-e yadgar-e imam*. Vol. II (Tehran, 1375 SH), pp. 139–261.

Khomeini, Seyyed Ruhollah, *Kashf al-asrar* (Qom, no date).

————, *Imam's Final Discourse* (Tehran, 1982).

————, *Islamic Government: The Guardianship of the Jurisprudent (Hokumat-e eslami: Velayat-e faqih)* (Tehran, 2003).

Montazeri, Hossein-Ali, 'Nazari bar zendegi kutah amma por az jehad va mobareze ostad shahid Mohammad Montazeri' (no date). Available at www.amontazeri.com/Farsi/article_read.asp?id=338.

————, 'Khastar tajdid-e nazar dar asl 8 qanun-e assassi shod', *Keyhan*, 3 Tir 1358.

————, *Mabani-e fehqi-ye hokumat-e eslami, Vol. I: Doulat va hokumat* (Tehran, 1368 SH).

————, *Mabani-e fehqi-ye hokumat-e eslami, Vol. II: Emamat va rahbari* (Tehran, 1369 SH).

————, *Mabani-e fehqi-ye hokumat-e eslami, Vol. III: Qava-ye se gane, amr be ma'ruf, hesbe va ta'zirat* (Tehran, 1370 SH).

————, *Mabani-e fehqi-ye hokumat-e eslami, Vol. IV: Ahkam va adab-e zendan-ha va estekhbarat* (Tehran, 1371 SH).

————, *Mabani-e fehqi-ye hokumat-e eslami, Vol. V: Ehtekar, siasat-e khareji, qavai nezami va ekhlaq-e kargozaran-e hokumat-e islami* (Tehran, 1374 SH).

————, *Didgah-ha: Payam-ha-ye va nazariat-e montashere-ye fagih aliqadr Ayatollah al-ozma Montazeri. Vol. I* (Qom, 1382 SH). Available at http://www.amontazeri.com/farsi/frame10.asp.

————, *Didgah-ha: Payam-ha-ye va nazariat-e montashere-ye fagih aliqadr Ayatollah al-ozma Montazeri. Vol. II* (Qom, 1385 SH). Available at http://www.amontazeri. com/farsi/frame10.asp.

————, 'Piravan-e ferqe baha'iyat va hoquq-e sharvandi' (25.03.1387 SH). Available at www.amontazeri.com/farsi/fhome.asp.

————, *Safir-e haq va safir-e vahi* (Tehran, 1387 SH).

————, *Az aqaz ta anjam: Dar goftogu-ye do daneshju* (Qom, 1388 SH).

————, *Pasokh be porsesh-ha-ye piramun majazat-ha-ye eslami va hoquq-e bashar* (Tehran, 1388 SH).

————, 'Pasokh-e Ayatollah al-ozma Montazeri be do porsesh piramun-e re'ayat-e qanun-e entekhabat' (12 and 13.03.1388 SH). Available at www.amontazeri. com/farsi/fhome.asp.

————, 'Payam-e Ayatollah al-ozma Montazeri be monasebat dehomin dure-ye entekhabat-e riasat-e jomhuri-ye eslami' (13.03.1388 SH). Available at www. amontazeri.com/farsi/fhome.asp.

————, 'Payam-e Ayatollah al-ozma Montazeri piramun-e natayej-e entekhabat-e riasat-e jomhuri-ye eslami va havadez-e pas az an' (26.03.1388 SH). Available at www.amontazeri.com/farsi/fhome.asp.

————, 'Payam-e Ayatollah al-ozma Montazeri dar eteraz be amalkard namonaseb-e ma'sulan va sarkub-e mardom' (03.04.1388 SH). Available at www.amontazeri. com/farsi/fhome.asp.

————, 'Pasokh-e feqhi-siasi Ayatollah al-ozma Montazeri be porsesh-ha-ye hojatoleslam va al-moslemin doktor Mohsen Kadivar' (19.04.1388 SH). Available at www.amontazeri.com/farsi/fhome.asp.

————, 'Payam-e Ayatollah al-ozma Montazeri dar eteraz be bargozari-ye dadgah-ha-ye farmayeshi' (13.05.1388 SH). Available at www.amontazeri.com/farsi/ fhome.asp.

————, 'Payam-e Ayatollah al-ozma Montazeri be maraj'e azam-e taqlid, olama' va huze-ha-ye elmi-ye' (22.06.1388 SH). Available at www.amontazeri.com/farsi/ fhome.asp.

————, *Didgah-ha: Payam-ha-ye va nazariat-e montashere-ye fagih aliqadr Ayatollah al-ozma Montazeri. Vol. III* (Qom, 1389 SH). Available at http://www. amontazeri.com/farsi/frame10.asp.

————, *Enteqad az khod* (Qom, 1390 SH).

————, *Democracy and Constitution* (11 February 2001). Available at www.am ontazeri.com/farsi/f1.asp.

————, *Matn-e kamel-e khaterat Ayatollah Hossein-Ali Montazeri* (Essen, 2001).

Mussavi, Mir Hossein, 'Matn-e kamel-e name Mir-Hossein Mussavi be Ayatollah Khamene'i' (11 June 2009). Available at www.bbc.co.uk/persian/iran/2009/06/ 090611_op_ir88_mousavi_khamenei_letter_text.shtml.

————, 'Matn-e bianiye Mir-Hossein Mussavi dar eteraz be natayej-e elam shode entekhabat' (13 June 2009). Available at www.bbc.co.uk/persian/iran/2009/ 06/090613_bd_ir88_mousavi_statement.shtml.

————, 'Matn-e kamel-e name Mir-Hossein Mussavi be olema va maraje'-ye Qom' (13 June 2009). Available at www.bbc.co.uk/persian/iran/2009/06/090613_ bd_ir88_mousavi_letter_qom.shtml.

————, 'Biyani-ye shomare 5 Mohandes Mir Hossein Mussavi' (30.03.1388 SH). Formerly available at http://www.rahesabz.net/section/archive/1388/3/30.

————, 'Matn kamel-e bianiye Mussavi pas az ta'yyid entekhabat tavassot-e shura-ye neghaban' (13.04.1388 SH). Available at www.bbc.co.uk/persian/iran/2009/07/090701_op_ir88_mousavi9_text.shtml.

Nuri, Abdollah, *Shukran-e eslah: Defa'yat-e Abdollah Nuri dar dadgah-e vize ruhaniyat* (Tehran, 1378 SH).

Peydar, Hamid, 'Paradoks-e eslām va demokrasi', *Kiyan*, No. 20 (1373 SH).

Qabel, Ahmad, 'Name be rahbar-e jomhuri-ye eslami-ye Iran' (10.03.1384 SH), Available at www.bbc.co.uk/persian/iran/story/2005/06/050601_ahmad-qabel-letter.shtml.

————, *Mabani-ye shar'iat* (1391 SH). Formerly available at www.ghabel.net/shariat/books.

Rafsanjani, Ali Akbar Hashemi, 'Khatbe-ha-ye namaz jom'e' (26.04.1388 SH). Available at www.hashemirafsanjani.ir/news_archive/1388.

Reyshahri, Mohammad Mohammadi, *Khatere-ha, Vol. IV* (Tehran, 1388 SH).

Sadri, Ahmad and Mahmud Sadri (eds), *Reason, Freedom and Democracy in Islam: Essential Writings of Abdolkarim Soroush* (Oxford, 2002).

Salahpur, Jahangir, 'Din-e demokratik-e hokumati', *Kiyan*, No. 20 (1373 SH), pp. 6–11.

Sane'i, Yussef, 'Javabi-ye Ayatollah al-ozma Sane'i dar pasokh be Mohandes Mir Hossein Mussavi' (25.03.1388 SH). Available at http://1saanei.org/?view=01,01,01,61,60.

————, 'Ebraz hamdardi Hazrat Ayatollah al-ozma Sane'i ba khanevade qorbanian-e fejai' akheir' (27.03.1388 SH). Available at http://1saanei.org/?view=01,00,00,00,0#01,01,01,62,60.

————, 'Bianiye marja'-e aliqadr Hazrat Ayatollah al-ozma Sane'i dar ertebat ba masa'el-e jari keshvar' (14.04.1388 SH). Available at http://1saanei.org/?view=01,00,00,00,0#01,01,01,63,60.

————, 'Bianiye marja'-e aliqadr Hazrat Ayatollah al-ozma Sane'i dar pi bargozari dadgah-ha-ye pas az entekhabat dahomin dure riasat jomhuri' (14.05.1388 SH). Available at http://1saanei.org/?view=01,01,01,67,50.

Shabestari, Mohammad Mojtahed, 'Mabani va mekanism-e sabat va tahul-e ma'refat-e elahi', *Kiyan*, No. 3 (1369 SH), pp. 3–4.

————, 'Naqd-e tafakkor-e sonnati dar kalam-e eslami', *Kiyan*, No. 10 (1371 SH), pp. 8–11.

————, 'Tchera bayad andishe-ye dini ra naqd kard?', *Kiyan*, No. 18 (1373 SH), pp. 16–21.

————, 'Motun-e dini va jahanbini-ye naqd-e tarikhi', *Kiyan*, No. 26 (1374 SH), pp. 22–5.

————, 'Vahy va azadi-ye aqli-ye ensan', *Kiyan*, No. 25 (1374 SH), pp. 16–22.

————, *Naqdi bar qora'at-e rasmi az din: bohranha, chaleshha, rahhalha* (Tehran, 1379 SH).

Soroush, Abdolkarim, 'Hokumat demokratik-e dini?', *Kiyan*, No. 11 (1373 SH), pp. 12–15.

————, 'Modara va modiriyat-e mo'menan – Sokhani dar nesbat din va demokrasi', *Kiyan*, No. 21 (1373 SH), pp. 2–14.

————, 'Horriyat va ruhaniyat', *Kiyan*, No. 24 (1374 SH).

————, 'Saqf-e ma'ishat bar sotun-e shari'at', *Kiyan*, No. 26 (1374 SH), pp. 25–31.

## Secondary Sources

Abdo, Geneive, 'Rethinking the Islamic Republic: A "Conversation" with Ayatollah Hossein Ali Montazeri', *Middle East Journal*, Winter (2001), pp. 9–24.

────── and Jonathan Lyons, *Answering only to God: Faith and Freedom in Twenty-First-Century Iran* (New York, 2003).

Abrahamian, Ervand, 'The Structural Causes of the Iranian Revolution', *Merip Reports*, No. 87: *IranRs Revolution: The Rural Dimension*, May (1980), pp. 21–6.

──────, *Tortured Confessions: Prisons and Public Recantations in Modern Iran* (Berkeley, 1999).

Adelkah, Fariba, *Etre moderne en Iran* (Paris, 1998).

Akhavi, Shahrough, 'The Thought and Role of Ayatollah Hossein Ali Montazeri in the Politics of Post-1979 Iran', *Iranian Studies,* December (2008).

Alsaif, Tawfiq, *Islamic Democracy and its Limits: The Iranian Experience since 1979* (Beirut, 2007).

Amirpur, Katajun, 'Reformen an theologischen Hochschulen in Iran: Revolutionäres Establishment contra religiöse Aufklärer', *Orient,* 09 (1997).

──────, *Die Entpolitisierung des Islam: Abdolkarim Sorushs Denken und Wirkung in der Islamischen Republik Iran* (Würzburg, 2003).

────── and Ludwig Amman (eds), *Der Islam am Wendepunkt: Liberale und konservative Reformer einer Weltreligion* (Freiburg, 2006).

──────, 'Wider die absolute "Führungsbefugnis des Rechtsgelehrten" (velayat-e motlaq-e faqih): Zur Rolle und Kritik des Hosein-Ali Montazeri', *Asiatische Studien,* 3 (2010), pp. 474–513.

Amnesty International, 'Iran: Election amid repression of dissent and unrest' (9 June 2009). Available at www.amnesty.org/en/library/info/MDE13/053/2009.

──────, 'Iran: Election Contested, Repression Compounded' (10 December 2009). Available at www.amnesty.org/en/library/info/MDE13/123/2009.

Ansari, Ali M., *Iran under Ahmadinejad: The politics of confrontation* (London, 2007).

Arjomand, Said Amir, 'Constitution-Making in Islamic Iran: The Impact of Theocracy on the Legal Order of a Nation-State', in June Starr and Jane Collier (eds), *History and Power in the Study of Law, New Directions in Legal Anthropology* (New York, 1989).

──────, 'Civil Society and the Rule of Law in the Constitutional Politics of Iran Under Khatami', *Social Research,* 3 (2000).

──────, 'Islam and Constitutionalism since the Nineteenth Century: The Significance and Pecularities of Iran', in Arjomand (ed.), *Constitutional Politics in the Middle East* (Oxford, 2007).

──────, *After Khomeini: Iran under his Successors* (Oxford, 2009).

Ashraf, Ahmad and Ali Banuazizi, 'Iran's Tortuous Path to "Islamic Liberalism"', *International Journal of Politics, Culture and Society,* Winter (2001), pp. 237–56.

Bashi, Golbarg, 'Eyewitness History: Ayatollah Montazeri' (3 August 2006). Available at http://www.payvand.com/news/06/mar/1067.html.

Behdad, Sohrab, 'Utopia of Assassins: Navvab Safavi and the Fadaiyan-e Islam in Prerevolutionary Iran', in Ramin Jahanbegloo (ed.), *Iran: Between Tradition and Modernity* (Oxford, 2004).

Behi, Kambiz, 'The "Real" in Resistance: Transgression of Law as Ethical Act', *Unbound,* 30 (2008), pp. 31–5.

272     THE DISSIDENT MULLAH

Behrooz, Maziar, 'The Islamic state and the Crisis of the Marja'iyat in Iran',
    *Comparative Studies of South Asia, Africa and the Middle East*, Vol. XVI, No. 2
    (1996), pp. 1–7.
——, 'Leadership and Legitimacy: The controversy among the clergy over who
    should lead the Islamic state', *Iranian* (2 January 1997).
——, 'Reflections on Iran's Prison System during the Montazeri Years (1985–
    88)', *Iran Analysis Quaterly*, Winter (2005), pp. 11–23.
Boroujerdi, Mehrzad, *Iranian Intellectuals and the West: The Tormented Triumph of
    Nativism* (Syracuse, 1996).
Bourdieu, Pierre, *Propos sur le champs politique* (Lyons, 2000).
——, *Das religiöse Feld: Texte zur Ökonomie des Heilsgeschehens* (Konstanz, 2000/2).
Brumberg, Daniel, *Reinventing Khomeini: The Struggle for Reform in Iran* (Chicago,
    2001).
Buchta, Wilfried, 'Die Islamische Republik Iran und die religiös-politische
    Kontroverse um die marja'iyat', *Orient*, September (1995), pp. 449–74.
——, *Die iranische Schia und die islamische Einheit 1979–1996* (Hamburg, 1997).
——, *Who rules Iran? The Structure of Power in the Islamic Republic* (Washington
    DC, 2000).
——, 'Die Inquisition in der Islamischen Republik Iran. Einige Anmerkungen
    zum Sondergericht für die Geistlichkeit', in Rainer Brunner (ed.), *Islamstudien
    ohne Ende* (Würzburg, 2002).
——, 'Mehdi Hashemi's Fall: An Episode of Intra Elite Struggle for Power under
    Khomeini', in Mohammad M. Ansari (ed.), *Iran Today: Twenty Five Years after the
    Revolution* (New Delhi, 2005).
Cottam, Richard, 'Inside Revolutionary Iran', *Middle East Journal*, Spring (1989),
    pp. 168–85.
Diaz-Bone, Rainer, *Kulturwelt, Diskurs und Lebensstil: Eine diskurstheoretische
    Erweiterung der bourdieuschen Distinktionstheorie* (Opladen, 2002).
Draper, Theodore, *A Very Thin Line: The Iran-Contra Affairs* (New York, 1991).
Foucault, Michel, *Archäologie des Wissens* (Frankfurt am Main, 1994).
——, *The Order of Things* (London, 2010).
Fourquet, Thomas, 'Le chiisme élitiste de l'ayatollah Mesbah Yazdi', *Maghreb-
    Machrek*, Winter (2006/2007), pp. 45–58.
Fürtig, Henner, *Liberalisierung als Herausforderung: Wie stabil ist die Islamische Republik
    Iran?* (Berlin, 1996).
——, 'Turbulente Wahlen in Iran: Die Islamische Republik am Scheideweg?',
    *GIGA Focus*, No. 6 (2009).
Ghamari-Tabrizi, Behrooz, *Islam and Dissent in Postrevolutionary Iran: Abdolkarim
    Soroush, Religious Politics and Democratic Reform* (London, 2008).
Goldberg, Jacob, 'The Saudi Arabian Kingdom', in Itamar Rabinovich and Haim
    Shaked (eds), *Middle East Contemporary Survey, Volume X: 1986* (London, 1988),
    pp. 543–73.
Hajatpour, Reza, *Iranische Geistlichkeit zwischen Utopie und Realismus, zum Diskurs über
    Herrschafts- und Staatsdenken im 20. Jahrhundert* (Wiesbaden, 2002).
——, *Realismus, Mehdi Haeri Yazdi interkulturell gelesen* (Nordhausen, 2005).
Heinrich Böll Stiftung, *Iran nach den Wahlen: Eine Konferenz und ihre Folgen* (Münster,
    2001).
Hermann, Rainer, 'Von der Wirtschafts- zur Legitimationskrise: Die Ära Khamenei/
    Rafsanjani in der Islamischen Republik Iran', *Orient*, 4 (1994), pp. 541–64.

Hooglund, Eric (ed.), 'In Search for Iran's Moderates', *Merip Reports,* No. 144, January/February (1987), pp. 4–6.

————, *Twenty Years of Islamic Revolution: Political and Social Transition in Iran since 1979* (New York, 2002).

Human Rights Watch, *'Like the Dead in their Coffins': Torture, Detention, and the Crushing of Dissent in Iran,* June (2004). Available at www.hrw.org/reports/2004/06/06/dead-their-coffins-0.

————, 'Ministers of Murder: Iran's New Security Cabinet' (2005). Available at www.hrw.org/reports/2005/12/15/ministers-murder-iran-s-new-security-cabi net.

————, 'The Islamic Republic at 31: Post-election Abuses Show Serious Human Rights Crisis', February (2010). Available at www.hrw.org/reports/2010/02/11/islamic-republic-31–0.

International Crisis Group, 'Iran: Discontent and Disarray', Middle East Briefing, No. 11, 15 October 2003. Available at http://www.crisisgroup.org/en/regions/middle-east-north-africa/iraq-iran-gulf/iran/B011-iran-discontent-and-disarray.aspx.

————, 'Iran: What Does Ahmadi-Nejad's Victory Mean?', Middle East Briefing, No. 18, 4 August 2005. Available at www.crisisgroup.org/en/regions/middle-east-north-africa/iraq-iran-gulf/iran/B018-iran-what-does-ahmadi-nejads-victory-mean.aspx.

————, 'Iran: Ahmadi-Nejad's Tumultous Presidency', Middle East Briefing, No. 21, 6 February 2007. Available at http://www.crisisgroup.org/en/regions/middle-east-north-africa/iraq-iran-gulf/iran/B021-iran-ahmadi-nejads-tumultuous-presidency.aspx.

Iran Human Rights Documentation Centre, *Deadly Fatwa: Iran's 1988 Prison Massacre,* September (2009). Available at www.iranhrdc.org/english/publicati ons/reports/3158-deadly-fatwa-iran-s-1988-prison-massacre.html.

————, *Speaking for the Dead: Survivor Accounts of Iran's 1988 Massacre,* January (2010). Available at www.iranhrdc.org/english/publications/reports/3160-speaking-for-the-dead-survivor-accounts-of-iran-s-1988-massacre.html.

————, *Violent Aftermath: The 2009 Election and Suppression of Dissent in Iran* (2010). Available at www.iranhrdc.org/english/publications/reports/3161-violent-afterm ath-the-2009-election-and-suppression-of-dissent-in-iran.html#.U0J9taYidKA.

Izadi, Mustafa, *A Glance at the Life Ayatullah Montazeri* (Tehran, 1984).

Jahanbakhsh, Forough, *Islam, Democracy and Religious Modernism in Iran (1953–2000): From Bazargan to Soroush* (Leiden, 2001).

Kamali, Masoud, *Multiple Modernities, Civil Society and Islam: The Case of Iran and Turkey* (Liverpool, 2006).

Kamrava, Mehran, *Iran's Intellectual Revolution* (Cambridge, 2008).

Keddie, Nikki R., *Modern Iran: Roots and Results of Revolution* (New Haven, 2006).

Kermani, Navid, *Iran: Die Revolution der Kinder* (Munich, 2005).

Khosrokhavar, Farhad, 'L'Iran, la democratie et la nouvelle citoyennete', *Cahiers internationaux de sociologie,* No. 111 (2001/02) pp. 291–317.

————, 'L'Iran de l'après Khomeini au postreformise', *Critique Internationale,* April (2004), pp. 23–31.

————, 'The New Intellectuals in Iran', *Social Compass,* 51(2) (2004), pp. 191–202.

Kian-Thiebaut, Azadeh, *Secularization of Iran a Doomed Failure? The New Middle Class and the Making of Modern Iran* (Paris, 1998).

Kramer, Martin, 'The Export of Islam', in Itamar Rabinovich and Haim Shaked (eds), *Middle East Contemporary Survey, Volume X: 1986* (London, 1988), pp. 127–56.

Künkler, Miriam, 'The Special Court of the Clergy (Dadgah-e Vizheh-ye Ruhaniyat) and the Repression of Dissident Clergy in Iran,' in Said Arjomand and Nathan Brown (eds), *Constitutionalism, the Rule of Law and the Politics of Administration in Egypt and Iran* (New York, 2012).

Landwehr, Achim, 'Das Sichtbare sichtbar machen. Annäherung an "Wissen" als Kategorie historischer Forschung', in Achim Landwehr, *Geschichte(n) der Wirklichkeit, Beiträge zur Sozial- und Kulturgeschichte des Wissens* (Augsburg, 2002).

——, 'Diskursgeschichte als Geschichte des Politischen', in Brigitte Kerchner and Silke Schneider (eds), *Foucault: Diskursanalyse der Politik: Eine Einführung* (Wiesbaden, 2006).

——, *Historische Diskursanalyse* (Frankfurt am Main, 2008).

—— (ed.), *Diskursiver Wandel* (Wiesbaden, 2010).

Martin, Vanessa, *Creating an Islamic State: Khomeini and the Making of a New Iran* (London, 2000).

Masserat, Amir-Ebrahimi, 'Blogging from Qom: Behind Walls and Veils', *Comparative Studies of South Asia, Africa and the Middle East*, 2 (2008), pp. 235–49.

Matsunaga, Yasuyuki, 'Kadivar, an Advocate of Postrevivalist Islam in Iran', *British Journal of Middle Eastern Studies,* December (2007), pp. 317–29.

Millward, William, 'Leadership in the Islamic Republic and the Hierarchy of Shia Islam', *Commentary,* January (1994).

Mirbagheri, Farid, 'Narrowing the Gap or Camouflaging the Divide: An Analysis of Mohammad Khatami's "Dialogue of Civilisations"', *British Journal of Middle Eastern Studies,* December (2007), pp. 305–16.

Mir-Hosseini, Ziba and Richard Tapper, *Islam and democracy in Iran: Eshkevari and the quest for reform* (London, 2006).

Mirsepassi, Ali, *Democracy in modern Iran: Islam, Culture and Political Change* (New York, 2010).

Moaddel, Mansoor, 'The Iranian Revolution and its Nemesis: The Rise of Liberal Values among Iranians', *Comparative Studies of South Asia, Africa and the Middle East*, No. 1 (2009), pp. 126–36.

Moin, Baqer, 'Questions of Guardianship in Iran', *Third World Quaterly,* January (1998), pp. 191–200.

——, *Khomeini: Life of the Ayatollah* (New York, 1999).

Moslem, Mehdi, *Factional Politics in Post-Khomeini Iran* (New York, 2002).

Mottahedeh, Roy, *Der Mantel des Propheten. Das Leben eines persischen Mullah zwischen Religion und Politik* (Munich, 1987).

Naji, Kasra, *Ahmadinejad: The secret history of Iran's radical leader* (Los Angeles, 2008).

Omid, Homa, *Islam and the Post-Revolutionary State in Iran* (London, 1994).

Posch, Walter, 'A Last Chance for Iran's Reformists? The "Green Struggle" Reconsidered', SWP Working Paper (May, 2010).

Rahimi, Babak, 'The Discourse of Democracy in Shi'i Islamic Jurisprudence: The two cases of Montazeri and Sistani', EUI Working Paper (2008).

Rahnema, Saeed, 'Lessons (not) learned: Reflections on a Failed Revolution', *Comparative Studies of South Asia, Africa and the Middle East*, No. 1 (2009), pp. 72–83.

Rajaee, Farhang, *Islamism and Modernism: The Changing Discourse in Iran* (Austin, 2007).

Rakel, Eva Patricia, 'The Political Elite in the Islamic Republic of Iran: From Khomeini to Ahmadinejad', *Comparative Studies of South Asia, Africa and the Middle East*, No. 1 (2009), pp. 105–25.

Randjbar-Daemi, Siavush, 'Building the Islamic State: The Draft Constitution of 1979 Reconsidered', *Iranian Studies*, 64.4 (2013).

Ranstorp, Magnus, *Hizb'allah in Lebanon: The Politics of the Western Hostage Crisis* (Basingstoke, 1997).

Richard, Yann, 'Hoseyn-'Ali Montazeri', *Orient*, September (1985), pp. 303–6.

———, 'L'islam politique en Iran', *Politique Etrangère*, Spring (2005), pp. 61–72.

Robertson, Geoffrey, *The Massacre of Political Prisoners in Iran, 1988* (London, 2011). Available at www.iranrights.org/library/document/1380/the-massacre-of-politi cal-prisoners-in-iran-1988-report-of-an-inquiry.

Roy, Olivier, 'The Crisis of Religious Legitimacy in Iran', *Middle East Journal*, Spring (1999), pp. 201–16.

Saffari, Said, 'The Legitimation of the Clergy's Right to Rule in the Iranian Constitution of 1979', *British Journal of Middle Eastern Studies*, Vol. 20, No. 1 (1993), pp. 64–82.

Said, Edward W., 'Irangate: A Many-Sided Crisis', *Journal of Palestine Studies*, Summer (1987), pp. 22–49.

Samii, Abbas William, 'Sisyphus' Newsstand: The Iranian Press under Khatami', *Middle East Review of International Affairs*, September (2001).

———, 'The Changing Landscape of Party Politics in Iran: A Case Study', *Journal of the European Society for Iranian Studies* (2005).

Sarabi, Farzin, 'The Post-Khomeini Era in Iran: The Elections of the Fourth Islamic Majlis', *Middle East Journal*, Winter (1994), pp. 89–107.

Savyon, A. and Y. Mansharof, 'The Docrine of Mahdism in the Ideological and Political Philosophy of Mahmoud Ahmadinejad and Ayatollah Mesbah-e Yazdi', *Inquiry & Analysis*, May (2007), pp. 4–10.

Schirazi, Asghar, *The Constitution of Iran, Politics and the State in the Islamic Republic* (New York, 1997).

Segev, Samuel, *The Iranian Triangle: The Untold Story of Israel's Role in the Iran-Contra Affair* (New York, 1988).

Sreberny, Annabelle and Gholam Khiabany, 'Becoming Intellectual: The Blogestan and Public Political Space in the Islamic Republic', *British Journal of Middle Eastern Studies*, December (2007), pp. 267–86.

———, 'Politics of/in blogging in Iran', *Comparative Studies of South Asia, Africa and the Middle East*, No. 3 (2007), pp. 563–79.

Taghavi, Seyyed Mohammad Ali, *The Flourishing of Islamic Reformism in Iran: Political Islamic Groups in Iran (1941–1961)* (New York, 2005).

Tellier, Frederic, 'La république islamique dans l'impasse', *Revues internationales et strategiques*, No. 49 (2003), pp. 44–55.

Towfigh, Ebrahim, 'Islamische Demokratie und "Restauration" der Theokratie: Diskursanalytische Betrachtung des Reformprozesses in der Islamischen Republik Iran', *Orient*, December (2004), pp. 521–47.

US Congress, 'The Iran-Contra Report' (1987). Available at www.presidency.ucsb. edu/PS157/assignment%20files%20public/congressional%20report%20key %20sections.htm.

Vahabzadeh, Peyman, 'Democratizing Shi'ism: The Theoretical Foundations of Iran's Reform Movement', *Humanitas*, Spring (2004), pp. 51–5.

Vahdat, Farzin, *God and Juggernaut: Iran's Intellectual encounter with Modernity* (Syracuse, 2002).

## Press articles

'Ayatollah Montazeri: Imam Khomeini riasat-e jomhuri nakhahand paziraft', *Etela'at*, 26 Khordad 1358.

'Payam-e tarikhi Imam Khomeini be majles barrasi-ye qanun-e assassi', *Etela'at*, 28 Mordad 1358.

'Bianat-e Imam khatab be nemayandegan-e majles-e khabregan', *Etela'at*, 28 Mordad 1358.

'Ejlas emruz majles-e khabregan', *Keyhan*, 2 Sharivar 1358.

'Velayat-e faqih tazvib shod', *Keyhan*, 22 Sharivar 1358.

'Bozorgtarin namaz jom'eh tarikh bar mezar-e shohada', *Keyhan*, 24 Sharivar 1358.

'Dustan-e Mohammad Montazeri pas az khal'-e selah afrad forudgah, u ra ba khod bordand', *Keyhan*, 24 Sharivar 1358.

'Ayatollah Montazeri khastar bazdasht va mo'aleje-ye Mohammad Montazeri shod', *Keyhan*, 30 Sharivar 1358.

'Ayatollah Montazeri: Aza-ye shura-ha ra az qashr-ha-ye mokhtalef entkehab konid', *Etela'at*, 31 Sharivar 1358.

'Ayatollah Montazeri be montaqedan-e majles khabregan pasokh dad', *Etela'at*, 4 Mehr 1358.

'Montazeri Jr to Send 17.000 Youths to Help Lebanese Struggle', *Tehran Times*, 6 December 1979.

'Montazeri's Teenage Army Occupies Airport Lounge', *Tehran Times*, 13 December 1979.

Tabarzadi, Heshmatollah, 'Ekhtiarat-e vali-ye faqih bayad be osul qanun-e assassi makhdud shavad', *Nimrooz*, 9 Aban 1376.

'Tazahorat vazi' zed velayat-e faqih dar Teheran', *Nimrooz*, 9 Aban 1376.

'Azari-Qomi az jame'eh modaressin houze elmi-ye Qom ejrah shod', *Nimrooz*, 23 Aban 1376.

'Mikhahand Montazeri ra be etteham tu'te aliye hokumat mohakeme konand', *Nimrooz*, 7 Azar 1376.

Jehl, Douglas, 'Iranian Clerics hint at Treason Trial for Critic', *New York Times*, 16 December 1997. Available at www.nytimes.com/1997/12/16/world/iranian-clerics-hint-at-treason-trial-for-a-critic.html.

'How Did Haj Ahmad Khomeini die?' (English translation), *Aftab-e Yazd*, 25 September 2000. Available at www.netnative.com/news/00/sep/1113.html.

'Freed Iran cleric vows to continue to fight for justice', *New York Times*, 31 January 2003. Available at http://www.nytimes.com/2003/01/31/world/freed-iran-cleric-vows-to-continue-to-fight-for-justice.html.

Worth, Robert F. and Nazila Fathi, 'Protests Flare in Tehran as Opposition Disputes Vote', *New York Times*, 14 June 2009. Available at www.nytimes.com/2009/06/14/world/middleeast/14iran.html?_r=2&.

Muhammad Sahimi, 'The Widening Divide among Iranian Clerics', *Tehran Bureau*, 30 June 2009. Available at www.pbs.org/wgbh/pages/frontline/tehranbureau/2009/07/the-widening-divide-among-irans-clerics.html.

'Qodrat nemai million mardom', *Rooz*, 22 December 2009. Available at www. roozonline.com/persian/archive/archivenews/news/archive/2009/december/22/ article/-d48f41cc22.html.

Qazi, Fereshte, 'Ta'zim-e donya be pedar-e ma'nvai jonbesh-e sabz', *Rooz*, 22 December 2009. Available at www.roozonline.com/persian/archive/archivenews/news/archive/ 2009/december/22/article/br-br.html.

'Sokhanrani Seyyed Hassan na-tamam mand', *Sharq*, 16 Khordad 1389.

Yazdan-Panah, Mohammad-Reza, 'Daftar-e Montazeri va Sanei takhrib va plomb shod', *Rooz*, 14 June 2010. Available at www.roozonline.com/persian/archive/ archivenews/news/archive/2010/june/14/article/-d6a1efa9e9.html.

# INDEX